# ESSAYS IN INDIAN HISTORY

Cuthbert Collin Davies

*(frontispiece)*

# ESSAYS IN INDIAN HISTORY

## In Honour of Cuthbert Collin Davies

*Edited by*

Donovan Williams
*and*
E. Daniel Potts

ASIA PUBLISHING HOUSE
LONDON

ISBN 0.210.22342.1

PRINTED IN INDIA
BY B. B. NADKARNI AT THACKER & CO., LTD. PRESS, BOMBAY AND
PUBLISHED BY P. S. JAYASINGHE, ASIA PUBLISHING HOUSE, 447 STRAND,
LONDON W. C. 2.

# PREFACE

The preparation of this commemorative volume for Dr. Cuthbert Collin Davies has been a labour of love which the editors were pleased to undertake. The essays have come from several branches of the academic world: lecturers, professors, research students and administrators. The contributors are representative of the many students who have benefited from the guidance and inspiration of Dr. Davies and who are now scattered from Britain to Australia, from Nepal to North America. This geographical distribution has made the task of editing difficult; that the difficulty has been overcome is a commentary on the high regard in which Dr. Davies is held by those who have passed through his hands.

The maps are reproduced from C. C. Davies's *An Historical Atlas of the Indian Peninsula*, by kind permission of Oxford University Press, Bombay.

DONOVAN WILLIAMS
E. DANIEL POTTS

# PREFACE

The preparation of this commemorative volume for Dr. Cuthbert Collin Davies has proved a pleasant task which the editors were pleased to undertake. The essays come from several branches of the academic world: lecturers, professors, research students and administrators. The contributors are representative of the many students who have benefited from the guidance and inspiration of Dr. Davies and who are now scattered from Britain to Australia, from Nepal to North America. This geographical distribution has added to the task of editing difficulties [illegible] difficulty [illegible]. Each essay is a contribution to the high regard in which Dr. Davies is held by those who have passed through his hands.

The maps are reproduced from C. C. Davies's *An Historical Atlas of the Indian Peninsula*, by kind permission of Oxford University Press, Bombay.

Donovan Williams
E. D. Potts

# CUTHBERT COLLIN DAVIES: A TRIBUTE

To celebrate his seventy-fifth year, former students and colleagues of Dr. Cuthbert Collin Davies have happily joined together in his honour to produce this volume of essays. Appropriately the subject matter is India and its history, to which through a lifetime of teaching and research he has single-mindedly devoted himself.

Collin Davies was commissioned in the 15th West Yorkshire Regiment in 1915 and was twice wounded during his service in France, 1916-1917. In 1918 he proceeded to India as Captain in the 2/1st Gurkha Rifles where he served on the north-west frontiers through the Third Afghan War and between 1921-1922 saw savage fighting in Waziristan. He also held command responsibilities in the relatively settled district of Peshawar, so that he was able to gain an intimate and varied knowledge not only of the general topography of the frontier areas but also of the way of life of the wild tribesmen themselves. As a good Welshman, he has always loved the mountains and had a sympathy for their peoples.

With his historical imagination stirred by what he had seen in India, he proceeded on his return to Britain to equip himself academically, taking a distinguished first degree in history in the University of Wales, then proceeding for a higher degree to Peterhouse, Cambridge, where he worked under Harold Temperley. It was natural that he should choose to turn to India and to the history of the north-west for his subject of study; and it was this nucleus of work which grew into his first, and, as most of his colleagues would probably agree, his best book *The Problem of the North West Frontier* (1932).

Making good use of his personal knowledge of the border country and its tribal peoples, reinforcing this with a characteristically thorough scrutiny of relevant manuscript and published sources, Collin Davies explored the modern defence problems of that area in the context of a beautifully clear presentation of its intricate history in the nineteenth century. The moral of history, the need not only for an intelligent defence system but also for a sympathetic policy towards the tribal peoples, is as pertinent for India and Pakistan today as for the Government of India at the time it was written.

The book reveals, too, his deep pride in the British frontier achievement. "The frontier problem", he said, "is not solved, the book of frontier war is not closed, but the British could have found a solution long ago. They could have made a solitude and called it peace. . . . But, on the whole, we have been merciful; tribal rights and customs have been respected; no attempts have been made to tamper with religious beliefs . . . every effort has been made to conciliate our trans-frontier neighbours."

Whatever their first point of contact, all students of British activities in India are sooner or later attracted to the remarkable career of Warren Hastings and to the whole subject of the making of the Indo-British empire in the closing decades of the eighteenth century. To these major themes Collin Davies has devoted himself, publishing successively *Warren Hastings and Oudh* (1939), *The Benares Diary of Warren Hastings* (1948), and *The Private Correspondence of Lord Macartney* (1950).

It was perceptive of him to choose to explore the question of Hastings's policy towards Oudh, because that subject formed one of the vital and yet neglected aspects of Hastings's work. The control of Oudh and its maintenance as a strong and friendly state were matters which, as Hastings perceived from the first, went to the very heart of the East India Company's position in India. On that depended the security of their revenues, and on their revenues depended their power. In his customary, careful and methodical fashion, using a wealth of private and official papers, Collin Davies produced a fresh and solid base on which to form a judgment on Hastings's policies. He provided new and weighty evidence further to discredit those inveterate antagonists of Hastings — Philip

Francis and General Clavering — and brought forward fresh material and argument to show that "the Benares charge", one of the most telling accusations against Hastings at the impeachment, rested on the misunderstanding that Chait Singh, the zamindar of Benares, was an independent prince. In this light Hastings's action in removing Chait Singh at once becomes more intelligible and capable of justification.

At this period when this book was being written, the myth of Warren Hastings's monstrous behaviour, created by the malevolence of Francis and the misguided oratory of Burke, was slowly and finally succumbing before the painstaking labours of scholars; and Collin Davies has enjoyed the great satisfaction of contributing in a significant respect to this process.

But on this anniversary occasion the thoughts of his colleagues and students will also naturally turn to his contributions as a teacher and counsellor, amply demonstrated first at the School of Oriental Studies between 1929 and 1936, and subsequently as Reader in Indian History at Oxford down to his retirement in 1965. His special course on "Warren Hastings and India" was yearly enjoyed by Oxford undergraduates; and his appreciation of their need for a clear guide to Indian history generally found expression in his *An Historical Atlas of the Indian Peninsula*, first published in 1948. Under his close, personal care and friendly guidance a very large number of students, the majority from the Indian sub-continent, proceeded to higher degrees by research. He was a strict taskmaster, insisting on an extensive use of first-hand materials, and a tight standard of accuracy and English usage, qualities which he continues to demonstrate, too, in his approach as an examiner for other universities. His reward is to have set many a grateful young man and woman on the path of scholarship, and to have taken a part in keeping alive the tradition of Indian studies in Britain. The devotion which he has inspired could not be better shown than by the way in which Dr. Donovan Williams, Dr. E. Daniel Potts and their colleagues have come together to produce this volume.

C. H. PHILIPS
*Director*
*School of Oriental and African Studies*
*University of London*

# THE CONTRIBUTORS

Sarvepalli Gopal
M. A., D. Phil. (Oxon.)
Reader in South Asian History
University of Oxford.

John Riddy
M. A. (Oxon.)
Assistant Secretary
University of Stirling
Scotland.

Bikrama Jit Hasrat
M. A. (Punjab), M.A., Ph.D. (Calcutta), D.Phil. (Oxon.), P.E.S.
Professor and Head of the Department of History
Tribhuvan University
Kathmandu, Nepal.

Kenneth Ingham
M. A., D.Phil. (Oxon.), O.B.E., M.C.
Professor of Modern History
University of Bristol.

Munir-ud-Din Chughtai
M. A. (Punjab), D. Phil. (Oxon.)
Reader in Political Science
University of the Punjab
Lahore, West Pakistan.

Eli Daniel Potts
B. A. (Iowa State College), M. A. (Iowa), D. Phil. (Oxon.)
Senior Lecturer
Department of History
Monash University
Victoria, Australia.

Gulammohammed Refai
M. A. (Baroda), Ph. D. (Cantab.)
Lecturer in History
University of California
Los Angeles, U.S.A.

Martin Gilbert
M. A. (Oxon.)
Fellow of Merton College
University of Oxford.

Richard John Bingle
M. A., D.Phil. (Oxon.)
Research Assistant in Charge of Western Manuscripts in the India Office Library (Commonwealth Relations Office)
London.

Amita Das
M. A. (Calcutta), D. Phil. (Oxon.)
Lecturer
Department of Modern History
Calcutta University, India.

Donovan Williams
M. A., Ph.D. (Rand), D. Phil. (Oxon.), F.R. Hist. S.
Professor
Department of History
University of Calgary
Alberta, Canada.

# CONTENTS

# GLADSTONE AND INDIA

SARVEPALLI GOPAL

While many books and monographs have been written on almost every aspect of Gladstone's thought and activity, his views on India have suffered neglect. Morley, in his Life of Gladstone, made no reference to them. Professor Paul Knaplund, in his book on *Gladstone and Britain's Imperial Policy*,[1] has almost nothing to say about India. Dr. Shannon, in a book published a few years ago,[2] goes so far as to say that Gladstone had no views on the subject. "India seems hardly to have entered his thoughts".[3] It is true that Gladstone was too preoccupied with first Italy, and then Ireland, to give much sustained attention to India. Yet he never completely forgot her. One can trace, down the years, an interest and a point of view which had been carefully thought out; and this interest and viewpoint, because they were Gladstone's, had an influence on British policy in India.

Gladstone's attention seems to have been first drawn to India by the fortuitous circumstance that the subject for the Newdigate Prize in 1831, Gladstone's last year at Oxford, when he was twenty-two years of age, was *The Suttee*. Morley refers to an unsuccessful entry for the Newdigate Prize in 1829

In this and the following essays, unpublished manuscript material from the India Office Library and the India Office Records, 197 Blackfriars Road, London SE 1, appears by permission of the Secretary of State for Foreign and Commonwealth Affairs.

[1] London, 1927.

[2] R. T. Shannon, *Gladstone and the Bulgarian Agitation 1876* (London, 1963).

[3] *Ibid.*, p.8.

but makes no mention of any second effort. Gladstone does not seem to have submitted a poem in 1831; but among the Gladstone papers in the British Museum there is to be found a draft of a poem on *The Suttee*.[4] It is clear that this was not meant to be the final version. It is not, in fact, good poetry; but it is of interest as indicating the early development of Gladstone's views on India. The poem runs into about 170 lines, but it is necessary to quote only a few lines as illustrative of Gladstone's outlook. A *sati* is a Hindu widow who immolates herself on her husband's funeral pyre. This practice of immolation, which had become a part of Hinduism in its days of decadence, was declared illegal by the Governor-General, Lord William Bentinck, in 1829. Gladstone, in his poem, first writes of the unity of mankind:

And voice serene of heav'ns unfading years
. . . gave to Time, his earth and sky and sea,
One frame divine, one living harmony.

Gladstone then commends the motives of the Hindu widow and asserts that she was not being forced to be a *sati* but was acting voluntarily:

She sate resolved — in death
Seal'd with a spouse's blood a spouse's faith,
And strove, nor vainly strove her soul, to prove
Tho' strong were torture, stronger yet was love.

Finally, Gladstone pays tribute to Bentinck:

Bentinck! 'Twas thine the bloodless crown to win,
Proud victor over deeds of death and sin!
Spirit of England's fame, no longer dim,
A voice of thunder, thou didst speak in him;
Echoed the glad command from shore to shore
And murder's ghastly flame ascends no more!

These three strands: an assertion that all men were equal, an appreciation of the motives and sentiments of Indians, and an

[4] Gladstone Papers, Add. MSS. 44721, folios 121 to 125, British Museum.

acceptance of British duties and obligations, together formed Gladstone's outlook on India throughout his public life.

For many years after 1831, however, India seems to have faded from Gladstone's view; and the mind of the young member of Parliament, when it looked beyond England, was seized of problems concerning other parts of the empire than India. Indeed, the promise of the Newdigate draft poem was shadowed by speeches in which Gladstone used the standard language of imperialism. For example, in 1837, speaking of Canada, he said: "the time when a separation on the part of Canada might be beneficial had not certainly arrived at the present period, when her population was divided into two parties of different origin, and inflamed by their passions into continual collisions with each other. In this state of things, this country was enabled by her power to act as a mediator and umpire, and thus prevented contests which might be found still more fatal."[5] On the other hand, he condemned the Opium Wars in China and appealed, to quote his words in the House of Commons in March 1857, "to that which is older than Christianity, because it was in the world before Christianity—to that which is broader than Christianity, because it extends in the world beyond Christianity — and to that which underlays Christianity, for Christianity itself appeals to it, — I appeal to that justice which binds man to man."[6]

In fact, in most problems concerning Britain's relations with other peoples, Gladstone was in these early years feeling his way; and India was no exception. "The test of a good colonial policy" he stated in a memorandum written sometime during the years 1848 to 1850, "is, that it shall prepare colonies for independence and self-government; as it is the test of a good academy or college, that it shall prepare its pupils for the world."[7] Nor was Gladstone inclined to apply this test only to colonies inhabited by people of the British race. He declared in Parliament in June 1858, at a time when public opinion in Britain had been excited by reports of atrocities in India and the whole basis of British rule in India was being re-examined, that the British went to India not to become

[5] 22 December 1837, *Hansard* (3rd Series), xxix, 1454. [6] *Ibid.*, cxliv, 1799.
[7] Gladstone Papers, Add. MSS. 44738, folio 247.

Indians and settle there permanently but to remain strangers with the only duty of bringing forward Indians; and any such advance, if it were to be a true advance, should not be limited to social progress but should also envisage political development.[8] He stated this more explicitly in a private memorandum written a month later, in July 1858. The object, he wrote, of the Crown taking over the administration of India was "to promote the practical equality before the law of the native population with the British, and to open to them impartially according to merit the honours and rewards of Government. India is to be governed for India; and as far as may be found practicable it is to be governed by India."[9]

How was this to be done? Gladstone from the start placed his faith primarily not in institutions or organization, but in men. He thought little more was required than to send out from Britain the right type of persons to govern India. His first experience in Cabinet strengthened this view. In 1843 the Governor-General, Lord Ellenborough, annexed the province of Sind without securing the assent of either the British Government or the Court of Directors of the East India Company. The Peel Ministry reluctantly acquiesced in the annexation but could not prevent the Directors from recalling Ellenborough for insubordination in this and other matters.[10] Gladstone saw in this further proof of the necessity of having reliable men at the head of the Indian administration. "It may almost, I think" he wrote in 1847 to Dalhousie, who had served under Gladstone at the Board of Trade and had been nominated to the Governor-Generalship, "be said that there is but one thing that can be done here for India, namely to send *just* and able men to govern it."[11]

This weightage given by Gladstone to character in the Viceroy was, to him, justified by the events of 1857 and 1858. In those years of mutiny and revolt, the Governor-General was Gladstone's close friend, Charles Canning (Viceroy, 1856-62); and the high statesmanship of Canning in disregarding the

[8] *Hansard* (3rd Series), cl, 1621.

[9] Gladstone Papers, Add. MSS. 44747, folio 180 ff.

[10] S. Gopal, "Lord Ellenborough and the Home Authorities 1843-44", *Proceedings of the Indian Historical Records Commission* 1953, Part II, pp. 32-5.

[11] W. Lee-Warner, *Life of the Marquis of Dalhousie* (London, 1904), i, 94.

fierce clamour for reprisals and asserting British power without surrender to vindictiveness delighted Gladstone. When in 1862, soon after his return to Britain, Canning died, Gladstone wrote, "Few men have had such an opportunity as he had in India, — of witnessing and striving for the things dearest to God, for justice, mercy and truth; fewer still have so used it."[12] And over thirty years later, in 1895, Gladstone, looking back over the half century of British rule in India in his time, stated that Canning was the greatest Viceroy he had ever known.[13]

Alongside Gladstone's interest in the social and political development of India under British guidance, which forms a consistent strand in his thought from 1831 to 1894, there was his deep interest in imperial finance. Hammond observed that Gladstone had Ireland in his heart, but he had in his brain a disturbing element of England, and of Treasury England.[14] The remark is pertinent to his attitude to India as well. He was convinced that the finances of India were mismanaged, and it was at his instance that Samuel Laing was sent out to India as Finance Member in 1860 to try to introduce sound principles of public finance.[15] Since Laing achieved little, Gladstone frequently, and throughout his years in office, suggested the extension of the principles of Treasury control to Indian finances by the appointment of a Treasury official to the India Council, the body of expert advisers attached to the Secretary of State for India. He believed that it was essential to import British rules and ideas into Indian disbursement.[16] Gladstone was also concerned to relieve the British taxpayer, whom he regarded as burdened unduly by the liabilities of India. This worried him from the time the Crown took over from the East India Company the administration of India. "The subject of English liability", he wrote in a private memorandum of 22

12 P. Knaplund (ed.), *The Gladstone-Gordon Correspondence 1851-1896* (The American Philosophical Society, 1961), p. 41.

13 Cited by Sir A. Godley to Lord Elgin, 19 Sept. 1895, Elgin Papers, corres. with persons in England, Vol. 2, 114, MSS. Eur. F. 84, Ind(ia) Off(ice) Lib(rary).

14 J. L. Hammond, *Gladstone and the Irish Nation* (London, 1938), p. 86.

15 Gladstone to Canning, 18 October 1860, volume of letters from ministers, 41, Canning Papers (in the possession of the Earl of Harewood).

16 See, for example, his letter to Lord Kimberley, 28 August 1893, Kimberley Papers E/6a (in the possession of the present Earl of Kimberley).

July 1859, "for the charges of the Government of India is one of the most formidable ever introduced to the notice of Parliament."[17] In 1867, when the allocation of expenses for the British expedition to Abyssinia was being debated, he commended the efforts to establish, in place of the existing system of 'give and take' between Britain and India, a greater strictness of account and a greater definiteness of relation.[18]

By the time Gladstone formed his first Government in 1868, he was too preoccupied with Ireland to take any direct interest in India. Indeed, if he thought of India at all, it was as the country which provided the model for tenancy legislation in Ireland. In 1869, Sir George Campbell, the chief Commissioner of the central provinces in India, visited Ireland and wrote a small book suggesting that the Bengal Tenancy Act of 1859, which recognized a right of occupancy for tenants and provided for compensation for improvements, could serve as a precedent for Ireland.[19] Morley revealed much later, in a private letter to Lord Ampthill in 1906,[20] that this book of Campbell first inspired the thought underlying the Irish Land Act of 1870, which recognized the tenant's right of occupancy in the form of a right to compensation for disturbance under certain circumstances. But apart from this, India did not figure at all in policy-making in London. Even the choice of the Viceroy in 1869 was not Gladstone's; for the Disraeli Government had, in their last days, appointed Lord Mayo as Viceroy (1869-72), and though Gladstone had considered cancellation of the appointment, he had refrained from doing so; and in India Mayo had carried out what was very much his own policy.[21]

The first Viceroy appointed by Gladstone was Lord Northbrook in 1872. "My own desires" Gladstone wrote to Northbrook soon after the latter's arrival in India, "are chiefly these, that nothing may bring about a sudden, violent or discreditable severance, that we may labour steadily to promote the political training of our native fellow-subjects, and that when we go, if we are ever to go, we may leave a good name and a clean bill

[17] Gladstone Papers, Add. MSS. 44748, folio 108.

[18] *Hansard* (3rd Series), cxc, 390 ff.

[19] *The Irish Land* (London, 1869).

[20] 9 January 1906, Ampthill Papers, vol. 13, MSS. Eur. E. 233, Ind. Off. Lib.

[21] S. Gopal, *British Policy in India 1858-1905* (Cambridge, 1965), p. 64.

of account behind us."[22] This, in a sentence, was the India policy of Gladstone: that while British rule might possibly be permanent, it was the chief duty of the British not to ensure that permanence but to train Indians to assume political responsibility. Gladstone believed, as did others like Macaulay and Munro before him, that the chief objective of an alien administration should be the teaching of its subjects to exercise authority. But Northbrook was hardly the man for the promotion of such a policy. A withdrawn and indeterminate personality, he sought to keep India static and to make no changes that were not absolutely necessary. Gladstone, as was to be expected, approved of Northbrook's decision to repeal the income tax which had been introduced by Mayo;[23] but on the other hand Gladstone was surprised at Northbrook's resistance — after the first Gladstone Ministry had resigned — to the abolition of tariffs and the restoration of free trade.[24]

All in all, Gladstone's first term as Prime Minister had seen little advance in the furtherance of his views on India. Mayo and Northbrook had not shared them. They had been more concerned with maintaining the empire than with training Indians in public life and administration; and Gladstone had made no effort to assert his own principles. But when the Liberal Party was in opposition, the policies of the Disraeli Government, and especially of the Viceroy (Lord Lytton, 1876-80), revived Gladstone's sense of obligation to India. In 1875, while he declared his displeasure at the British propensity to push financial generosity towards India beyond the bounds of reason and justice, he stressed that unless the British presence in India was beneficial to the people of India, the British had no business there at all.[25] Speaking in March 1876 on the Royal Titles Bill, he referred to the Imperial power in India as "that vast and curiously constructed fabric of which we are the stewards, and which it is our duty to maintain so long as any obligation connected with that power remains to be fulfilled."[26] It was what seemed to be a gross abuse of this power by Lytton in passing the Vernacular Press Act that led

22 15 October 1872, Northbrook Papers, vol. 20, part I, p. 74, MSS. Eur. C144, Ind. Off. Lib. 23 *Ibid.*

24 Gladstone to Northbrook, 20 September 1875, Northbrook Papers, vol. 23, folio 248 ff. 25 *Hansard* (3rd Series), ccxxv, 1499. 26 *Ibid.*, ccxxvi, 1739.

Gladstone to raise the matter in the House of Commons in July 1878. Lytton's Government had suspended the standing orders of the Indian Legislature, secured approval by telegraph from the Secretary of State and, in the course of a single day, enacted a measure imposing stringent restrictions on newspapers published in Indian languages. Gladstone condemned the Press Act as a betrayal of trust. He believed that the sole justification for British rule in India would be that India was governed in the interests of the Indians and not of the British. The people of India, he said, realized this and that was why, despite sporadic dissent, their attitude was basically loyal. However, Lytton and his masters acted on the premise that the people of India resented British rule; and this was the basic flaw in their policy.[27] The issues involved in the Vernacular Press Act seemed to Gladstone of such importance that he insisted that the House vote on them.

Soon after, Gladstone expounded in detail his conception of England's mission in India. He emphasized the difficulties of the task. The British were in India travelling on a journey to which honour and duty inexorably bound them but on a route which plainly led into the unknown. It was "a tutelage, unexampled in history." Over a large population inhabiting a vast territory, the British held "a dominion entirely uncontrolled, save by duty and by prudence, measured as we may choose to measure them." But this dominion was exercised by a very few officials, and in Britain there was little interest. However the truth as to India could not too soon be understood. The Conservatives treated India as a possession to be defended, whereas in fact it was a trust to be fulfilled. If the masses of India could be convinced that the British were in their country with a mission and not merely to further their own interests, then there would be a chance of consolidating British rule. Indeed, this would form the best defence of the empire.[28]

In the Midlothian campaign of 1879 and 1880, Gladstone called upon British electors to choose between these rival conceptions of foreign and imperial policy; and he made the war in Afghanistan, on which the Conservative Government had embarked, and Lytton's administration of India, two of the

27 *Ibid.*, ccxlii, 48 ff.

28 "England's Mission", *The Nineteenth Century*, September 1878, pp. 578, 580

main issues of contention. The Afghan war Gladstone described as, among other things, unjust, foolish, frivolous, dangerous and wanton, and he said the pulpit rather than the platform was the proper place from which to condemn it. He asserted that all men, British or Afghan, were equal and had the same rights and that in Afghanistan the British were in conflict with the sentiment of a free people. As for Lytton's administration, "I cannot tell you" said Gladstone, "how dishonouring to England I consider to have been the government of India during the last three years." He accused Disraeli and Lytton of having failed to fulfil Britain's task in India — "the most arduous and perhaps the noblest trust that ever was undertaken by a nation." The assumption of the higher title of Empress of India should have been accompanied by an increase of franchise or of privilege, by augmentation of benefits and by redress of grievances. Instead, the Indian people had been distrusted, the press had been gagged and funds, raised ostensibly for famine relief, had been spent on a ruinous war. By these means, said Gladstone, the Conservatives had impaired the foundations of the empire and had forsaken their duty "to consecrate the Empire to the Almighty by the strict application of the principles of justice and goodwill, of benevolence and mercy."[29]

So in the four years of Lytton's Viceroyalty Gladstone put forward the same principles which had inspired his Newdigate Prize poem of 1831 — that the peoples of India and Asia had the same rights as those of Britain and Europe, that the sentiments and needs of the Indian people should be respected and that Britain had a mission in India. These principles had by now become the policy to which the Liberal Party was committed and, with the Liberal victory in the 1880 elections, the policy to which the new Government were committed. This was certainly the way in which Indian opinion regarded it, and Gladstone was aware of this. "I know" he told the electors of Midlothian, "the news of these elections has passed to India, reached the mind and the heart of many millions of your Indian fellow-subjects and I will venture to say that it has

[29] *Political Speeches in Scotland* (Edinburgh, 1880), i, pp. 199-203.

gladdened every heart among them."[30] The new Viceroy, therefore, would be regarded as the personal representative of Gladstone, sent out to give expression and effect in India to the new temper and energy of British Liberalism. So the selection of the right man seemed to the Prime Minister of more importance than ever, and it was only as a third choice that he selected Ripon (1880-84), a man who deserved well of the Liberal Party but had irritated Gladstone by becoming a Roman Catholic.[31]

Ripon, however, was the right choice in so far that he whole-heartedly shared Gladstone's views. He withdrew British troops from Afghanistan and established friendly relations with its ruler. Acting on what was virtually a specific mandate from the Prime Minister, he repealed Lytton's Vernacular Press Act. Gladstone also suggested to Ripon that he should amend the Arms Act of 1878, which stipulated that no Indian could possess firearms without a licence, for Gladstone believed that such special laws restricting the possession of firearms indicated, as did the Vernacular Press Act, a lack of trust in the people. But, despite the Prime Minister's support, Ripon's amending bill was smothered by official resistance.

This failure of Ripon to have his way on the Arms Act was a warning of what was to come in his handling of more important issues. The Afghan settlement and the repeal of the Press Act were only part of what Gladstone termed the "great undoing process which the late Government bequeathed to us."[32] When Ripon proceeded to undertake constructive measures, his efforts were virtually destroyed by lack of resolution. The Viceroy sought to strengthen local self-government in the hope that it would serve as a means of political education, promote self-confidence among the educated classes of India and train them for participation in government. Ripon thought also that the gradual admission of Indians to a larger influence in the administration, and a training to exercise that influence, would do more to secure the continuance of British

[30] 2 April 1880. W. E. Gladstone, *The Midlothian Campaign* (Edinburgh, 1880), p. 194.

[31] S. Gopal, *The Viceroyalty of Lord Ripon* (Oxford, 1953), pp. 2-3; Gopal, *British Policy*, p. 129.

[32] 13 March 1882, cited in Gopal, *British Policy*, p. 145.

rule in India than any policy of repression. It was not merely, therefore, the duty of Britain, but in her interest, to train educated Indians for public life and seek their support. Gladstone was cordially in favour of this policy of local self-government. It was in accordance with his theory that local responsibilities prepare men for national tasks; as he phrased it, it is liberty alone which fits men for liberty.[33] He was in sympathy also with Ripon's belief that the support of educated Indians would strengthen British rule and with the doctrine that it was Britain's duty to train Indians for self-government. "We are pledged to India," he wrote to Ripon,[34] "I may say to mankind, for its performance; and we have no choice but to apply ourselves to the accomplishment of the work, the redemption of the pledge, with every faculty we possess." But Ripon's local self-government policy was not a great success. The officials showed little enthusiasm and Indians, while they appreciated the spirit of Ripon's endeavour, displayed scant interest. The policy only served to frighten the British community in India as being one more effort to introduce into India what they regarded as the subversive principles of Gladstone.

Ripon's Government then introduced a bill removing racial discrimination in the sphere of criminal jurisdiction. Indian judges in the districts, i.e. outside the towns, were disqualified from hearing cases in which the accused were Europeans; and the Government sought to remove this anomaly. There was an immediate storm of protest, not so much because this was a major matter, as because it formed a convenient issue round which the British community's dislike of Ripon and of Gladstone could crystallize. To ignore and overcome the opposition would, of course, have been the right thing to do. Gladstone told Ripon that his interest in the matter was great and that his "prejudice or conviction as to principles" was wholly and warmly with the Viceroy — "wholly as to my understanding of the general view; warmly because in that general view great interests of the future seem to me to be at stake."[35]

33 Letter to W. E. Forster, 12 April 1882, R. Morley, *The Life of William Ewart Gladstone* (London, 1903), iii, 58.

34 24 November 1881, cited in Gopal, *British Policy*, p. 147.

35 1 June 1883. Ripon Papers, Add. MSS. 43515, no. 26, British Museum. The number of the manuscript is as of 1951, when the papers were consulted.

But again Ripon showed himself lacking in determination. He believed in Gladstone's ideals but lacked Gladstone's moral stamina and reserve of underlying strength. Setting aside considerations of principle, he offered to reduce the scope of the bill. The Prime Minister was not pleased with this anxiety to compromise. He assured Ripon that he would accept whatever the Viceroy decided, because it was for him to deal with the matter; but, Gladstone added, "There is a question to be answered; where, in a country like India, lies the ultimate power, and if it lies for the present on one side but for the future on the other, a problem has to be solved as to preparation for that future, and it may become right and needful to chasten the saucy pride so apt to grow in the English mind towards foreigners, and especially toward foreigners whose position has been subordinate."[36] Gladstone could never find any justification for racial arrogance; and he wrote to his son Henry, who was at this time in Calcutta and was one of the three or four Englishmen who supported the bill, that he had no patience with the "narrow and domineering" spirit of the British community in India.[37]

On learning of Gladstone's staunch views on the subject, Ripon, in his weakness, sought to transfer responsibility to the Home Government; and he asked the Cabinet either to take a decision on the bill or to submit the matter to the House of Commons. Gladstone sharply refused to do either. The Cabinet was unanimous and firm in its general support of Ripon and the Prime Minister repeatedly gave expression to this in the House. But he was unwilling to go beyond such general assurances of confidence in the Viceroy and to take a specific decision on pending Indian legislation. In fact, the question was not even brought up before a full meeting of the Cabinet. The principle, said Gladstone,[38] was beyond dispute; what was under discussion was a problem of Indian administration which had been initiated in India and should be settled there.

[36] 17 April 1883, cited in Gopal, *British Policy*, p. 151.

[37] 6 February 1884. See F. W. Hirst, *Gladstone as Financier and Economist* (London, 1931), ch. xix.

[38] Gladstone to Granville, 28 September 1883 and Granville to Gladstone, 1 October 1883. A. Ramm, *The Political Correspondence of Gladstone and Granville 1876-86* (Oxford, 1962), ii, nos. 1106 and 1107.

Ripon could not, therefore, evade a decision and virtually surrendered to the opposition. The bill was so modified as to become almost meaningless. Because of the personal failure of the Viceroy, the principles of Gladstonian Liberalism suffered a severe reverse in India.

Ripon's successor was also chosen by the Gladstone Government; but Dufferin (Viceroy, 1884-88) was only nominally a Liberal and he had no intention, as he described it,[39] of 'Midlothianizing' India. Gladstone too had, in these years, no time for Indian details; and the experiment of administering India according to his principles, which had begun under such favourable auspices in 1880, petered out.

However, in the years that followed, Gladstone was able to perform a few minor services for India. Dufferin had suggested that the legislative councils in India should be given the right of interpellation and authority to discuss the budget, and that the principle of election, in however dilute a form, should be utilized in the formation of these councils. The Salisbury Government were opposed to this, and even Northbrook, who had served as one of Gladstone's viceroys, advised against any such legislation lest Indian and Irish politics get mixed and Gladstone use what Northbrook termed "dangerous" language.[40] Finally, in 1892, for fear that if Gladstone returned to office he might introduce a far more radical measure, the Salisbury Ministry went ahead with legislation for Indian Council reforms. Their bill permitted the Government of India to nominate non-officials "on the basis of recommendations" and empowered the authorities in India to make rules enabling the discussion of the annual budget and the asking of questions. The Indian National Congress, which had been formed some years earlier as the organization of politically conscious Indians, sent to Britain a delegation which sought Gladstone's support for the introduction of the principle of elections.[41] Gladstone promised to help, and his speech in the House was cleverly designed to secure this. He did not

[39] To Sir Fitzjames Stephen, 28 July 1885, Reel 525 of Dufferin Papers (microfilm copy), Ind. Off. Lib.

[40] Northbrook to Lansdowne, 1 March 1889, Lansdowne Papers, VIII/1, no. 42, MSS. Eur. D558, Ind. Off. Lib.

[41] S. N. Banerjea, *A Nation in Making* (Calcutta, 1963), p. 105.

criticize the Government for failing to provide explicitly for elections and assumed that the term "nomination on the basis of recommendations" was a euphemism for elections. It would not, he said, be well or wise for Parliament to proceed to particulars. "It is not our business to devise machinery for the purpose of Indian Government; it is our business to give ample information as to what we believe to be sound principles of government.... What I wish is that these first steps shall be genuine, and whatever amount of scope they give to the elective principle shall be real. What we want is to get to the real heart and mind — at the most upright sentiment and the most enlightened thought of the people of India. We may be justified in expecting something more than a merely nominal beginning in this great and magnificent undertaking."[42] Gladstone's speech delighted the Government in that it had prevented a division in the House; but it satisfied Indian opinion in that it drew from the Government a commitment to the principle of elections.

In 1892 Gladstone was back as Prime Minister. Lord Lansdowne (Viceroy, 1888-94), described it as "a very serious misfortune" for India, because he expected Gladstone to resume his efforts of the eighteen-eighties.[43] In fact, Gladstone's mind was far from India. He sent out as Viceroy an unimaginative person, Lord Elgin (1894-99), primarily on the ground that he was a close friend of Lord Rosebery. There was only one occasion when Gladstone in his last term showed a flicker of interest in India. It had for long been a demand of the Indian National Congress that examinations for recruitment to the Indian Civil Service should be held both in Britain and in India, so as to enable more Indians to compete and qualify without having to travel overseas. In 1893 the Liberal back-benchers in the House of Commons took the whips by surprise and passed a resolution recommending that examinations be held simultaneously in both countries. Gladstone desired that the Government of India should be warned against displaying a hostile spirit to this resolution.[44] He seems to have been

42 28 March 1892, *Hansard* (4th Series), iii, 78 ff.

43 Lansdowne to Lord Cross, 19 July 1892, Lansdowne Papers, corres. with Secretary of State, vol. 4, no. 33.

44 Gladstone to Kimberley, 3 June 1893, Kimberley Papers, vol. E/6a.

genuinely anxious to meet the wishes of the House and of the Congress; but it was commonly believed that he wished merely to appease all sections of the Liberal Party in order to ensure the success of his Irish Home Rule Bill. "When", wrote the Duke of Argyll to Lansdowne,[45] "*shall* we get rid of this fanatical octogenarian, who has no interest in the future? He never did care for India, and, I *suspect*, would argue in private that it does us no good to keep it!"

Gladstone did not achieve much in India. The Viceroys selected by him were men of slight calibre; and he himself was preoccupied elsewhere. Nor did he modify his ideas on finance even during Ripon's term. No critic of the Disraeli Government had been more vehement in condemning British aggression in Afghanistan and the foisting of unnecessary expenditure on the Indian treasury; but when in office he was unwilling to sanction more than five million pounds as a grant from the British Exchequer[46] — a sum which was less than half the total expenditure. In 1882 the Government of India were directed to despatch at their cost a contingent of troops to Egypt. When Ripon in India and Henry Fawcett in London protested, Gladstone yielded only to the extent of sanctioning a grant of £500,000 out of a total expenditure of nearly 1.3 million pounds; and he silenced Ripon and Fawcett in order to secure a majority in the House on what he treated as a vote of censure.[47] But despite the lack of results and his rigidity in financial matters, Gladstone succeeded in winning the confidence and affection of the Indian people. The experiment in Ripon's time to govern India in accordance with Gladstone's principles came, in practical terms, almost to nothing; but the immediate failure led to a later and more eventful triumph. For it kept alive the conviction that political and social advance in India should be a co-operative adventure of the rulers and

45 14 June 1893, Lansdowne Papers, VIII/5, no. 58.

46 Gladstone to Lord Hartington, 23 October 1880 and 8 February 1881, and Hartington to Gladstone, 9 February 1881. Gladstone Papers, Add. MSS. 44145, folios 135, 200, and 202.

47 Fawcett to Gladstone, 15 September 1882, Gladstone Papers, Add. MSS. 44156, folio 139; Gopal, *Ripon*, p. 217; Gladstone's speech, 27 July 1883, *Hansard* (3rd Series), cclxxxii, 806 ff; Gladstone to Granville, 28 July 1883, Ramm, *The Political Correspondence of Gladstone and Granville 1876-86*, ii, no. 1072.

the ruled. The emotional memory of Gladstonian Liberalism remained a prominent and a fertile element of the Indian scene right down to our own times.

# SOME OFFICIAL BRITISH ATTITUDES TOWARDS EUROPEAN SETTLEMENT AND COLONIZATION IN INDIA UP TO 1865

JOHN RIDDY

"The want of permanent residence among the British Population tells against it. It is a fleeting population always looking ultimately to home. Its permanent affections and interests are not here, and there is a feeling of sadness about it all."[1] Thus Lord Minto (Viceroy, 1905-10) wrote to the Secretary of State on 28 May, 1906. "We all feel we are mere sojourners in the land, only camping and on the march."[2] Minto was repeating, in vivid form, a sentiment which lurked in the minds of almost all Britons called to rule India, whether as servants of the East India Company or of the Crown. More than fifty years before, Sir Charles Wood, President of the Board of Control, had voiced the same sentiment to Lord Dalhousie:

> I hope we shall govern India for many years; but it is clear to my mind that we shall always govern it as aliens, not settling in the country or having much in common with the mass of the people whom we govern.[3]

[1] Quoted by Mary, Countess Minto, in *India: Minto and Morley* (London, 1934), p. 29.

[2] *Ibid.*, p. 153. Minto was quoting Morley, who had said that British India was "the most fleeting society in the world."

[3] Dalhousie to Wood, Letter Book of India Board, iv, 12, MSS. Eur. F. 78. (This and all subsequent MS. references are to the India Office Library collection.)

In the development of this sentiment the Mutiny marks no watershed. Even those who spanned the Mutiny, and who thought the most clearly and deeply about the problem of restoring British power on a permanent basis were infected by this underlying pessimism. Lord Canning, corresponding with Wood on the difficulty of getting the 'unofficial' European community to cooperate in the task of rebuilding after the shattering effects of the Mutiny, said:

> We have the great disadvantage that nineteen-twentieths of the Englishmen who come here have no tie or permanent interest in the country and desire none. They come to make their money and be off.[4]

It is rare indeed to find in the writings of those responsible for the maintenance of British government in India any thought that a physical settlement by people of British extraction could or should be other than transitory. Certainly no British administrator was to match the bright optimism of that great Portuguese Viceroy, Albuquerque, writing to his sovereign in 1512: "In the eyes of the peoples of India it is an assured thing that we have come to stay in this land, since they see our men planting trees, building houses of stone and lime, and rearing boys and girls."[5] Perhaps the closest that the British Administration ever came to Albuquerque's vision was in the writings of J. M. Thorburn, who allowed himself the luxury of seeing India clear in centuries to come as a British dominion.

A Madras Civil Servant, Thorburn travelled widely in India. In *The Great Game*[6] he issued a frank appeal to imperial acquisitiveness. He quoted with evident approval a contemporary commentator in the *Fortnightly Review* who believed that wherever Europe showed herself in the East, "Whether as missionary or in. . .her warlike power, she brings only blessings in her train, and scatters the seeds of a new order of things."[7] He thought "Hindus have rights in their country; but so has mankind."[8] In the Indian uplands "There are tens of thousands

[4] Canning to Wood, 8 October, 1860, MSS. Eur. F. 78, Box 2, bundle 6.

[5] Quoted by C. R. Boxer, "Golden Goa", *History Today*, November, 1954, p. 756.

[6] 2nd edn., Madras, 1875. [7] *Ibid.*, p.1. [8] *Ibid.*, p.66.

of fertile square miles. . . [where] even the poorest Englishmen may live. . .healthily and far more comfortably than in their birthplace; and raise. . .vigorous sons of the soil."[9] He recognized that to deflect the flood of emigrants from Britain then settling in North America, South Africa and Australasia, the Government of India would need to invest money in assisted passages and in providing guaranteed protection, political privileges and economic concessions. Weighted pensions might encourage military pensioners to retire to the Indian hills, their offspring forming a reserve force of sturdy Englishmen ready to crush any insurrection. Leadership would come from a class of wealthier settlers, exploiting the *zemindaris* (large, landed estates, frequently sequestrated and sold for arrears of land revenue payments) and the vacant waste tracts in Burma, Assam, the Central Provinces, Sind, Kashmir and even Malwa, available at modest cost. A "lavish bestowal of. . . Baronetcies" might attract this class. However, a few years later, in a study entitled *India Solvent*,[10] Thorburn makes no mention of European settlement as a solution to India's financial problems; *The Great Game* may have been written with tongue in cheek.

The problems of European settlement and land purchase, of marriage and the raising of children were with the Company from the earliest days. In the 1670's Gerald Aungier, Governor of Bombay, had suggested to the Company Directors in London that "English women of the meaner sort, but of honest reputation" be shipped out to Bombay, because his soldiers "do frequently converse with the country women, whom we force them to marry for the preventing of sin and God's judgement thereon."[11] But the few Englishwomen willing to go out to India had refused to marry anyone of lower rank than a gentleman, had carried on disgracefully and had generally reduced English prestige.

By the time of Lord North's Regulating Act of 1773, the transitoriness of the English community in India was considered a *sine qua non* of the survival of the Company's trading monopoly. It was so widely accepted that secular colonization would

[9] *Ibid.*, p.73. [10] J. M. Thorburn, *India Solvent* (Madras, 1880).

[11] Quoted in Sir Charles Fawcett, *The English Factories in India* (*The Western Presidency*), *1670-1677*, New Series (Oxford, 1936), i, 73.

be followed by the disaffection of the natives, the disturbance of the land revenue collections, the overthrow of established custom and law and the disappearance of profitable trade in India, that there was little or no discussion. The historian looking for material on European colonization before 1833 has to be content with shreds of evidence and with comments in the margins, as it were, of more important debates on the continuance of the Company's trade monopoly. It was possible for the Company's champions to assume unchallenged that colonization was, like missionary activity, an evil accident, to be prevented by the simple repetition of the fears of the Company's officers, without there being any need for supporting material evidence. The discussion, what there was of it, was conducted almost as monologue until 1813. The Company's belief that colonization was unfortunate, undesirable or impossible was accepted even by the enemies of the Company's monopoly.[12] This belief is first apparent, understandably enough, in the period of the American Revolution. It is perhaps no mere coincidence that the earliest contribution to a collection of minutes and memoranda defining the Company's case against European colonization[13] is a Bengal Revenue Consultation dated 12 May, 1775, a day on which General Gage was involved in the preliminary skirmishes of the American War of Independence. On the question whether it was in the interest of Great Britain to colonize India, Philip Francis, Counsellor to the Governor-General, Warren Hastings, argued that arrears of land revenue could easily be collected from natives through the Diwani Court, but that Englishmen would have to be sued in the Crown Courts; he concluded that the "collections would universally fail." George Monson, minuting on the same question, pointed to the "few wants of the natives. . .satisfied with the mere necessities of life. . .allowing them to pay larger taxes to Government from the same

12 For example, see J. C. Marshman's review of S. Wheatley, "Letter to His Grace the Duke of Devonshire, on the state of Ireland and the general efforts of Colonisation", *Friend of India* (Quarterly Series), No. XII, May 1825. Marshman, missionary and champion of missionary endeavour, thought that America and Australia would absorb all British emigration.

13 *Papers relating to the settlement of Europeans in India* (Calcutta, 1854), India Office Library Tracts, dlxxiv, 11.

quantity of land in the same state of culture than an European can afford to do."[14] The Company's servants in India believed that while the Indians could be governed by the Company, Europeans could not; furthermore, the latter would prove an unsettling influence on the normally docile natives. In a Bengal Revenue Consultation of 18 May, 1785, John Shore expressed fears that increased contact with Europeans would lessen respect for British rule. These fears recur. "I feel...the utmost delicacy is requisite in guarding against unrestrained intercourse with the natives of India",[15] said Henry Dundas, when President of the Board of Control in 1793. And on 7 December Dundas received from Lord Cornwallis (Governor-General, 1786-93), who had (by Regulation XXXVIII of 1793) taken power to control the residence of Company Europeans more than ten miles from a Presidency town, the opinion that "Europeans should be discouraged and prevented as much as possible from colonising and settling in our possessions of India."[16] Lord Cornwallis pointed out the need to relieve European troops often, and to secure their return to Europe at the expiry of their service by making pensions and allowances payable only in Europe. Henry Dundas later reaffirmed this stand: "No principle ought ever to be tolerated or acted upon that does not proceed on the basis of India being considered as the *temporary* residence of a great British Establishment."[17] On 4 February, 1801, the Court of Directors resolved against colonization.[18]

The Company's attitude was not changed by the successive breaches in its monopoly. Indeed, it almost seems that as the laws regulating missionary activity and trading in India by Europeans not in the Company's employ relaxed, so the attitude of both Directors and Administration against colonization hardened. Dundas, in his letter to the Company Chairman of 2 April, 1800, explained: "Nothing certainly can be more just or natural than...that the capital of the British subjects resident in India should be brought home...where

14 *Ibid.*, p.13. 15 *Ibid.*, p.16. 16 *Ibid.*, p. 17.

17 *Ibid.*, p. 19; also in Montgomery Martin (ed.), *The Marquess Wellesley's Despatches, Minutes and Correspondence during his Administration in India* (London, 1837), v, 121 ff. My italics.

18 *Ibid.*, p. 20.

it is desirable that all capital should ultimately settle."[19] In a summary of applications for licences under the 1813 Charter Renewal Act, dated 27 February, 1818, the Directors informed the then President of the Board, George Canning, of their agreement with the "opinion among the many eminently distinguished persons who...have acted a prominent part in the Company's affairs in India" that

> India has never been considered and administered as a British Colony.... The system applied to this species of dependency has always been regarded as singularly ill-adapted to a country rich, populous and powerful in itself, and the inhabitants of which are so dissimilar from Europeans in their manners and customs, social institutions and religious beliefs.[20]

The antipathy towards colonization may be seen in a large measure as an expression of well-bred disgust at the excesses of which the English lower orders were thought capable. There was a fear of disturbances caused by persons not restricted by the Company's covenant (which stated that the natives should be treated well), and indirectly of the disruptive political example likely to be set by Englishmen aggressively aware of their rights and liberties.[20a] The baneful influence of the English lower orders upon Indians was to be a recurrent theme in any discussions of colonization in India, there being in many of the Company's officers a sense that those not reared as gentlemen would unnecessarily complicate the task of maintaining order among the Indians. For instance, John Jacob believed as a result of his 30 years' Indian experience that "the native Indian soldier should never be associated with any Europeans but Gentlemen... [and]... never see an European in any but a superior position."[21] This opinion was shared by Hervey Harris Greathed, Commissioner in Meerut in May, 1857; while H. W. Reeves, Revenue Commissioner of the Southern Division of the Deccan, wrote: "I should expect as the first fruits of European colonization a great amount of

19 Martin (ed.), *Wellesley's Despatches*, v, 123.

20 *Papers...Settlement of Europeans...*, dlxxiv, 8. 20a *Ibid.*, pp. 8-9.

21 Quoted by H.T. Lambrick, *John Jacob of Jacobabad* (London, 1960), p. 357.

evil to natives from the vicious example and tyranny of the settlers; we should also have European pauperism to contend with; our criminal and civil business would increase."[22] On 12 July, 1859, Sir John Lawrence was questioned by the Chairman of the Select Committee on European Colonization and Settlement in India on the advantage to the notoriously inefficient Indian police of having British military orphans serve as petty police officers and junior superintendents. He replied: "I would be for employing native officers over natives in preference to Europeans . . . first of all, because there is a great antagonism between the two races". Although aware of the immense influence of the "well-educated, moral Englishman", he did not "think that the majority of men in the class of life of N.C.O.'s would answer that description" and thus that the "best kind of native" was not prepared to serve under them.[23] The great fear was that the discovery by Indians that Britons could be other than gentlemen would undermine morale and discipline.

The desire to protect Indians from making this discovery was a strong factor behind the objections to rendering Europeans amenable to the ordinary Mofussil courts and to native justice. Contact with these courts would bring out the worst in the unofficial European, making him censorious, venal or tyrannical; and at the same time the sight of the European at his less than perfect would diminish that mysterious power, 'European prestige'. Lawrence was strongly against making Europeans amenable to native magistrates, and was "quite certain it would work badly."[24]

The inadequacy of local justice became another argument against promiscuous European settlement. In the course of the 1833 Charter Renewal debate Charles Grant the younger, as President of the Board of Control, repeatedly made the point, the essence of which was to recur during the hearings of the Select Committee on colonization in 1858-59, that:

> If the Provinces are to be thrown open to the British settler, let it be universally understood, that no doubt may remain,

22 *Parl(iamentary), Papers, H(ouse) of C(ommons)*, 1857-58, xlii, Paper 180, 21.
23 *Ibid.*, 1859, v, Answers to questions 347-349.
24 *Ibid.*, question 459.

> nor any ground for subsequent reproach, that they go to live under a despotic and imperfect but strong government — that they carry with them no rights but such as are possessed by the natives themselves; and that it is impossible at present to give them either that security and easy enjoyment of landed property or those ready remedies for private wrongs which more regularly constituted governments afford.[25]

It is worth recalling that the European was in a privileged legal position, in that native courts had a strictly limited jurisdiction over him. Except for petty civil cases, where he could enter into a bond to recognize local jurisdiction, and those matters in which the local Collector was competent to pronounce, most civil and criminal cases were referred by writ of *certiorari* to the Supreme Courts in the three main Presidency capitals, where hearings were before British judges. The law-enforcement machinery, depending on underpaid agents, was slow, inefficient and corrupt, as acknowledged in the report of the Select Committee of 1858-59.[26] The lack of an effective police system especially in Bengal and Assam, at least until the legal and police reforms of the 1860's, reinforced in the settler his sense of self-reliance, and his willingness to take the law into his own hands. This is amply illustrated by the history of the indigo disputes, and by the labour troubles that beset the early efforts at establishing the tea industry in Assam, especially in the 1860's.[27]

India was not a country in which the shock of financial failure could, for Europeans, be easily cushioned by the social structure, and this was especially true of those parts of India which climate and availability of land made attractive to settlers.[27a] Act XXI of 1869 was directed against the indigent,

25 *Hansard* (3rd Series), xviii, 738. Grant was quoting Sir Charles Grey.

26 See B. B. Misra, *The Central Administration of the East India Company 1773-1834* (Manchester, 1959), 298-377, for a review of the police system under the Company.

27 For example, see Dunne's case, covered at length in *Parl. Papers* (*H. of C.*), 1867, Paper 124, pp. 357-384.

27a See for example the description by the Special Commissioner for the Assam Tea Districts, J. W. Edgar, on the ruin and starvation of numbers of "young gentlemen . . . engaged in England" who were turned adrift by the collapse of many tea companies in the slump of the late 1860's in *ibid.*, 1874, xlviii, *Report on the Tea Cultivation in India*, p. 1, *et seq.*

vagrant European. The Indian police were empowered to bring any Englishman apparently a vagrant before a police magistrate or J.P. for committal to a workhouse.[28] Perhaps it is not surprising that the official fear that the unofficial settler would somehow snap the thin thread of miraculous, hypnotized respect by which the British maintained their position is also evident in the legislation by which, when the principle of settlement was eventually conceded, the right to purchase and hold land was restricted in such a way that only the man of means, by implication a gentleman, could venture successfully.

Before 1813, the law, backed up by distance, dangers and disease, largely prevented the immigration of the unofficial European. The first major breach in the Company's exclusive legal control was Clause 33 of the Charter Renewal Act of 1813, which made provision for persons to settle in India under licence given by the Company's Court of Directors, refusal of licence being subject to appeal. Clauses 34 to 39 placed anyone going to India under the Company's rules and regulations, and gave discretionary power to the Governor-General or any President Governor to revoke the licence. Clause 93 made pensions payable to officers only in England; Clause 104 confirmed the power of the Governor-General to deport illicit residents to Britain; and Clause 108 made necessary the possession of a separate licence for those residing more than ten miles from the Presidency towns. No legal contract would be enforceable unless such a licence was deposited in the local civil court. This clause contributed, along with the general difficulty of registration and record-keeping in India, to that feeling among Europeans, especially indigo planters, that obligations and contracts were only to be maintained by illegal force. Although a high proportion of applicants were successful — of 1547 applications made between 1813 and 1831, 1324 were granted[29] — the restrictive nature of the licensing,

[28] It is amusing that at the time of the Ilbert Bill furore in 1883, Mr. Justice Dosabhoy Framji, a Parsi and one of the few 'natives' to have been appointed Justice of the Peace, ordered a group of Salvation Army missionaries in Bombay to be confined under this Act, on the grounds that they were vagrants. *Friend of India*, 27 March, 1883.

[29] J. Crawfurd, *Notes on the Settlement or Colonisation of British Subjects in India*, 2nd. edn. (London, 1837), p. 19.

the high cost of the passage to India,[30] and the very nature of that country repelled most private settlers.

By the late 1820's, under the Governor-Generalships of Lords Amherst (1823-28) and Bentinck (1828-35), a genuine debate on colonization had emerged, and for the first time the case for colonization, albeit on a very limited scale, was heard. The greatest obstacle was felt to be the difficulty facing Europeans wishing to hold cultivable land in leasehold or freehold. The land available and opened up by communication and settled administration was densely populated; in the areas of the Permanent Settlement the relationship between the *ryot* (peasant) and the *zamindar* appears to have been close, and the latter unwilling to sublet to Europeans; the extent of the waste land at the disposal of Government close to the Presidency towns was undefined, dangerous to health, and often subject to native rights of grazing and firewood. Above all, there was the sustained antipathy of Leadenhall Street to the settler-farmer. When Bentinck proposed to approve leaseholds for European indigo farmers in 1829, the Directors replied in language which, for all its discretion, cannot hide the rebuke to Bentinck and their aversion to the notion :

> You well know that the authorities in England as well as your predecessors in the Government of India have always regarded the question whether the European should be permitted to hold any permanent interest in land as one of the most serious in Indian policy; nor has there been any measure, in their opinion, which required more mature deliberation and cautious proceeding than one by which Europeans would be . . . entitled to mix themselves with the natives.[31]

30 £100 first class, £60 second class, £35-40 steerage. It is perhaps worth recalling that the emigration flow from the British Isles was by 1832 over 100,000 a year, and that in the fifty years from 1815 it was well over 5,500,000. (See, for example, *Parl. Papers* (*H. of C.*) 1863, xxxviii, 2-3.

31 *Papers. . .Settlement of Europeans. . .*, dlxxiv, 28-9; see also p. 95, H. T. Prinsep's memorandum opposing European landholding as opening the door to land jobbing.

Englishmen intending to farm had therefore to resort to subterfuge; holding land through 'front' nominees; or by making private arrangements with individual farmers. Until after the Mutiny by far the most popular crop cultivated was indigo.[32] The European entrepreneur usually established a factory to process the plant grown by the local *ryots* who received cash advances on the crop. Such advances could rarely be redeemed and came to be a permanent and increasing burden on the peasant, often descending from father to son. From the legal inability to hold land, and from the difficulty faced by investors — usually retired Company factors or Civilians — in finding suitable qualified and licensed European managers (which compelled the employment of individuals illegally resident,— "Frenchmen, ships' carpenters and ships' cooks", as Alexander Forbes branded them[33] — prepared to take risks within and without the law to obtain a quick return on investment) arose evils which were to cloud the issues in the debate on European immigration for settlement in India.

Thrice at least in the 1820's the Government of India attempted to liberalize the system and to increase India's attractiveness to the European farmer of means. In 1824, Lord Amherst, and in 1829 Lord Bentinck, during their periods as Governors-General, attempted to produce rules of conduct and tenure which might afford the wealthy European a chance to establish a foothold in the lands of the Permanent Settlement; and in 1825 an effort was made to open the waste lands of the Sunderbans, the fertile but unhealthy area at the mouth of the Ganges, to permanent European enterprise.[33a]

32 Although the Assam Tea Co. began operations in the later 1830's and was followed by other experimental tea companies in the 1840's, it was not until after the Canning-Wood tenurial reforms of 1861-62 that the industry really took root. See *The Imperial Gazetteer of India* (Oxford, 1931), vol.3; and H. A. Antrobus, *A History of the Assam Company, 1839-1953* (London, 1954), *passim*.

33 *Parl. Papers* (*H. of C.*) 1859, v, question 2357.

33a This unsuccessful attempt gave way to fresh terms of 16 March 1830, under which any amount of land in the Sunderbans could be taken up rent-free for 20 years. However, malaria and the difficulties of clearing the land and finding labour brought the pioneers down; in January 1842 a petition from all the early grantees who had not already thrown in their concessions asked the government to extend the rent-free tenure to 30 years. The Sunderbans were to be the wreck of many fortunes (see e.g. evidence to Select Committee on Colonization, 1858-9, *ibid.*, 1859, v, *passim*).

Coffee had been grown in Calcutta in the 18th century, and high prices in European markets led Lord Amherst in 1824 to prescribe regulations for land tenure by Europeans as the best means to revive cultivation in Bengal. He pointed to the advantages that might be expected.[34] Recognizing that there was a speculative element in the enterprise, he thought only European acumen and intelligence were up to the task.[35] The interest of Indian farmers and Europeans alike would be protected by making leases registrable by the appropriate Collector, who would have the final ruling on matters of registration. On matters concerning the adjustment of boundaries and rent, there was right of appeal to the Board of Revenue. Of particular interest was his view that: "It appears for several reasons desirable that the tenure of the European planters should be that of leaseholders; not that of proprietors of the land." He laid down in his rules that all parties possessing an interest in the soil had to give consent. One clause provided that a European disturbing his contract or the peace might have his lease sold up by order of the Governor-in-Council. Coffee had to be the main crop, although some land for household needs might be allowed. In spite of the extension of these rules to encourage the growth of sugar cane and cotton,[36] only five parties had taken advantage of them by 1829,[37] the leases amounting to some 6,000 acres in all.

The indigo interests pressed hard to have the concessions extended to cover indigo cultivation, and in 1829 the argument was taken a step further by Lord Bentinck, strongly supported in his Council by Sir Charles Metcalfe. Fourteen Calcutta merchant houses presented a Memorial in January, 1829, which laid heavy stress on the difficulties the indigo 'planters' had in making the system of advances, on which two-thirds of all the indigo grown in Bengal depended, work; the other third being grown on land leased indirectly through nominees.[38]

34 Bengal Revenue Consultations, 7 May, 1824, quoted in *ibid.*, 1843, xxxv, 21.

35 *Ibid.*, p. 3. 36 *Ibid.*, p. 6.

37 *Papers. . .Settlement of Europeans. . .* ,dlxxiv, 56.

38 The unhappy relationship between planter/merchant and *ryot* is neatly epitomised by Bengal Regulation VI of 1823 which gave legal cover to indigo 'planters' who wanted to put their own guards round fields sown with indigo against the very *ryots* who had farmed the land.

Bentinck, in Resolutions dated 17 February, 1829, extended to indigo planters the leasehold concession granted to coffee growers. Two days later, Metcalfe concurred: "I have long lamented that our countrymen in India are excluded from the possession of land and other ordinary rights of peaceable subjects."[39]

He continued that he was "further convinced that our possession of India must always be precarious, unless we take root by having an influential portion of the population attached to our government by common interests and sympathies"; and that British settlers would "conduce to the stability of our rule."[40] He looked forward to the production of codified rules to govern the relations between British settlers and Indians, and to the unification of the legal and judicial systems, currently governing the behaviour of the two groups.

Even more significant was Lord Bentinck's spirited defence of his Government's Resolutions.[41] He noted first the failure of Indian commerce and industry to match European competition. In 1828 the Company's Directors had announced the abandonment of the only remaining portion of their monopoly trade from India, in cotton piece goods, owing to the unsaleability of the Indian hand-woven product in Britain.[42] Bentinck looked to British enterprise to make good the deficiency by setting up, for example, cotton-spinning and weaving plants. Similarly, he saw nothing but benefit from the introduction of European agricultural enterprise; having now decided that "the occasional misconduct of the planters is as nothing compared to the sum of good they have diffused around them."[43] Indeed he foresaw, from the proposed extensive settlement of Europeans and their free admission to the possession of landed property, improvement in everything from communication and public works to the availability of ready money, and scoffed at fears that it would lead to a revolution such as had occurred in British North America.[44] Bentinck thought that such a view was based on the misconception that the ordinary British manual worker would thrive in India, whereas "India offers no advantage to the

[39] *Papers. . .Settlement of Europeans. . .*,dlxxiv, 33.

[40] *Ibid.* [41] *Ibid.*, p.34. [42] *Ibid.*, p.36. [43] *Ibid.*, p.39. [44] *Ibid.*, p.40.

European who has only his labour to bring to the market." Instead, "The climate must in almost all our districts confine the European husbandman to the work of general superintendence."[45] Only Britons of property could find a profitable place in India, and of these only the hardiest and best in character would survive. So limited were the prospects that no encouragement the Government could afford would attract enough men of this sort.

The Directors were none the less prompt to express their disapproval at what Bentinck had done, saying that "What had been done in 1824 for coffee cannot and must not be drawn into a precedent."[46] More seriously, they noted that in promulgating his Resolutions Bentinck appeared to have committed a serious indiscretion by omitting Clause 19 of the previous Resolutions which had allowed control over the unruly planter with the threat of confiscation of his property. Only the ultimate deterrent — the right of withdrawing the residence licence and deportation of the individual — was left, and this was thought too drastic. The Directors ordered that the 1824 Resolutions be adhered to *in toto*, with an additional provision that no lease could be held for longer than 21 years.[47]

Bentinck retaliated that Clause 19 of the Amherst Regulations seemed needlessly harsh, and indeed altogether unnecessary. Law and order were already protected by adequate safeguards, in the rules requiring compulsory registration of title and of any transfer; and of course there was always the Governor's power over the residence licence. The required limitation on the length of tenure he hotly opposed. Indigo needed a heavy investment in capital equipment; assured tenure and long leases ought to be offered to the investor. Insecurity of tenure Bentinck correctly identified as one of the great obstacles to European settlement.[48] The Governor-General pressed the point that a system which permitted no rights over the land, and which forced the planters to depend on subterfuge, or remote control through advances, was pernicious.[49] Sir Charles Metcalfe and W. B. Bayley, both

[45] *Ibid.*, p. 41. [46] *Ibid.*, p. 28. [47] *Ibid.* [48] *Ibid.*, pp. 56-57.
[49] *Ibid.*, p. 59.

members of the Governor-General's Council, agreed with Bentinck; but the Directors adamantly replied that "We are not disposed to suggesting any other course than that communicated in our dispatch of 8 July, 1829."[50]

Bentinck's faith in the benefits of European settlement was in part vindicated by a contemporary judicial enquiry into the behaviour of the indigo 'planters', and by the Charter Renewal Act of 1833. A "survey of European Indigo planters . . . and all cases of affray" and judicial opinions thereon, ordered by a Judicial Dispatch of 6 August, 1828, revealed no evil that could not be solved by wider settlement. The local officers generally entertained a very agreeable opinion of the character of the planters. The magistrates of 32 Districts of the Bengal Presidency reported favourably on 432 planters in their area, and their views were summed up by Alexander Ross, a man of great administrative experience. He went on record as having the opinion that British residents outside Calcutta should be subject to the same criminal laws as "the Natives . . . . In the very few cases that [he presumed] would occur . . . a jury composed half of natives and half of Europeans or descendants of Europeans might even now be assembled; and . . . any difficulty in assembling a jury so composed" would be overcome providing Europeans settled freely in the country.[51] Ross's survey formed part of the favourable evidence for permitting free admission of Britons to India considered by the Select Committee of the House of Commons set up to review the case for the renewal of the Company's charter.

The 1833 Charter Renewal Act might have marked a watershed in the history of European settlement in India. Clause 81 opened India to the European adventurer, within the limits of the territories under the Company's Government on 1 January, 1800 and within "any part of the countries ceded by the Nabob of the Carnatic . . . without any licence whatever."[52] In January 1800 the Company's territory had consisted of little more than, approximately, East and West Bengal, part of Orissa, and the immediate hinterland of the Presidency towns of Bombay and Madras. At the committee stage, the clause

50 *Ibid.*, p. 60. 51 *Ibid.*, p. 67.

52 A. Berriedale Keith (ed.), *Speeches and Documents on Indian Policy, 1750-1921* (Oxford, 1921), i, 272.

had made provision for free access to territories under the Government of India at the date of the expiry of the 1813 Charter (22 April, 1834); but, for reasons that remain obscure, this was deleted, and the result was that all the vast territories acquired since January 1800, including the hill territories of Assam, Darjeeling and the Dun, and the Western Ghats,—all potentially attractive—remained legally inaccessible, except under licence or to Company servants. And the Governor-General never exercised his power (Clause 83) to declare any parts of India acquired after the beginning of 1800 open to all Britons. In the final Report of the Select Committee on the Colonization and Settlement of India of 1859, Clause 3 ran: "It appears even now to be doubted by legal authorities whether Europeans can enter without a licence those parts of India which have been acquired within the present century."[53]

The 86th clause of the 1833 Act, put into effect in India by Act IV of 17 April, 1837, made it lawful for any subject of Her Majesty to acquire and hold in perpetuity or for any number of years property in land or emoluments issuing out of land. The way was clear. But the flood of adventurers did not materialize. In February, 1840, Mr. William Ewart, M.P. for Wigan, moved for papers showing the extent of settlement by British subjects in India since 1833, as he thought "A great number of persons, both British and European, have been induced to settle in India and to purchase lands."[54] He wanted the figures published as encouragement to others. The result must have surprised Mr. Ewart. Although there was no information on the overall extent of landholding by Europeans in India at India House, and the periodic statements of lands held by Europeans made by collectors of land revenue had been discontinued in 1836, it appeared that only nine grants had been made in Bengal; one of them, interestingly, to a Mr. Bruce for a tea plantation at Sudya in Assam, which marks the foundation of the Assam Tea Company. In Madras five grants had been made in the same period and in Bombay eleven, mostly small holdings ranging from less than an acre to twenty acres.[55]

53 *Parl. Papers* (*H. of C.*), 1859, v. 54 *Hansard* (3rd. Series), lii, 133.
55 *Parl. Papers* (*H. of C.*), 1840, xxxvii, 453.

In a debate on the tenure of land in the Madras Presidency in the Commons on 11 July, 1854, John Bright quoted the Secretary of the East India Company as saying that there were no more Englishmen engaged in the cultivation of the soil in India in 1857 than there had been in 1834.[56] An "Analysis of the Evidence given before the Select Committee of both Houses of Parliament on the Renewal of the East India Company Charter", published in 1853, found little change during the previous fifty years:

> The number of Europeans in India . . . has scarcely increased at all . . . India is not like Australia or America where there is plenty of vacant space for foreigners . . . there is a dense population in many parts. Many of the natives are active, skilful and industrious, in agriculture quite equal to the European . . . only in the hilly districts would it be at all possible to keep up the British race for three generations without deterioration.[57]

The question of colonization was evidently to the forefront in the late 1850's, when two surveys were made, one by the Government of India in 1856 and the other by Parliament in 1858-59, the two divided by the Mutiny which is so often taken to be a great watershed in British sentiment towards India. Significantly, both came to the conclusion that India was not the place for the labouring Englishman, but that, provided he had plenty of capital, the middle-class rentier-investor could with luck find a return on his money.

In September 1856, the Indian Administration was asked to comment on the practicability of inducing retired officers and soldiers to remain as settlers.[58] The enquiry pointed out the advantages to all concerned accruing from the offers of Crown lands overseas on favourable terms, and that Crown lands in other colonies had, since 1836, been offered for settlement by Indian Army officers; that in June, 1856, the offer had been extended to Natal; but that the amount of waste land available for settlement outside India was fast diminishing as local

[56] *Hansard* (3rd. Series), xxxv, 77. [57] p. 153.

[58] *Parl. Papers* (*H. of C.*), 1857-8, Paper 180, xlii, 1. According to *Friend of India*, 17 June, 1858, this letter was inspired by Sir George Clerk.

legislatures in New South Wales, Victoria, New Zealand, South Australia, and the Cape of Good Hope took over responsibility from the Imperial Parliament for the disposal of local lands. The answers were familiar. Health hazards, the difficulties to be expected in providing protection and in the administration of law created by the presence of European settlers, the high cost of individual settlement: these are arguments that had an ancestry going back at least as far as George Monson 90 years before.[59] Major A. P. Phayre, Commissioner of the Provinces of Pegu, pointed out that though there was abundant waste land in Pegu and the health hazards were low "the province cannot be expected to attract Europeans as colonists" because of the cost of importing labour.[60] The Punjab was written off as too densely populated and unhealthy.[61] (In the light of subsequent developments, it is a little surprising how much of the hill territories were deemed by their administrators to be unsuitable.) The western Dun had seen an experimental venture in colonization by "Portuguese and Anglo-Indians discharged from Scindiah's military service . . . but it languished and failed."[62] Only one European land speculation was a success.[63] Kumaon was reputed to be too unhealthy. Although there was no exact knowledge of the Nilgiris available to the Madras Board of Revenue,[63a] it was thought that those hills were within the fever range. Major-General D. Macleod, Commissioner of the Ceded Districts, reiterated the sentiment that it was impossible for Europeans to pare costs "to compete with the natives." The Secretary to the Madras Medical Board noted the healthy condition of American missionaries in the Nilgiri and Palni hills, but also the ravages of fever among the Anglo-Indians in the Shevaroy hills. Brigadier P. Thomson, a veteran of 40 years with the Madras Army, Officer-Commanding in Malabar and Canara, declared that neither hills nor seaside offered any hope for European settlement: the offspring of Europeans would be sadly degenerate.[64] The length of service of these corres-

59 *Ibid.*, xx, 2. 60 *Ibid.*, p. 3. 61 *Ibid.*, p. 2. 62 *Ibid.*, p. 5.

63 That of Major F. C. Elwall, who had retired in 1848 after 25 years with the Bengal Army and who had rented *zemindari* lands.

63a *Parl. Papers (H. of C.)*, 1857-8, Paper 180, xlii, 13.

64 *Ibid.*, pp. 15, 16 and 17.

pondents of Government seems in singular disaccord with the implications of their pronouncements about the health hazards of India.

In Bombay there was much the same story. The Governor, Lord Elphinstone (1819-27), assured the Government of India that "there are no tracts suitable for settlement by Europeans under this Presidency," while James Grant Lumsden, a member of Council, and for 31 years in the Bombay service, condemned the climate.[65] The Collector and magistrate in Dharwar believed that, particularly with regard to cotton cultivation, it would be "as purchasers of produce rather than as producers that settlers would succeed . . . as merchants rather than as farmers."[65a]

Some voice was given to the need to encourage settlers. Captain James, Officiating Superintendent of Darjeeling, drew attention, in a letter of 20 December, 1856 to the Military Secretary, to the advantages of his charge where there were 281,673 acres of waste hill land available for distribution, where the climate was mild and the health record excellent. He quoted Mr. B. H. Hodgson, a retired civilian who had settled there in 1844, as saying that "the encouragement of colonisation . . . is one of the highest and most important duties of the Government . . . [to insure] . . . the stabilisation of British power in India."[66] According to him, settlers would be attracted by assisted passages and the news that the hills of India offered a "certain prospect of comfort, a full belly and a warm back and a decent domicile such as would be a perfect godsend to the starving peasantry of Ireland and the Scottish highlands."[67] Major-General J. W. Cleveland, with the Madras Army since 1807, pointed out the possibility of success in coffee plantations in Mysore and Coorg on which "Many steady old European soldiers might find employment."[68] Even harsh critics like Henry Wilson Reeves noted that many pensioners were thriving as mechanics and traders in towns like Belgaum and Poona.

The arguments of those who would protect the Indian peasant against exploitation and who were against letting

65 *Ibid.*, pp. 19 and 26. 65a *Ibid.*, p. 21. 66 *Ibid.*, pp. 8-10.
67 *Ibid.*, p. 10. 68 *Ibid.*, p. 16.

Europeans put themselves in positions where discredit could be brought upon the English name won the day.[69] Colonization would merely lead to the creation of "a community of pauperism and vice".[69a]

The Mutiny seems to have affected hardly at all the contempt of the Government of India for the colonizing ability of the British soldier or the British working classes. Although some lip service was paid to the theory that English settlers would learn to know and like the Indian people — in a way in which Government administrators, however gifted linguistically, however well-intentioned, never could — nothing was done to make the place more attractive to the colonist. Lord Elphinstone, Governor of Bombay in this period, was typical in his inflexibility. Three years of reflection on the Mutiny and its causes did nothing to change his opposition to military colonization. He declared that "the best part of the land is already occupied. . . . It will not pay to buy out the natives, and they cannot be turned out to accommodate settlers".[70] He still thought Australia and New Zealand to be the best places for the British colonist.

There was to be no scheme for free or assisted passages for the poor; no free land grants; no advances towards the high cost of jungle clearance, irrigation and road-cutting to encourage settlement by the Englishman without means. On the other hand, after the Mutiny, India did become an easier place for the capitalist to exploit. The Mutiny tilted the debate in favour of British upper middle-class colonization. An attempt to exploit the vast waste lands[71] at the disposal of the Government by accurate survey and by fixing settled terms under which colonists might hold land securely slowly opened up the hill lands of Assam and Darjeeling in the north, and the Nilgiris in the south, to the moneyed investor.

On 16 March, 1858, Mr. W. Ewart, by now M.P. for Dumfries, and long a poser of questions on India, rose to call attention to "the propriety of colonisation in India, and the extension of our trade with Central Asia". He wondered

69 For example, see *ibid.*, p. 21, Henry Wilson Reeves's Memorandum.

69a *Ibid.*, p. 24. 70 *Ibid.*, 1862, xl, 687 ff.

71 For extent, see Returns printed in *ibid.*, 862, xl.

why both British capital and British labour had not flocked to settle the vast unclaimed tracts after the relaxation of terms of entry in 1833. He believed that "colonists only would settle and keep the country".[72] Mr. H. J. Baillie, M.P. for Inverness and Secretary to the Board of Control, opposed Ewart with the familiar hostile arguments, some of which had been used by members of the Board at least since Dundas's time. Ewart, however, was supported by the strong 'cotton faction', who had long been pressing for the opening of western India to improved cotton-farming methods,[73] and on 21 March a 15-man Select Committee was appointed (later increased to include an Irish member).[74] Sitting for almost eighteen months, and receiving a vast amount of evidence, the Committee finally agreed with the opponents of large-scale European colonization of India. The Committee began its report, ordered to be printed on 9 August, 1859, by pointing out that "the term colonisation must clearly be limited to a class of superior settlers who shall by their enterprise, capital and skill set in motion the labour and develop the resources of India."[75] Again and again this refrain comes through the evidence before the Committee. Ross Donnelly Mangles summarized prevalent opinions when he said that "the evidence . . . showed what indeed most of us were well aware of . . . that mere labour colonisation, as in America or Australia, is not applicable to India."[76]

In fact this appears to have been a misinterpretation of the situation. One of the greatest problems facing the tea planters in Assam, Cachar and the Dun was the difficulty in finding satisfactory labour.[77] Dr. J. B. Barry of Sylhet testified that

72 *Hansard* (3rd. Series), cxliv, 269.

73 Wood to Dalhousie, 24 March 1853; Wood to Sir Henry Pottinger, 24 March 1853, MSS. Eur. F. 78, Letter Book of India Board, iii, 40 and 46.

74 The hearings were recorded in *Parl. Papers* (*H. of C.*), 1857-8, vii, and 1859, iv and v. For a "Statistical Memoir of a Survey of the Neilgherry Mountains", laid before the Committee in 1858, and containing a most interesting account of hill lands studied from the point of view of the potential British settler, see *ibid.*, 1861, xliii, 403, *et seq.*

75 *Ibid.*, 1859, v, *Report*, clause 1.

76 *Ibid.*, question 1080. Mangles, a member of the Committee, had been in the Bengal Civil Service between 1820 and 1839.

77 *Ibid.*, question 3400.

Chinese coolies were still being imported through Calcutta at 30 to 40 shillings a head;[78] he discounted the argument that the European could not survive hard labour under the Indian sun.[79] The 1859 Report indeed accepted the evidence "that the dangerous effect of the climate of India has been considerably exaggerated." Clause 8 drew attention to the number of healthy planters living even in the low-lying miasmal areas of lower Bengal and Bihar. The health hazard was not the weather, but the Englishman himself. Had the European working-man been able to abstain from alcohol the Indian climate could not have been the danger it was: "Drunkenness is the great obstacle to working class settlement."[80]

For the five years after the Mutiny the tide ran, albeit sluggishly, in favour of measures to open India for settlement by the wealthy. A correspondent of *The Times of India* of 10 February, 1859 wrote :

> In the suppression of crime, the superintendence of police, the opening out of roads for country produce, in enterprises of all kinds, and lastly in ascertaining the spirit of the people, what better coadjutors could we have than European Zamindars? . . . [He] . . . has the means of endearing himself to the people of the country which not all the official acts of a century will ever bring about.

The administration of Lord Canning (1856-62) saw then a brief intensification of interest in European colonization. The Lancashire cotton manufacturing interests, long aware of the possibility of India as an alternative source of cotton to America, clamoured with increasing insistence for any measure that would increase the yield of good quality fibre. Lord Canning, well aware of the hostility of his senior subordinates towards the colonists,[81] was himself not averse to colonization. He feared that those in England "overrate[d] the amount of Waste Land through which the railways [and the Grand Trunk Road] pass . . . one of the mistakes of the agent of the

[78] *Ibid.*, questions 3271-7.

[79] *Ibid.*, questions 3342-4; and *Report*, clause 45. [80] *Report*, clause 45.

[81] Canning to Wood, 1 October 1860, MSS. Eur. F. 78, Box 2, bundle 6.

[Lancashire] Cotton Supply Association was to assume that the country he saw from the road was all Waste Land."[82] Yet he favoured a generous settlement of the rules by which waste land might be opened up.[83] In a dispatch to Wood dated 17 October, 1861, he proposed Resolutions for the disposal of waste land and the redemption of the Land Revenue. Indians and the Government of India, as well as British immigrants, might be expected to benefit from permission to redeem the Land Revenue, which "would tend to create a class which although composed of different races and creeds will be peculiarly bound to the British rule."[84] The terms Canning proposed were broad. Resolution 29 put a price of half a crown an acre on uncleared land, and double that on cleared land, in all cases when a plot attracted only one bidder; competition for plots was to be settled by auction. Purchasers were to have the right to hold, bequeath or otherwise control the land in perpetuity, subject to the payment of the Revenue, and without obligation to plant within a given time.[85] Canning thought that a limitation on the size of grants would be necessary, especially in the potential tea areas of Bengal, Assam and Cachar, to discourage land speculation. But the limit proposed was 3,000 acres,[86] and a settler might take an option on adjoining tracts for a period of up to five years. Grants could be staked by overseas bidders, final survey and settlement awaiting the settler's arrival. Finally, Canning proposed that the Land Revenue demand should be redeemed at twenty years' purchase, subject to certain rights and restrictions by Government.[87]

Canning's policy,[88] although in retrospect a logical development of Waste Land Settlement rules laid down by his predecessors,[89] found little favour with Sir Charles Wood, Secretary

[82] Canning to Wood, 3 January 1862, MSS. Eur. F. 78, Box 6, uncatalogued, bundle 108.

[83] *Ibid.*, Paper 15; and see *Parl. Papers* (*H. of C.*), 1862, xl, 674, *et seq.*

[84] *Ibid.*, Paper 15, *Resolutions*, clause 5.

[85] *Ibid.*, clause 15. [86] *Ibid.*, clause 21. [87] *Ibid.*, Section II, clause 41.

[88] It is interesting that Canning's Administration also devised regulations acceptable to Whitehall for the acquisition of land by Indian Civil Servants in 'Atherton's Case': see *Parl. Papers* (*H. of C.*), 1862, xl, 676, *et seq.*

[89] *Cf.*, the Waste Land disposal regulations for Assam, *ibid.*, 1843, xxxv, **11**; and the 1854 Assam rules, *ibid.*, 1874, xlviii, 14.

of State, who rejected his vision of the European settler mingling harmoniously with the Indian. He saw the Indians as "passionately attached . . . to their ancestral lands", looking upon the intrusion of strangers as an encroachment and likely to lead to quarrels, affrays and bloodshed, and to the costly "necessity of an armed force for their suppression". Wood reminded the Government of India of the "recent unhappy occurrences in New Zealand", and foresaw an identical situation arising in India, with the new settler gravitating to precisely those fertile hill regions where he would be "beyond the reach of the ordinary agencies of Government."[90] Wood was none the less under pressure to ameliorate the lot of the British settler in India, and agreed to the necessity for settled waste land rules. His modifications were important: all grants applied for were to be put up for auction only after accurate survey and demarcation, regardless of the number of bidders; no lands were to be reserved for any settler. He discounted the attractiveness to the European settler of sinking the amount of money that would be required into the redemption of the Government revenue assessment, but rather looked to a permanent settlement of the rate of assessment as providing all the security the settler might need.

Despite his caution, his modification of Canning's proposals and his reluctance to allow Britons advantages over Indians on the land, Wood was criticized in some quarters for being too generous. The press in London and India were less convinced than the Manchester cotton manufacturers of the desirability of European settlement. A *Times of India* leader accused Wood of profligacy, claiming that valuable land was being sold at ridiculous prices to private speculators.[91] The *Homeward Mail* declared that:

> The White Zamindar may be in every respect a Christian gentleman liberal to his tenants, kind to his dependents, a strict observer of other men's rights, a mild observer of his own . . . he would still in the eyes of the people of the soil . . . be an alien and an usurper, and Britain could not hope to

90 Wood to Canning, 9 July 1862, MSS. Eur. F. 78, Box 6, bundle 108, paper 16.

91 27 December, 1862.

> retain power by refusing to interfere with the Indian peasants' ancient rights in the soil.[92]

The London *Times* cautioned against assimilating "the question of waste lands *in a colony* to the question of waste lands *in India.* In a colony *waste lands* and *land lying waste* are convertible terms. In India they are by no means so." The *Times* charged the Lancashire cotton interests with seeking by "unfair abuse" to hide "their own remissness in providing for a supply of cotton in the case . . . of a failure in the produce of the Southern Plantations".[93]

Wood was obviously worried by these criticisms, and caused C. J. Wingfield, who had recently been Commissioner in Oudh, to prepare two memoranda in rebuttal. Neither bears any date, but from their position among the Wood papers would appear to have been written late in 1863.

Wood need not have worried. The demand from the Lancashire cotton interest died down with the end of the American Civil War, and resulted in the collapse of numerous cotton-buying agencies and banks in Western India which had speculated in cotton advances. It rapidly emerged that there was little demand for land for permanent, personal settlement: rather the British interest appeared to become increasingly an affair for Managing Agencies, opening up hill lands for tea, coffee and cinchona, and employing European managers who looked forward to retirement in Britain; or for speculators buying to acquire a title, and then selling at an enhanced rate when the price of land rose. By the mid-1880's the pattern was clear: the *Report on the Moral and Material Progress of India* for 1884-85 records:

> The waste land grants in Assam are taken up almost exclusively for tea gardens . . . of late years the available waste [has been] taken up by persons not purposing to cultivate [it] themselves, but to hold against an increase in value.[94]

The 1891 Census found only 168,158 Europeans in India, including the service personnel, the mercantile population, and the civil servants.[95]

92 15 January, 1863. 93 10 April, 1863. My italics.

94 *Parl. Papers* (*H. of C.*), 1886, xlix, 422.

95 *Imperial Gazetteer of India* (Oxford, 1909), i, 477.

# GENERAL SIR HUGH GOUGH AND THE PUNJAB CAMPAIGN, 1848-49

BIKRAMA JIT HASRAT

## *War*

If there be a war, Lord Dalhousie (Governor-General, 1848-56) wrote shortly after the defection of Sher Singh to Mulraj at Multan on 14 September, 1848, it would be a very different one from the last one. On paper, he said, the Sikhs had an army of 25,000 men, scattered all over the country and likely to be swelled by the disbanded soldiery, but the fighting power of the Khalsa was gone for ever. "The Sikh strength," he concluded with benign complacency, "was in their guns, and most of them are reposing placidly at my elbow in the arsenal of Fort William!"[1] The unsuccessful actions of Ramnagar, Sadulpur, and Chillianwala with which the Punjab campaign opened soon dispelled this illusory belief.

The British Government was the protector and guardian of the ruler of the Sikhs, whose government under the treaty of Bhyrowal was presided over by a British Resident. A declaration of war against the State of Lahore would, therefore, amount to a declaration of war against the Government of India. "Our acts," declared Dalhousie, "require no explanation."[2]

[1] Dalhousie to Sir Geo. Couper (Private), 18 September 1848, Dalhousie Papers (Coulston House).

[2] Dalhousie to Hobhouse, 30 October 1848, Broughton Papers (British Museum), Add. MSS. 36476.

However, this bold statement did not ring true at Lahore, where an explanation for the sudden presence in the Punjab of the British army under General Sir Hugh (later Lord) Gough was given. Sir Frederick Currie, the Resident, issued on 18 November a Proclamation exhorting the subjects of Maharaja Dalip Singh to remain loyal to their sovereign.[3] The British army, they were told, came not as an enemy but to punish insurgents and restore order and obedience on behalf of the Maharaja. To give public credence to this deception, Misar Sahib Dayal, a Lahore Darbar official, was deputed to accompany the Commander-in-Chief.[4]

Thus the Punjab Campaign opened under these false colours. It amounted to a surreptitious invasion of the Punjab by the *de facto* rulers of the Punjab and the protectors of the young Maharaja, in direct contravention of the political and moral obligations imposed upon them by the treaties of Lahore and Bhyrowal. To designate it as the Second Anglo-Sikh War as is usually done is therefore a misnomer.

In the meantime, Dalhousie did not mince words with the Home Government. He reported the British invasion of the Punjab in rather clear and unambiguous terms: "Unwarranted by precedent, uninfluenced by example, the Sikh nation has called for war, and on my word, Sirs, they shall have it with vengeance!" He branded the Sikhs, the Darbar, and their sovereign as treacherous, and accused them of being opposed to the presence of the British. There was, he complained, no alternative for the British Government but to declare war on the Sikh dynasty. Its power in that State, he concluded, must be destroyed.[5]

## *Reaction in London*

The vigour and vehemence exhibited by Dalhousie in his public and private despatches was not a surprise, but in London eyebrows were raised at his determination to prosecute an illegal war to end a rebellion. He wrote to Sir George Couper on 8 October:

[3] *Parl(iamentary) Papers, H(ouse) of C(ommons)*, 1848, xli, Paper 42, Doc(ument) 8. [4] *Ibid.*, Doc. 1.

[5] Dalhousie to Hobhouse, 28 October 1848, Broughton Papers.

> If it please God to grant me success, I will make a clean job of it this time. I declare it before Heaven I have done all men can do to avert the necessity; but since they will force war on me, I have drawn the sword, and have this time thrown away the scabbard. If the Sikhs, after this is over, rise again, they shall intrench themselves behind a dunghill, and fight with their finger-nails, for if I live 12 months they shall have nothing else left to fight with.[6]

Both at Whitehall and Leadenhall Street allowances were made for these "wild outbursts," but Dalhousie's fantastic accusations and drastic conclusions cut no ice with statesmen closely associated with the political affairs of the Punjab. Along with Lord John Russell's Government they agreed to the necessity of putting down a rebellion, but pointed to the absolute immorality of holding the Darbar and the young Maharaja responsible. The India Board tersely reminded Dalhousie that since the entire control over the civil and military matters in the Punjab was vested in the Government of India, it could not escape its responsibility: "As the real supreme authority was vested in our Resident and the Army of Occupation, it is fair to say that the British functionaries are to the full accountable as the Sikh Darbar for any mismanagement that may have led to the present revolt."[7]

General opinion in England, in the press and both the Houses of Parliament, also seemed averse to the course suggested. The British Cabinet, going into the whole question of relations with the Punjab, decided that although the treaty of Bhyrowal allowed room for changes in policy, it did not favour deposing the son and heir of Ranjit Singh, despite the prospect of rebellion.[8] The Home authorities informed Dalhousie in unequivocal terms that his proposal to overthrow the Sikh dynasty was premature, immoral and unjustified.[9]

[6] Dalhousie to Couper, 8 October 1848, Dalhousie Papers. Sir George Ebenezer Wilson Couper, 2nd Bart., 1824-1908. Bengal Civil Service 1846; Punjab Commission 1849.

[7] Hobhouse to Dalhousie (India Board Letter), 7 February 1849, Dalhousie Muniments (Section 6, 55-58) (Scottish Records Office, Edinburgh).

[8] *Ibid.*, 24 November 1848. [9] *Ibid.*, 7 December 1848.

### *The Sikh Response*

Sher Singh had soon been disgusted by the suspicious behaviour of Mulraj, and had left Multan on 9 October with 900 infantry and 3,400 horse. He proceeded northwards to join his father at Gujrat. It seems surprising that not the slightest attempt was made either by General Whish with his 7,200 men or Lieutenant Edwardes with his 20,000 Muslim mercenaries to bar his passage, to attack or to follow him.[10]

Initially, it had been believed that Sher Singh's revolt had been on personal grounds. He had resented British affronts to his father and had been aggrieved by the Resident's refusal to allow the marriage of his sister to the young Maharaja. He probably had no idea that his defection would lead to that of others. But as he marched northwards, Mulraj's troops deserted and joined his force. Motley crowds of malcontents and disbanded soldiers also swelled his ranks, proclaiming him the leader of the Khalsa. Once his spirits were aroused, he began to believe this himself. He whipped up enthusiasm for the Khalsa, proclaiming himself to be its servant and that of the Maharaja (Dalip Singh) and calling the people to rise in arms and expel the *firangees* from the Punjab.[11]

Simultaneously in the northwest the rising under Sardar Chattar Singh had gained momentum. The Sikhs responded well to his call to arms. In the Sind Sagar Doab multitudes of disbanded soldiers flocked to his standard. The soldiers of the Khalsa crossed the Ravi in large numbers out of the Manjha to join him. He wrote to Gulab Singh, telling him to move his troops from Jammu into the Rechna Doab. An offer of Peshawar was made to Amir Dost Muhammed Khan, of Kabul, to obtain Afghan support.[12]

News of the disaffection spread rapidly and widely. Very soon the Sikh troops in the northern districts heard of the rising of the Khalsa. The contingent at Bannu revolted, murdered their European officers, and marched to join Sher Singh.[13] The Sikh force at Peshawar also revolted and added

[10] Dalhousie to Hobhouse, 30 October 1848, Broughton Papers.

[11] *Ibid.*, 10 October 1848. [12] *Ibid.*, 7 and 19 September 1848.

[13] Dalhousie to Couper, 31 October 1848, Dalhousie Papers.

their numbers to the cause. Major George Lawrence and other British officers stationed there fled for their lives to Kohat in the southwest[14] where Sultan Muhammad Barakzai, its fickle governor, was hobnobbing with the rebels. But in Hazara Captain James Abbott, who had by his stupidity and arrogance raised the storm, continued the game of inflaming the Muslim population against the Sikh 'infidels'. Attock held out precariously under Lieutenant Herbert's hard-pressed Muslim mercenary garrison.

The north was seething with revolt. Currie sent the frantic report: "All I believe are disaffected-Chiefs, Darbar officials, army and the Sikh population."[15] The rebellion of the Sikh nation, Dalhousie wrote, had at last become open, flagrant, and universal.[16]

### *The Army of Invasion*

The main column of the Army of the Punjab under the command of General Gough consisted of 2 Infantry Divisions (14,419 men), a Cavalry Division (3,369 horse) and an Artillery Division with 66 guns, including ten 18-pounder batteries and six 8-inch howitzers drawn by elephants. In addition, there were 6 troops of Horse Artillery, 3 light and 2 heavy batteries. Its total strength amounted to 24,404 men (6,396 Europeans) of all arms and 66 guns.

At the same time, three other columns were in simultaneous operation throughout the Punjab. At Lahore, in the centre, Brigadier-General Wheeler's Occupation Force, 10,000 strong, held firmly the capital of the Sikhs. In the extreme south, before the citadel of Multan was the 1st Infantry Division (7,600 men) under Major-General Whish, with 93 field and siege guns. The arrival of the Bombay Column under Brigadier-General Dundas had augmented its strength to 21,000 men of all arms. In addition 6,200 men of the Lahore Infantry were under British control at Multan. This brought the total regular force at the disposal of General Whish to 26,330 men. The cavalry force at Multan amounted to 10,173

14 Dalhousie to Hobhouse, 20 November 1848, Broughton Papers.

15 Currie's Report, 2 September 1848, *ibid.*

16 Dalhousie to Hobhouse, 1 October 1848, *ibid.*

horse — 1st Division, 2,173; Bombay Column, 3,000; and Edwardes's irregular horse, 5,000. And above all, there were the irregular Muslim levies and mercenaries raised by the British to fight the Sikhs. At Multan, Edwardes had the largest number, 20,000 men inclusive of 9,000 Bahawalpur Baloch troops; at Hazara, Abbott had got together 8,000 irregulars; at Attock, Herbert had raised 3,000; at Peshawar, George Lawrence had raised another 3,000; and at Bannu, Taylor had amassed 4,000 — an overall total of 38,000 mercenaries, Muslims, Afghans, Balochs and tribesmen with over 5,000 horse and camel corps.

And finally, on the frontier at Gobindghar, Jullundur, Hoshiarpur and Bodipur had been left a force 5,962 strong, with 22 guns.

Taken in all, these figures add up to the staggering total of 104,666 men — 61,366 of the regular British army, 5,300 of the Lahore army, and 38,000 irregular troops; 13,542 cavalry (exclusive of 10 troops of horse artillery), 123 field guns and 22 heavy guns — all deployed at various points.[17] Another crucial factor to remember is that with the exception of the frontier force (5,962) and the Lahore Column (10,000), the entire regular army of the Punjab — 45,404 men, 13,542 horse and 145 guns ultimately converged on Shadewal for the final battle of Gujrat.

### *The Rebel Force*

In sharp contrast to these figures, the numerical superiority of the Sikhs, as claimed by the British, appears to be a myth.[18] The Sikh force which ultimately mustered could not even be equivalent to the shadow of the Khalsa republican army which fought the British at Ferozeshah, Aliwal and Sobraon.

[17] These and the following approximate figures are based on various official British papers, published and unpublished: *Parl. Papers* (*H. of C.*), 1849, xli; The Lahore Political Diaries; Private papers of Lord Dalhousie in the Broughton Papers; and Dalhousie Muniments, Section 6, among which No. 366 (1849) is particularly informative.

[18] Lord Gough's despatches enumerate the strength of the Sikh force at Ramnagar and Chillianwala to be 30-40,000, and at Gujrat, 60,000 men and 60 guns; see *Parl. Papers* (*H. of C.*), 1849, xli, Paper 44, Doc. 51 and Paper 49, Doc. 3.

The army of the late Ranjit Singh, a powerful resurgent force between 1842-45 and once in control of the State, was completely broken up after its capitulation at Sobraon in 1846. Lord Hardinge (Governor-General, 1844-48) had meticulously seen to the complete annihilation of the military power of the Sikhs. The treaties of Lahore and Bhyrowal had broken the back of the Khalsa republican army of 92,000 men, 31,800 cavalry with over 384 guns; and the Peace Settlement of 1846 had envisaged its systematic destruction. Its soldiers had been disbanded and dispersed, its generals discharged or won over, its *jagirdari* force starved to extinction, and the pride of its artillery—36 guns of the highest calibre—dismantled and carted away to the arsenal of Fort William. The claim that the Army of the Khalsa or of the entire Sikh nation opposed and fought the British in the military operations of the Punjab Campaign of 1848-49, therefore, is hardly admissible for the simple reason that no such force existed. A skeleton army of 25 battalions (20,000 men) and 12,000 cavalry permitted to the State of Lahore under the treaty of March 1846 was a mere reflection of the Khalsa, and the British were its masters. Dispersed to far-flung districts for garrison duty under the observing eyes of the British political officers, it possessed neither will nor effective fighting power. Lahore had a garrison strength of 6,500 men, but the citadel was under British military occupation. Peshawar had a garrison of 3,000 men, Hazara 3,000 men, the fortress of Gobindgarh 2,000 men, Bannu and Tank 1,300 men, Attock 700 men and Kohat 500 men; the remaining 3,000 men of the entire force were at numerous small posts throughout the Punjab.

Now, the contingents of the Lahore army which ultimately revolted and joined the rebels were those of Hazara, Peshawar, Tank and Bannu, Kohat and Attock—9,400 men inclusive of Sher Singh's force defected at Multan (900 infantry and 3,400 horse). The garrison at Gobindgarh had been disarmed and the fort occupied. Allowing that the 3,000 men stationed at various isolated places throughout the Punjab could get through and join those in the north, the obvious strength of the regular Sikh force could hardly exceed 13,000 men and 9,000 horse.

Disbanded soldiers and the Khalsa freelance which flocked to it could scarcely exceed 10,000 men. With Lahore and Amritsar in the hands of the British and the passage to the Rechna Doab blocked by Wheeler's force, the trickle of unarmed soldiery of Gobind from the Manjha and Malwa regions, the home of the late republican army, could hardly exceed the above figure. The disbanded soldiery would merely augment the strength of the Sikh force, which had few generals and fewer arms; it had no access to the state arsenals situated in the British occupied area, and no means of procurement of arms or supplies in the predominantly Muslim districts, the population of which was already aroused against the Sikhs.

The above figures show that the strength of the entire Khalsa force could hardly exceed 23,000 men; at any rate, it is hardly possible to accept the statement of Lord Gough that the Sikh army which fought the British at Gujrat was 60,000 strong.[19] That these figures are highly exaggerated is evidenced by the fact that the whole Sikh army under Sher Singh and Chattar Singh which, a few days after the battle, surrendered to General Gilbert at Rawalpindi amounted to 16,000 men.[20]

Perhaps the most curious phenomenon was the intervention of the Afghans on the side of the Sikhs. The Barakzai Amir, having almost forgotten the lessons of defeat and humiliation of a decade earlier, still cherished a desire to repossess the Afghan northern provinces. Lured by Chattar Singh with an offer of Peshawar, still a key to the Afghan national pride, Dost Muhammad Khan marched down from the hills of Kabul as an ally of the Sikhs, and declared a limited *jehad* on the *firangees*. He was met at Peshawar by Chattar Singh, but what transpired between them is not known. His revived claims to the other former Afghan possessions, Kashmir, the Derajat, and Hazara frightened the Sikhs; and his exhortations to the Kandahar Chiefs to march on Sind annoyed the British.[21] Although he wavered in his allegiance to the Sikhs,[22] he fought the British at Gujrat and fled northwards.

19 *Parl. Papers* (*H. of C.*), 1849, xli, Paper 49, Doc. 3.

20 Dalhousie to Hobhouse, 24 March 1849, Broughton Papers.

21 Dalhousie to Couper (Private), 5 February 1849, Dalhousie Papers.

22 For Abbott's negotiations with Dost Mohammed, see Broughton Papers, and Lahore Political Diaries, vol. iv, 30 December 1848 ff.

*The 'Sad Affair' at Ramnagar*

General Gough crossed the Ravi on 16 November. He marched on rapidly into the Rechna Doab towards Ramnagar, where on arrival on 22 November, he discovered Sher Singh's entire force on the right bank of the Chenab. But in the rapid forward movement heavy field artillery had been left behind, and immediately afterwards an action had to be fought with the Sikhs which was neither brilliant nor complete. In fact, it was " a sad affair with distressing results."[23]

Anticipating the difficult situation which might arise, Gough had, a day earlier, ordered Brigadier-General Campbell to move out the 3rd Infantry Division from Saharun to disperse the Sikh force reported to be in the vicinity of Ramnagar. A cavalry division and three troops of horse artillery under Brigadier-General Cureton, the Commander of the Cavalry, accompanied Campbell's force.[24]

On arrival at Ramnagar, Campbell found the Sikh force in position on the opposite bank of the river, though small parties of Sikh soldiers were observed retreating from the town towards the ford to the Sikh encampment. Cureton had numerous cavalry but no guns, and as the situation was pressing, he ordered the horse artillery to charge the retreating parties. Lieutenant-Colonel Lane, who commanded the horse artillery, in his eagerness to overtake the withdrawing Sikh troops through the deep and heavy sand of the river, met with a disaster. The Sikh artillery on the opposite bank of the river opened up with disastrous effects; and Lane hastily attempted to withdraw the horse artillery, leaving stuck in the sand a heavy gun and two ammunition wagons, which the Sikhs captured.

At the same moment, the Sikhs sprung a surprise on Cureton. A column of their cavalry had crossed the river under cover of the artillery, leaving him the choice between an immediate engagement or the disgrace of retirement. Acting on the spur of the moment, the Commander decided to lead a squadron of H.M. 14th Light Dragoons in support of the

[23] Dalhousie to Hobhouse, 7 December 1848, Broughton Papers.

[24] *Parl. Papers* (*H. of C.*), 1849, xli, Paper 42, Doc. 3; Campbell to Adjutant-General, 24 November 1848, Broughton Papers.

light infantry and in the short swift action was himself shot dead. The commander of the Light Dragoons was reported missing, and 90 officers and men with 140 horse were lost. The only British gain was "a handsome silk standard" captured by a Muslim trooper who was commended for the Order of Merit by Gough, an eye-witness of the battle.[25]

The action at Ramnagar was a signal defeat for the British. Dalhousie apportioned the blame between Campbell and Gough for the "sad affair" from which "there was no objective to be gained"; and the home government expressed their utter inability to understand why the battle was fought at all.[26] Gough, on the other hand, claimed it as a victory. "The enemy", he announced in a General Order, "was signally overthrown on every occasion, and only saved from utter annihilation by their flight to the cover of their guns on the opposite bank."[27]

### *The Sadulpur Debacle*

For about a week after the British reverse at Ramnagar, the two armies faced each other across the river. Gough waited impatiently till his heavy guns came up. On 30 November, he detached a force under Major-General Sir Joseph Thackwell to make its way across the river and take the Sikh army in the flank.[28] In the meantime he pushed British batteries and breastwork to the bank of the river and opened up a cannonade upon Sher Singh's front in order to divert his attention from the flank.[29] At the same time, another brigade of infantry under Brigadier Godby was detached from the main army and ordered to ford the river 6 miles from Ramnagar and give support to Thackwell's force.[30]

25 *Parl. Papers* (*H. of C.*), 1849, xli, Paper 42, Doc. 6.

26 Hobhouse to Dalhousie, 24 January 1849, Dalhousie Muniments.

27 *Parl. Papers* (*H. of C.*), 1849, xli, Paper 42, Doc. 3.

28 Thackwell's force consisted of Brigadier White's 1st brigade of cavalry, the 24th and 61st Foot, 5 regiments of native infantry under Campbell: 7,827 men, 1,425 horse and 32 field guns.

29 *Parl. Papers* (*H. of C.*), 1849, xli, Paper 42, Doc. 10.

30 Godby's force: 2nd brigade of infantry, 2nd European Light infantry, 31st and 70th native infantry (2,543).

Sher Singh's entire force — 12,000 men and 28 guns — lay strongly entrenched. So far Chattar Singh had not joined forces, and consequently its strength, enumerated between 30,000-40,000 men in Gough's despatch, seems not only improbable but imaginary.[31] As the numerous fords were vigilantly guarded by the Sikhs, Thackwell's force had to move 22 miles up the river to Wazirabad, where on 2 December, it made the crossing. Godby's brigade had crossed the river 16 miles below, and so Thackwell hastily marched southwards. At mid-day on 3 December, he arrived at Sadulpur, barely 4 miles from the Sikh encampment. Here he halted, giving well-earned rest to his men, who were in a state of complete exhaustion from 5 days' continuous march.[32]

The Sikhs realized that danger was imminent. Sporadic artillery fire from the British guns on the Ramnagar embankment had continued on their centre. Two British columns had successfully crossed the river and threatened their flanks and the rear. Sooner than expected, heavy Sikh artillery opened up on Thackwell's position, while the Sikh cavalry barred the passage of Godby's force. Thackwell's instructions were not to engage the enemy till united with Godby's brigade. For some time, the British guns remained silent; they opened up tardily and desultory fire continued for two hours on both sides. But Godby could not form a junction in time, with the result that Thackwell could attack neither the enemy's flank nor the rear.

As the dusk fell, the guns on both sides became silent; and as the darkness enveloped Sadulpur, the entire Sikh army crossed over to the left bank of the river Jehlum. Sher Singh's action thus nullified the British manoeuvre; it also made it possible for Chattar Singh's force to join him later.

The British general claimed a victory without a battle. He reported a meagre loss of 40 men at Sadulpur and claimed that the noble army under his command had upheld its tradition of valour. The Sikhs, he said, were in full retreat, leaving behind some 60 boats which had been captured.[33]

The news of the ineffective action was received by Lord Dalhousie on 7 December at Ambala. He scoffed at the

[31] *Parl. Papers* (*H. of C.*), 1849, xli, Paper 42, Doc. 10.

[32] *Ibid.* [33] *Ibid.*

Commander-in-Chief's suggestion of firing a salute for the victory: "I will not do so for I do not like that sort of practice-bravado, and shall reserve salutes for real victories which this is not!"[34] To the home authorities he complained that it was neither a victory, nor even a success; and that Gough had not complied with his instructions regarding the crossing of the Chenab. He blamed General Thackwell for lack of initiative, despite the fact that the Sikhs had suffered heavily, and had finally retired in disorder: "Every one was in the act of advancing when the General ordered a halt. However, notwithstanding the eagerness of the troops and the entreaties of all who had a right to speak, General Thackwell would not advance a yard!"[35]

Lord Gough's "victories" of Ramnagar and Sadulpur surprised military and political circles at Whitehall. In both Houses of Parliament disappointment was shown at the mode in which the Punjab campaign had been opened. Referring sarcastically to Gough's "Waterloo Letter" about the action at Sadulpur, the President of the Board wrote to the Governor-General:

> We have kept our thoughts to ourselves, unless indeed you think the way in which the Punjab war is mentioned in the Queen's Speech is sufficiently indicative of our disappointment. In fact, it is no wonder that all confidence in Lord Gough, if ever it was entertained, should have been entirely lost.[36]

Hardinge had reposed the fullest confidence in General Gough, and perhaps his finest gesture as a soldier-statesman was his offer to serve under him at Ferozeshah and Sobraon. Compared to this, Dalhousie's treatment of the grand old veteran of the Peninsular War appears to be full of pettiness and arrogance, and charged with unnecessary petulance. In this sordid affair, the conduct of Gough seems to be more dignified than that of Dalhousie. Private correspondence of the two men, the Duke of Wellington and Sir John Hob-

[34] Dalhousie to Hobhouse, 7 December 1848, Broughton Papers. [35] *Ibid.*

[36] Hobhouse to Dalhousie (Private), 7 February 1849, Dalhousie Muniments.

house, reveals that the Commander-in-Chief received shabby treatment at the hands of both the Government of India and the home authorities.[37]

From the outset, Dalhousie had been averse to the prolongation of Gough's command when it expired in August 1848, and before leaving for India, he had expressed his anxiety for a new appointment to the Duke of Wellington and Lord John Russell.[38] The suggestion, however, had carried little weight and the British Cabinet had extended Gough's term mainly on the recommendation of the Duke of Wellington. Dalhousie had accepted the reappointment without murmur, though later on he complained that his wishes had been ignored in the matter. Such being the case, a clash between the highly taciturn military commander and the equally overstrung Governor-General occurred soon after the Multan affair, when Dalhousie strongly disapproved the movements of European troops by Gough to Ambala and Ferozepur in May 1848. Herbert Edwardes's valiant action at Multan and its approbation by the Court and the Home authorities against Dalhousie's wishes, and the Commander-in-Chief's acquiescence in Currie's movement of a British column to support him were highly displeasing to the Governor-General.[39] Seeds of discord sown by these events created further disagreements. Gough's refusal to dismiss General Whish for raising the ineffective siege of Multan, his christening of the army assembled at Ferozepur as "the Army of the Punjab", and his order for moving up the Bombay Column to Multan had earned the Governor-General a sharp rebuke from the Secret Committee.[40]

37 For fuller details, see Broughton Papers; Dalhousie Muniments, Section 6, particularly Letters from India Board (London), Nos. 55-58, and Letters from Lord Gough, Nos. 71-72.

38 Dalhousie to Hobhouse (Private), 20 April 1849, Broughton Papers.

39 Dalhousie to Hobhouse, 11 May 1848, Broughton Papers; Hobhouse to Dalhousie, 24 August 1848, Dalhousie Muniments. Writing to Couper on 31 October 1848, he complained: "The despatches of the Court by the last mail are not satisfactory. Mr. Edwardes's successes have made them cock-a-hoop; they crow loudly, and manifest strong intention of throwing this Government over."

40 Hobhouse to Dalhousie, 7 July 1848, Dalhousie Muniments.

The breach widened with the disillusionment which came soon after the actions at Ramnagar and Sadulpur. Charging openly the Commander-in-Chief with incompetency, Dalhousie blamed him for incomplete actions and enormous losses. From that time onwards, interference in the direction of operations became open and flagrant. Relying mainly on the information supplied by political officers, particularly Major Mackeson, the Governor-General's political agent at the Commander's headquarters, he dubbed Gough's despatches as untruthful,[41] and peremptorily forbade him to cross the Chenab.[42] Gough acquiesced, though with protests against this unwarranted interference, and complained to the home authorities and the Duke of Wellington.

### *Disaster at Chillianwala*

Such was the state of affairs when Lord Gough fought the battle of Chillianwala. Resentful of intervention and under orders not to cross the Chenab for over a month, his force remained where it was. His headquarters were at Loah Tibbi and a bridge had been thrown across the river in front of Ramnagar. Attock had fallen and Chattar Singh had gone to Peshawar to meet Dost Muhammad Khan, his entire force having joined Sher Singh's army. "What His Excellency's plans are", Dalhousie reported of his forced inactivity, "or whether he has any plans at all, I am unable to tell you!"[43] However, by now Dalhousie realized, though never admitted, his mistake, and seeing danger imminent he ordered Gough to strike an effective blow at the enemy immediately.[44] When these orders came, the General marched his men from Loah Tibbi to Dhingee, 12 miles distant, leaving behind a small force at Ramnagar to blockade the river and to protect the bridge.

The main Sikh force was at Lollianwala, its left flank resting in the north at Rasul, on the river Jehlum. In the south, the villages from Lucknawala to Chak Fateh Shah were in their firm possession. In short, the interval of British inactivity had allowed Sher Singh to occupy a strongly entrenched position, completely commanded by the Sikh artillery.

41Dalhousie to Hobhouse, 20 January 1849, Broughton Papers.
42 *Ibid.*, 7 December 1849. 43 *Ibid.*, 4 January 1849.
44 *Parl. Papers* (*H. of C.*), 1849, xli, Paper 44, Doc. 51.

In the front of the Sikhs was a dense jungle eight miles wide, which could only be crossed by two narrow paths.[45]

A day later, on 13 January, the British approached the village of Chillianwala, where the Sikhs had a strong picket line. Beyond the village lay the ugly and dense jungle whose southern extremity of a low range of rugged hills was intersected by ravines, and in these hills were the Sikhs.[46] It is, however, doubtful that their total strength could have exceeded 10,000 men. The British took the village, but their preparations for encampment were rudely interrupted by sharp artillery fire. From a mound outside the village, Gough obtained an extended view of the Sikhs drawn out in battle array;[47] they had moved out of the hills into the dense jungle in front, their artillery bearing upon Chillianwala, to the left the hills and to the right thick jungle.

The British general at once decided upon an immediate engagement. But to his surprise, Henry Lawrence and Major Mackeson, on Dalhousie's orders, strongly objected. Here is Dalhousie's own account of his dramatic obstruction just before the battle:

> The Commander-in-Chief had resolved not to attack that day, but to reconnoitre and attack early next morning. The enemy, however, opened a distant fire, on which His Excellency forgot or abandoned all his plans and resolved to attack forthwith. Every one about him — his Staff, my Agent Sir Henry Lawrence pointed out to the inexpediency of this step. His answer was that he would attack. He told my Political Agent that he was the Commander-in-Chief of that army and desired him to be silent.[48]

45 *Ibid.*

46 *Ibid.*; Dalhousie to Hobhouse, 4 January 1849, Broughton Papers.

47 In his official despatch of 16 January 1849 (*Parl. Papers* (*H. of C.*), 1849, xli, Paper 44, Doc. 51), he estimated the Sikh force between 30-40,000 strong, which seems highly exaggerated, even if we presume that Chattar Singh's force had joined Sher Singh's army — a presumption belied by the evidence available. Moreover, the Sikh force was not concentrated, but spread on the right bank of the Jehlum in a wide arch from Rasul in the north to Lucknawala in the extreme south.

48 Dalhousie to Hobhouse (Confidential), Camp Mukho, 22 January 1849, Broughton Papers.

Few examples of such gross and unwarrantable interference by a Governor-General *in absentia* can be produced from British military annals in India.

The enemy was poised for attack. The Sikh guns had started a cannonade. Postponement of action on grounds of the lateness of the day, the exhausted state of the troops, or the general unfamiliarity with the terrain would have amounted to cowardice. Gough acted like a seasoned soldier. Completely unruffled by the chatter of protestations around him, he drew up the order of the battle. Any delay in the trial of strength would allow the enemy time to bring up his heavy artillery within the range of the British encampment. Following a conservative pattern, Gough placed Gilbert's 2nd Infantry Division on the right, flanked by Pope's cavalry brigade, and further strengthened by the 14th Light Dragoons and three troops of horse artillery under Lieut.-Col. Grant. To the left was Campbell's 3rd Infantry Division, flanked by White's cavalry brigade, with three troops of horse artillery under Lieut.-Col. Brind. In the centre were placed heavy 18-pounders and 8-inch howitzers, while the numerous field batteries were assigned to the two Infantry Divisions.

The British heavy guns opened up on the Sikh centre, their destructive fire supported by the field batteries of the left and right Infantry Divisions. The cannonade lasted for about an hour, when both the divisions were ordered to advance simultaneously.

But disaster resulted. The density of the jungle made it impossible to preserve order and formation; every British brigade was separated from its neighbour, and regiment parted from regiment. The Sikhs fought with determination and daring, and their artillery took a heavy toll. Campbell formed a line to his right, ordering Pope to protect his flank and movement. But the ground proved unsuitable for cavalry action and the artillery having failed to provide cover, the advancing British infantrymen were mowed down by the terrific fire of the Sikh musketry. The Sikh *ghorcharas* were on familiar ground; and in successive onslaughts broke up the British cavalry line. All was confusion. There was disorder in British ranks. They were fighting front, flanks, and rear at the same time. In vain they swept through the jungle, captured and spiked Sikh batteries, only to be driven helter-skelter at bayonet point by individual Sikh soldiers.

While Campbell's charge failed to dislodge the Sikhs from their position, towards the right, Pope's cavalry brigade, which included H.M. 14th Light Dragoons, H.M. 9th Lancers and the Bengal Regular Cavalry, advanced to meet some hundred Sikh horse swiftly advancing in their direction. The Sikh *ghorcharas* swept the field like lightning, yelling the dreadful Khalsa war cries. The entire British brigade took fright. On came the Khalsa horsemen sweeping the field like an avalanche. Suddenly, to their amazement, the enemy took to their heels, as if they had seen a ghost. They fled, galloping over their own horse artillery and turning it topsy-turvy, leaving their comrades to be slaughtered by the Sikhs. Four British guns were lost and nearly half a regiment wiped out. Dalhousie records that:

> The cavalry on the right disgraced their name and the colours they carry. They galloped on into the Field Hospital, among the wounded and never stopped till they were brought up by the Chaplain, who was administering to the wounded, and who pistol in hand, declared he would shoot at the first man who passed him.[49]

In another direction misfortune overtook a brigade led by Brigadier Pennycuick, which had moved in double time and precipitately advanced through the jungle. Again confusion followed: the regiments were separated, as were the officers from their men, and they arrived in complete disorder at a belt of the thick forest. Here the Sikh artillery waited. From within the jungle, the guns opened up with devastating effect. Lieut.-Col. Brookes, leading the 24th Foot, was killed between the enemy guns. Trapped, the brigade turned to flee in the face of the destructive fire of shot and shell. It left behind its commander, along with other field officers of the 24th, and nearly half the regiment slaughtered remorselessly.[50] The most serious disaster, however, befell Gilbert's division. The plight of Pope's cavalry had arrested Brigadier Godby's

49 *Ibid.*

50 *Parl. Papers* (*H. of C.*), 1849, xli, Paper 44, Doc. 51.

attention. He halted in utter bewilderment and a large body of Sikhs surrounded his 2nd Infantry Brigade. Now Gilbert's force had neither the cover of guns nor the support of cavalry. In the hand-to-hand fight, the brigade was repulsed and driven back with heavy loss.

The battle lasted over three hours. When darkness fell, Gough left the battlefield, ordering a retreat towards the village, and the Sikhs retired to Tupai, carrying away with them the 40 guns which the British later claimed to have captured. British casualties in the action amounted to 2,446 men, with 132 officers killed and 4 guns lost.[51] For some days after the battle, heavy gloom prevailed in the British camp.[52] The Commander-in-Chief claimed a victory,[53] which claim the Governor-General dubbed as "perhaps poetical".[54] "We have gained a victory," he observed ruefully, "like that of the ancients; it is such an one that 'another such would ruin us!' "[55]

Dalhousie now came out openly in his bid against the General. He informed the home authorities that Gough's ineptitude to command had been the main cause of the signal reverse at Chillianwala, and that "The army officers and men have lost confidence in their C-in-C and his own confidence is utterly gone. He flees from the excess of tumidity to the excess of timidity, and has no mind or plan — nothing but a will, an obstinate and jealous will."[56]

And yet, publicly salutes were fired and General Orders issued to celebrate a victory, and losses sustained were minimised.[57] In private it could not be concealed that the so-called victory was incomplete, and losses sustained quite incommensurate. Another such victory would compel the Governor-General to place the command in abler hands.[58] "He has won me a victory such as it is", reported Dalhousie.

51 *Ibid.*, 'The Return of Killed and Wounded at Chillianwala'.

52 Dalhousie to Hobhouse, 22 January 1849, Broughton Papers.

53 *Parl. Papers* (*H. of C.*), 1849, xli, Paper 44, Doc. 51.

54 Dalhousie to Sir John Russell, 20 April 1849, Broughton Papers.

55 Dalhousie to Couper, 20 January 1849, Dalhousie Papers.

56 Dalhousie to Hobhouse, 7 February 1849, Broughton Papers.

57 *Ibid.*, 22 January 1849.

58 *Ibid.*

> I have placed in the field in the Punjab a noble army — a nobler army never was assembled in India. With ordinary confidence it is fit to sweep India from Peshawar to Cape Comorin. If this army shall be repulsed, if its confidence lost, and the war protracted, it will be by the incompetency of the officer who has been retained in the command. I beg also respectfully to add that I will not submit to the Government of India being condemned and my reputation destroyed in silence, but will not conceal the fact that such a result will be attributable to the incapacity of the instrument by which I have been compelled to act.[59]

The news of Chillianwala and Multan[60] reached London at the same time. Whitehall informed Dalhousie that "the disaster [at Chillianwala] has thrown the success [at Multan] into shade — and the impression made upon public mind has been stronger than that caused by the Cabul massacre. . . . The result has been, that, in eight and forty hours, after the arrival of the mail, it was decided to send Sir Charles Napier to command the Indian Army."[61]

### *The Battle of Gujrat: "the Battle of Guns"*

Dalhousie's interference in Gough's campaign which had left him little independence of action and initiative was not taken into account. The India Board charged the General with incompetency; the Duke made the cryptic observation for his failure to employ the artillery in the battlefield: "they are not masters of their game"; and the critics at home dubbed him as "a superannuated general, who could not mount his horse without assistance, and who was irascible [*sic*] and wedded to ancient notions of cavalry manoeuvres." While these charges were in the air, the report of Sir Charles Napier's appoint-

59 *Ibid.*

60 In discussing the fate of Mulraj after his unconditional surrender, Hobhouse had agreed that "It would be better to send him across the seas for life than to hang him." As no convincing evidence of his guilt could ever be established he was deported for life, "a fate perhaps as terrible as death." Mulraj died on his way to the Andamans in August, 1851. (Hobhouse to Dalhousie, 14 July 1849).

61 Hobhouse to Dalhousie (Private), 7 March 1849, Dalhousie Muniments.

ment reached Dalhousie. Private advices from Sir John Hobhouse, the Duke of Wellington and Lord John Russell encouraged him to continue unabated his private war against the Commander-in-Chief.[62] The tenor of further complaints made to the Home Government was that whereas the Sikh army was regrouping on the banks of the Jehlum, the British operations were still confined to the Chenab.[63] The Sikhs were on the move — a large force with 40 guns had pushed forward north of the Porneu Pass and had steadily moved to Khoree on the left of the British flank. On 12 February the rest of the Sikh troops with 25 guns left Rasul to join the force at Khoree. "On the morning of 15th, the Sikh army was at Goozrat and Wuzeerabad, with a portion of their force across."[63a]

Gough had no direct knowledge of these accusations, but he refused to be browbeaten by the Governor-General. He listened to the representations made by the Governor-General's political officers, but replied firmly that it was his intention to wait for the large scale reinforcements ordered from Multan, which would give him a decided superiority over the enemy. On the 13th Whish's Column (13,400 men and 30 pieces of heavy artillery) reached Ramnagar. The Bombay Column (12,100 men and 3,000 cavalry) joined the Army of the Punjab a few days later. Thus assured of an overwhelming superiority of men and heavy artillery, Gough ordered the entire force forward, and four days later reaching the village of Shadewal, 5 miles south of Gujrat, he came face to face with the Sikh force.

The Commander-in-Chief's sudden movement surprised Dalhousie, but he threw this last barb at him. Writing in the most discourteous manner he threatened him with summary dismissal if, "in his persistent obstinacy", he failed to use his guns and fought an incomplete action. "I shall not leave him," he reported to the India Board angrily, "to demoralise the army he commands, and this he is rapidly doing". He

62 "After what happened," wrote the British P.M. confidentially to the G.-G., "I should advise your Lordship, if you have not already done so, to place the command in the hands of some officer in whom the troops should have full confidence." Dalhousie Muniments.

63 Dalhousie to Hobhouse, 21 February 1849, Broughton Papers.

63a *Ibid.*

further forbade him to cross the Jehlum, nominating Gilbert to be in command of the force which would cross that river.[64] Gough stopped all private communications with the Governor-General and proceeded forthwith to Jehlum.

Sher Singh's army now reinforced by Chattar Singh's force and an Afghan contingent of 3,000 horse under Akram Khan had encircled the strategic town of Gujrat.[65] The regular Sikh troops were placed in the centre, between the town and the deep dry bed of the river Dwara which passed round nearly two sides of the town and then ran south through the centre of the ground at Shadewal. The Sikh position on the right was greatly strengthened, the *nullah* giving cover to their infantry in front of their guns. Another deep and narrow watercourse falling eastwards in the Chenab towards Wazirabad covered their left, where in the village of Burra Kalra a large body of infantry was concentrated. The four-mile-wide open ground between the two watercourses was well suited to all forces; the Sikh artillery was stretched on the *nullahs*, their cavalry on both the flanks.

The battle of Gujrat fought on 21 February, 1849 must be regarded as one of the most memorable in the annals of British warfare in India.[66] Never perhaps had the British amassed so many guns and men in any single battle.[67] Lord Gough placed on the extreme left the Bombay Column (Dundas) supported by a brigade of cavalry and Sind Horse, troops of horse artillery covering the infantry. On its right was the 3rd Infantry Division (Campbell) covered by light field batteries and a brigade of infantry in reserve. To the right stood the 2nd Infantry Division (Gilbert). The heavy field guns having been dispersed between the two divisions, the

64 *Ibid.*

65 Dalhousie to Hobhouse, 6 March 1849, Broughton Papers. The Sikh intention of crossing the Chenab and marching on to Lahore cannot be accepted for the simple reason that Whish's force barred their passage below Wazirabad, and with the arrival of the Bombay Column all hopes, if any, of their entry into the RechnaDoab were lost. A portion of their force was separated from the rest, having crossed the Jehlum, while their main army 20,000 strong moved upon Gujrat.

66 G.-G. to Secret Committee, 7 March 1849, Bengal & India Secret Letters, No. 13, Ind(ia) Off(ice) Lib(rary).

67 The total British army inclusive of the Lahore force amounted to 56,636 of all arms, 11,569 cavalry, 96 field and 67 siege guns.

line was prolonged by the 1st Infantry Division (Whish) and a second line formed in support of the whole covered by troops of horse artillery. The cavalry brigades (White and Pope) and the horse artillery protected the right; the light cavalry with Bombay light field batteries protected the rear and baggage.

At half-past eight the whole British army advanced with the precision of a parade movement.[68] The Sikh guns opened up, disclosing their position and range. The British general brought the three divisions to a sudden halt and ordered the advance of the whole line of artillery — left, right and centre. The cannonade of 100 guns which now opened up was described as "magnificent and terrific in its effects."[69] The Sikh artillery replied with its accustomed rapidity, but the terrific fire of British 18-pounders and 8-inch howitzers broke up their obstinate resistance. No infantry movement took place for nearly two hours. The batteries of the 1st and 2nd Divisions inched forward to within 600 yards and heavy field guns to within 800 yards of the Sikh lines, breaking up their ranks and taking up forward positions.[70]

When the guns on both sides had spent their fury, the British infantry line advanced rapidly and drove the Sikhs before it. The Sikh positions at Burra Kalra and Chota Kalra, where their infantry was concentrated, were quickly captured and the Sikhs driven out of cover. Within an hour the battle was over.[71]

The Sikh loss was estimated between 3,000-5,000 men and 53 guns; the British casualties were 96 killed and 700 wounded. "The Sikhs," commented Dalhousie afterwards, "displayed the skill, the courage and activity which belong to their race."[72] At long last the British General had retrieved his reputation by a decisive and complete victory. "I think," wrote Dalhousie grudgingly, "that the C-in-C of the army may justly feel that he has gained a victory calculated, as much as any that has ever been won in India."[73] Soon afterwards, General Gough resigned his command.

68 *Parl. Papers* (*H. of C.*), 1849, xli, Paper 49, Doc. 3.

69 *Ibid.* 70 *Ibid., Doc.* 6.

71 G.-G. to Secret Committee, 7 March 1849, Bengal & India Secret Letters No. 13, Ind. Off. Lib.

72 Dalhousie to the Queen, 7 March 1849, Broughton Papers. 73 *Ibid.*

## APPENDIX

### THE ARMY OF THE PUNJAB (21 FEBRUARY, 1849)

| | | | |
|---|---|---|---|
| 1. *1st Division* (Whish) | | | |
| inclusive of the Lahore force under Courtland and Imam Bux | | | 13,400 |
| Cavalry | 5,000 | | |
| Artillery | 67 siege and 30 field guns | | |
| 2. *2nd Division* (Gilbert) | | | 5,248 |
| 3. *3rd Division* (Campbell) | | | 8,171 |
| 4. *Bombay Column* (Dundas) | | | |
| 4 reg. of Eur. Infan. | 4,000 | | |
| 9 reg. of N.I. | 8,100 | | |
| 5 reg. cav. | 3,000 | | 15,100 |
| 5. *Troops at Ramnagar* | | | 1,837 |
| 6. *Cavalry Division* | | | |
| 1st Brigade (White) | 2,006 | | |
| 2nd Brigade (Pope) | 1,563 | | 3,569 |
| 7. *Artillery Division* (Tennaut) | | | |
| 6 troops horse artillery | 36 guns | 420 men | |
| 3 field batteries | 18 guns | 180 men | |
| 2 heavy batteries | 12 guns | 120 men | |
| 8. *Force at Lahore* | | | |
| 5 reg. N.I. | 4,321 | | |
| 1 troop horse art. | 131 | | |
| 3 cos. F. art. | 311 | | |
| 1 co. Pioneers | 115 | | |
| irr. cav. | 659 | | 5,537 |
| *Under Wheeler* | | | |
| 2 reg. N.I. | 1,937 | | |
| 1 troop horse art. | 126 | | |
| Lt. cav. | 197 | | |
| F. art. | 973 | | |
| Lt. cav. | 541 | | 3,774 |
| TOTAL: | Infantry | 56,636 | |
| | Cavalry | 11,569 | |
| | Artillery | 96 siege and 67 field guns (inclusive of 10 18-pounders and 6 8-inch howitzers drawn by elephants). | |

# SEPARATED BY A CENTURY: EDUCATION IN INDIA AND EAST AFRICA

KENNETH INGHAM

A study of educational developments in India in the late eighteenth and early nineteenth centuries and in East Africa a century later reveals interesting contrasts and some rueful parallels. The general situation in both regions was very similar. Order was maintained with the good will of local princes and chiefs and by the presence of a handful of troops with European commanders. After a series of campaigns to establish their authority, the East India Company in the one instance and the British Government itself in the other were reluctant to involve themselves in expensive administrative exercises. Officials in the countries concerned frequently showed more enterprise in a number of directions than their supporters at home would have approved, but in the end considerations of economy inevitably exercised a stultifying influence upon their efforts. The idea of educating the whole population was, in both cases, far beyond the financial competence of the local administration, even if in the late eighteenth century such a policy had not been far in advance of popular opinion. In both India and East Africa, however, Christian missionaries were present to provide the enthusiasm and the talent which made it possible, if not to educate the whole population along western lines, at least to bring the idea of such education to all conditions of men.

The basic difference between the two situations lay initially in the attitude of Europeans towards the people they were called upon to govern. These attitudes were largely uninformed even among those living in the countries concerned. In India, Islam commanded the respect if not always the approval of the Company's servants. Hinduism, too, with its classical Sanskrit literature, captured the interest of the more scholarly-minded administrative officers. However unreliable and scheming they may have seemed in their relations with the Company, the Indian princes had a measure of dignity and style. They were the descendants of ancient civilizations, corrupt perhaps, but no more so than many of the petty monarchies of Europe. "Darkest Africa", by contrast, was not so called simply because it was unknown to the nations of Europe, but also because in the eyes of the latter its people were deeply submerged in the darkness of ignorance, insecurity and want. The efficient organization of the Buganda kingdom under its ruler, Mutesa I, startled the earliest European visitors, but the other peoples of East Africa were thought to lack all vestiges of worthwhile culture. Mwanga, too, Mutesa's son, who succeeded his father in 1885, quickly defaced the image Mutesa had created in the minds of the Englishmen who knew him, and although a number of his subordinates performed bravely in their relations with the British this did not make up for the fairly obvious deficiencies to western eyes of the people of the surrounding region.

To the British in India, then, it came as no surprise in 1780 when "a considerable number of Mussulmen of Credit and Learning" in Bengal attended upon the Governor-General with the request that he should try to prevail upon a Muslim stranger lately arrived in the Residency to remain and instruct students in Muhammadan Law and "in such other Sciences as are taught in the Mahametan school". The petitioners' arguments appealed directly to the pride, the civilization and the common sense of the Company's officials. They represented that it was a favourable occasion to establish a Madrassa, or College, that Calcutta was already the seat of a great empire and the resort of people from all parts of Hindustan and the Deccan. It had been the pride of every polished court and the wisdom of every well-regulated government both in India and

Persia to promote the growth and extension of liberal knowledge by such means, but there had been a serious decline in learning accompanying that of the Mugal empire. Finally, the numerous offices of government required men of trained ability to fill them and care must be taken to select people of eminence in science and jurisprudence to fill them.[1]

This was no request for widespread education but a petition from the old aristocracy to their new overlords asking them to foster the scholarship of the formerly dominant class. As such it stirred the interest of the rulers both in India and England who, though they may have been businessmen, were also gentlemen. The Governor-General readily gave his assistance to launch the project and appealed to the Court of Directors of the East India Company for a more adequate and permanent endowment.

The initiative for the founding of a Hindu College in Benares came in 1792 from a British official, Jonathan Duncan, Resident at Benares, but the appeal was based on identical grounds. To the Governor-General Duncan recommended that a part of the surplus revenue from Cornwallis's Permanent Settlement should be devoted to the establishment of a Hindu College "for the preservation and cultivation of the Laws, Literature and Religion of that Nation at this centre of their faith". This would, he thought, endear the Government to the Hindus while making possible the collection of "a precious library of the most ancient and valuable general learning and tradition now perhaps existing in any part of the Globe". At the same time it would directly benefit both the people and the Government by disseminating the knowledge of Hindu law and by providing a training ground for Hindu scholars who would assist the European judges in administering the law.[2]

The important factor in both these instances was that the measures proposed would be pleasing to the leaders of the Indian people and would therefore contribute towards the maintenance of order. More questionable, therefore, was the proposal made by John Sulivan, Resident in Tanjore, that schools

[1] Extract of Bengal Public Consultations, 18 April 1781, Home Misc(ellaneous) Series, cdlxxxvii, 1-5, Ind(ia) Off(ice) Lib(rary).

[2] Extract of Bengal Revenue Consultations, 13 January 1792, Home Misc. Series, cdlxxxvii, pp. 29-32, Ind. Off. Lib.

should be established in his district for the teaching of English. Although he argued that this might prove the most effective means of communicating the Government's aims to the Indian population and that with the aid of a Danish missionary named Christian Freidrich Schwartz he had prevailed upon the Rajah of Tanjore to accept the plan, the Court of Directors remained cautious.[3] They realized that the action might be interpreted by the Indians as an attempt to interfere with their customs, but they comforted themselves with the assurance that in all other respects their rule could be clearly seen to be superimposed upon the existing social structure rather than attempting to supplant it, and that it was aimed solely at protecting the rights and happiness of the people.

The missionary link in the project was conceived to be much more dangerous since it might entail an attempt to convert the people to Christianity and so stir up resentment. The Directors therefore required a firm assurance that this was not the intention before they would give their support.[4] At this stage their fears were probably without foundation. Only a few years later the arrival of the first representatives of the more evangelical Protestant missionary societies put a new complexion on the whole situation. These men had one overriding aim, to win the people of India from the darkness of what they believed to be superstition and idolatry to the light of the Christian faith. The chief means of succeeding in this aim lay in providing the Gospels and the means of reading them. This was just as important for the poor and the simple as for the rich and the scholarly. With their energy and determination the new missionaries presented a challenge to Hindu society at every level.

The Baptist missionaries established a college at Serampore in Bengal where instruction in Sanskrit was combined with the study of European ideas and methods of thinking, and in 1820 the Anglicans founded Bishop's college in Calcutta where Indians received instruction in Christian theology. At these centres Hindu and Muslim philosophies were

[3] Court of Directors' Letter, 16 February 1787, Box C, India II, 2, no. 15a, S(ociety for the) P(ropagation of the) G(ospel).

[4] John Sulivan to Schwartz, 29 January 1787, Box C, India II, 2, no. 14, S.P.G.

challenged by liberal western ideas. At the village level the challenge was equally vigorous though the missionaries' techniques differed. In the indigenous village schools, where they existed, instruction was given in the elements of the Muslim or Hindu religions while children learned by precept and by practice the customs and traditions of the society in which they lived. Improvement, indeed change of any kind, was not envisaged. Among the Hindus in particular the caste system provided a solid framework within which, provided the rules were obeyed, society could move along its inevitable road without disturbance. To these traditions the missionaries presented not the contrast of a liberal critical education but the challenge of an alternative tradition, no less dogmatic even if it was deemed by the missionaries themselves to be more enlightened in content. Nor did they limit their teaching to the children who came to their schools. When manpower permitted, preaching took place to adults in bazaars and other public places.

These open and aggressive methods of proselytization were not at all to the liking of the Court of Directors. Yet their caution was probably excessive since there is plentiful evidence to suggest that the poorer Indian families at least were often more than willing to risk the dangers of conversion in order to enjoy any form of instruction which might confer the skills required to open the gateway to government employment in a clerical capacity. The bolder among the Company's servants in India recognized this, and it is significant that the Company's policy towards the missionaries' activities varied with successive Governors and Governors-General without any noticeable change in the degree of unrest in the country.

East Africa a century later provided the same picture of an administration strictly limited by financial considerations from undertaking any adventurous policy. By contrast with the situation in India, however, the attitude of both the British Government and of the administrators in East Africa was uniformly friendly towards the activities of the missionary societies once protectorates had been declared. Interest in the abolition of the slave trade had given the British presence in East Africa a benevolent aura even if the actual declaration of the protectorates had been primarily a diplomatic move to forestall the overseas expansion of rival European powers. There was, therefore, a sense of moral responsibility towards the African people although the administrators themselves could see little prospect of any large-scale improvement as a result of their own limited efforts. In any event, government responsibility for mass education was still a new idea even in England.

The missionaries were in a different category. In Buganda they had begun to teach boys to read more than a decade before the Protectorate was declared. They were willing to undertake educational work, and so far as the administrators could see nothing but good was likely to come from their efforts. It did not seem possible that their teaching would conflict with any indigenous scholarship for, except among the Arabs of the coast, reflective study seemed non-existent. For the Africans of the interior instruction of the children took a practical form. In the household of the ruler of Buganda young pages, sons of chiefs, were brought up to understand the functions of the offices of state. While the hereditary principle scarcely existed the association of certain families with the country's administration was perpetuated by these means and the stability of the society assured. Similarly, among the non-monarchical Jaluo of western Kenya young men and boys learned the rules of their community and acquired a theoretical knowledge of such basic skills as farming and how best to make war by listening to discussions among the elders in a social assembly called *chir*.[5] Again this was essentially the product of a conservative system demanding obedience to custom rather than encouraging young minds to question what went on around them. It was by their results that these and similar systems were judged by contemporary western observers and to them the results were not impressive except, perhaps, in Buganda where a high degree of organization existed. Administrators and missionaries were equally confident that education to a higher moral code and instruction in more effective methods of making a living would not only be beneficial to the Africans but would be readily seen by them to be so. Experience in Buganda appeared to bear out this view. There was

[5] B. A. Ogot, "The Social History of the Jaluo, 1870-1890," Makerere College Arts Research Prize Essay, 1950. Unpublished.

consequently little of the uncertainty regarding the effects of interference in the religious and social order of the people which had encouraged caution in India.

The German rulers in what was later to become Tanganyika took a more exclusively practical line, concluding that their main aim must be to train selected Africans to carry out the orders of the Administration. Education, at least in the 99 government schools which had been opened by 1914, was simply a question of learning a new routine, a process which would probably be expedited by acquiring some degree of literacy.[6] With the exception of an industrial school opened by the Kenya Government in Machakos in 1914 the administrators of the British East African territories were content to leave African education entirely in the hands of missionaries without questioning either their aims or methods. The missionaries were themselves limited by lack of funds, so that a uniform programme was difficult to implement and individuals tended to develop their own educational ideas with whatever talents they possessed. Nor with most of the human material at their disposal could they hope to make much progress initially. Following traditional practice instruction was given in reading to provide the foundations upon which elementary Christian teaching could be built, but wherever possible an attempt was made to go further and to develop "the whole man". The Catholic Mill Hill missionaries in Uganda started a school in 1901 where pupils not only read in English but also studied mathematics, geography and music. Two years later and only a few miles away the Church Missionary Society founded King's College, at Budo, to carry students beyond the stage of learning the three R's.[7]

The administrators of both the British East African Protectorates were pleased with what they saw. In 1904 Sir James Hayes-Sadler, His Majesty's Commissioner in Uganda, gave sincere praise to the missionaries' educational activities in his annual report on the Protectorate, and the Government gave £10 scholarships to the mission schools to promote

[6] Judith Listowel, *The Making of Tanganyika* (London, 1965), p. 48.

[7] Kenneth Ingham, *The Making of Modern Uganda* (London, 1959), p.123.

secondary education.[8] In the neighbouring East Africa Protectorate, later Kenya, the Government only paid the missionary societies capitation grants of £5 per head for boys who reached a satisfactory standard in various skills such as carpentry, masonry and agriculture, but official approval of missionary achievements was certainly not limited to their successes in these purely practical subjects.[9]

Thus, in the early years of European administration western education in both India and East Africa remained the responsibility of Christian missionaries, but in atmospheres which differed widely in so far as official attitudes were concerned. In both regions, however, although a hundred years separated events, the second decade of the century saw the beginnings of a change in the attitude of the European rulers towards educational matters. The provision in the Charter Renewal Act of 1813 for an annual expenditure on education of at least £7,500 from the East India Company's surplus revenue was the result of the efforts of evangelicals in England to influence members of Parliament rather than of any initiative from the Company itself. In any case such a sum was never available until 1823. Nevertheless, in 1815 the Company began to advance Rs. 600 a month, later increased to Rs. 800, to support the schools set up in Chinsurah by Robert May of the London Missionary Society, after being assured that no attempt would be made to convert the children to Christianity.[10] Shortly afterwards the Governor-General, Lord Hastings, who had been responsible for initiating assistance to Robert May, gave money to the Baptist missionary, Jabez Carey, to open schools in Rajputana, and both the Calcutta School Society and the Calcutta School-Book Society, founded by a group of private individuals, received an annual grant as a result of Hastings's intervention.[11]

More significant was the change in the outlook of the Court of Directors towards the encouragement of Hindu

[8] "Colonial Policy and Education in British East Africa, 1900-1950," *The Journal of British Studies*, vol. V, no. 2 (May 1966), p. 119.

[9] *Cd. 6007. East Africa Protectorate Annual Report, 1911-12*, pp. 57-8.

[10] Bengal Despatches, xxc, 627-9 and xxcvi, 603-5, Ind. Off. Lib.

[11] The Marchioness of Bute (ed.), *The Private Journals of the Marquess of Hastings*, 2nd edn. (London, 1858), ii, 346-7.

and Muslim learning. While still prepared to admit that there were "few objects more worthy of the attention of a liberal and enlightened Government, than the protection and encouragement of Science and Literature", they were unimpressed by reports on the achievements of the Hindu College at Benares. In an attempt to improve the standard there and in two similar colleges more recently established at Nadia and Tirhut they suggested that an incentive should be provided by offering the best students posts in the courts of justice. They were opposed to the establishment of further colleges for the study of Persian and Arabic since this would not only give the Muslim population an unfair proportion of the country's educational opportunities but would also serve to perpetuate among the Hindus the memory of a past domination.[12]

These doubts about the success of the Muslim and Hindu colleges did not yet betoken a complete change of heart among the Court of Directors. They were, too, quite happy to look to the indigenous village schools to achieve a general improvement in the character of the people. In 1819 they were still anxious to avoid all interference with the religious prejudices of the people.[13] This continuing caution in England was in contrast with the attitude of one of the Company's servants, the Resident at Allepey in Southern India, who was openly in favour of making proficiency in English compulsory for all who hoped to obtain a good situation. He persisted in this view although the C.M.S. missionaries in the district made no secret of their belief that education would help the spread of Christianity and in spite of the fact that it was rumoured in the bazaar that the local people were doubtful of the benefits of the instruction and were nervous that their children might be converted to Christianity.[14] His confidence was quickly justified, for even the preaching of the missionaries aroused no unrest.

But greater changes were on their way. In 1823 a General Committee of Public Instruction was set up by the Govern-

[12] Bengal Despatches, lxvi, 232-50, Ind. Off. Lib.

[13] *Ibid.*, xxc, 631.

[14] Copy of correspondence, South India etc., i, 24-8 and 35, Church Missionary Society.

ment of Bengal to investigate the state of education in the Presidency and to submit recommendations for its improvement. It was not anticipated that any large-scale programme would be the outcome, nor did such a programme emerge. In 1824, however, the Court of Directors, who had previously expressed their disappointment with the work of the Hindu College and the Madrassa, openly denounced the whole philosophy upon which those colleges had been established. In a forceful letter which the Board of Control attempted unsuccessfully to modify the Court stated that "With respect to the Sciences it is worse than a waste of time to employ persons either to teach or to learn them, in the state in which they are found in the Oriental Books. As far as any historical document may be found in the Oriental Languages, what is desirable is, that they should be translated, and this it is evident, will best be accomplished by Europeans who have acquired the requisite knowledge. Beyond these branches, what remains in Oriental Literature is poetry, but it never has been thought necessary to establish Colleges for the cultivation of poetry". The Court were still filled with "zeal for the progress and improvement of education among the Natives of India" and were prepared "to make sacrifices to that important end", but they now believed that the whole plan of the colleges had been "originally and fundamentally erroneous". The great end should not have been "to teach Hindoo learning or Mahomedan learning, but useful learning."[15] Here at last emerged the explanation for the Court's change of heart. The Directors have succumbed to the doctrines of the Utilitarians.

The Directors' change of view became still more evident a year later in a letter commending the activities of the Vidyalaya, a college which had been founded in Calcutta in 1816 on the instigation of a number of wealthy Indians. The aim of the college had been to enable the sons of the founders to receive instruction in English language and literature and in European science, as well as in Asiatic languages, and willing use was made there of scientific equipment provided by the British Indian Society. Seizing upon the news of the college's success the Directors urged the Governor-General to continue

15 Bengal Despatches, xcv, 1069-73, Ind. Off. Lib.

to stimulate the acquisition of useful knowledge by offering preferment in the Company's service to those Indians who attained the highest standard of proficiency in the subjects taught at the college.[16] Two years later they were even prepared to assert that a little skill and address was all that was necessary in most cases to remove the prejudices of the Indians which they believed were not particularly strong as far as education was concerned.[17]

This new-found confidence in the superiority of western education over the teaching of the Orient did not affect the official attitude towards Christian teaching. Jabez Carey, who had used the Scriptures as a school book when he first started work in Ajmer, was subsequently forbidden to do so or to use any religious tracts which might arouse jealousy among the parents of his pupils.[18] About the same time the Governor-General, Lord Amherst, rescinded a decision taken in his absence by the members of his Council to support the efforts of the Ladies Society for Native Female Education to build a central school. Some of the patrons of the Society, Amherst claimed, had expressed an intention to propagate Christianity, and on learning this the Court of Directors gave their full support to the Governor-General's decision.[19]

The Court's new educational policy was finally enunciated in 1827. In view of the limited resources available to the Company, they stated, their most effective contribution to Indian education would lie in the centres of greatest importance and among the upper and middle classes whose influence upon their fellow countrymen was strongest. In addition to providing sound education along western lines for these groups they must also endeavour to prepare a body of men whose ability and probity would fit them for the discharge of public duties.[20] For the vast majority of the people whose only immediate concern was the daily routine of village life their own indigenous languages and their own indigenous schools were thought to provide adequate instruction.

16 *Ibid.*, xcix, 167-74. 17 *Ibid.*, cv, 313.

18 Jabez Carey to the Rev. John Dyer, 22 October 1824, Baptist Missionary Society.

19 Bengal Despatches, ciii, 447-56, Ind. Off. Lib.

20 *Ibid.*, cv, 324-6 and 361-2.

All the colleges supported by the Government appeared to be working satisfactorily towards the Directors' target by 1830. In that year the Court noted the progress in the study of the English language in both Muslim and Hindu colleges and also recorded that work was being carried on in the field of anatomy along western lines and involving both the handling of human bones and the dissection of animals. It was now openly recognized, the Court stated, that a knowledge of English was essential as a means of access to this broader field of knowledge.[21] Not all the Company's servants were so confident that the growing emphasis upon English teaching was beneficial, and a number of the more influential among them began in the 1830s to stress the importance of building upon indigenous cultures. They were running against the tide of public feeling in England and the growing confidence of the Victorian era was soon to sweep aside their misgivings.

In the meantime Christian missionaries continued as they had begun, providing such all-round education as their pupils were willing and able to accept and finding for the most part that their teaching won readiest acceptance among those who believed it would benefit them most, whether by giving them access to better paid employment or, in the case of the untouchables, by giving them a status they could not otherwise have dreamed of acquiring. Among the better educated and wealthier classes who earlier had been most critical of the missionaries acceptance was slow. Many, however, saw that the best answer to the missionaries was to revive their own beliefs rather than simply to oppose those of the Christians. In some cases this resulted in a conservative reaction, but more often Hinduism, with its genius for absorbing the ideas of others and adapting them to its own ends, returned the challenge of the West by assimilating such elements of western scholarship as it deemed necessary while apparently resisting all attempts at western encroachment.

It was not the bold spirit of a new age of material prosperity which brought changes in the attitude of the rulers of East Africa towards the education of those under their protection. The First World War had exhausted the peoples of the region,

[21] *Ibid.*, cxiv, 359-90.

setting back economic development for almost a decade and laying waste the whole of former German East Africa. But the struggle had shown Africans in a new light to many Europeans who had come to recognize their latent abilities for the first time. In the councils of the Great Powers consideration was being given to the advancement of subject peoples who had contributed so nobly to the white men's war. These charitable sentiments, however, were almost always tempered with a powerful element of paternalism, so that the growth of public interest in African education resulted in a mixture of liberal sentiment and mundane practices.

It was the latter element which predominated immediately after the war when local schemes held the field before the Government in England had had time to promulgate their plans. British administrators were at one with the old established trading concerns and the most recently arrived settlers in their anxiety to stimulate as quickly as possible the territories' run-down economy, and to do this they believed there was an urgent need for a trained African labour force. In their view, therefore, education of a purely practical kind was the prime necessity. In 1919 the Governor of Uganda appointed a Development Commission which recommended that technical schools should be founded without delay to train carpenters, masons and motor mechanics. The report continued, "We are opposed to any extensive literary education for the general native population, and we consider that it should not proceed beyond a standard which will enable a native to learn a trade by which he can earn a living. Unless literary education is complete, or is accompanied by technical training, the native is apt to regard himself as a superior being for whom the ordinary duties and responsibilities of life have no significance. He is not advanced sufficiently to obtain employment as a clerk and he will not demean himself by manual work. Too often, therefore, he becomes a loafer, and degenerates."[22]

The Director of Education in Kenya, J. R. Orr, and a number of missionaries were able to exert a more liberal influence upon the deliberations of the committee set up at

[22] *Report of the Uganda Development Commission, 1920* (Entebbe, 1920), paras. 220-31.

about the same time by the Convention of Associations, the "settlers' parliament", with a view to urging the Kenya Government to initiate a policy of technical education for Africans. While recommending that European craftsmen should be encouraged to train African artisans in various skills they also suggested that evening classes should be opened in African locations to teach elementary reading, writing and arithmetic. Among the Jaluo and Kikuyu, from whom there had been many requests for education, the Government should combine technical and general education in new government schools while assisting the mission schools to do the same.[23] Most of these recommendations were accepted by the Government, but eighteen months later the Education Department was unguarded enough to comment in its Annual Report that "it will be readily admitted by most educationists that literary education *per se* is harmful to the ordinary native of Africa". *The Leader of British East Africa*, a Nairobi newspaper which claimed to voice the opinions of the white settlers, was quick to underline the statement and to declare "what is wanted is technical education in excelsis with a good knowledge of English to supplement it".[24]

In England a broader-based interest in the problems of African education resulted in 1923 in the appointment of an Advisory Committee on Native Education in the British Tropical African Dependencies. The Chairman was the Hon. W. G. A. Ormsby-Gore, Parliamentary Under-Secretary of State for the Colonies, and among the nine members were two bishops, Dr. J. H. Oldham, Secretary of the International Missionary Council, and a number of others, including Lord Lugard, who possessed a wide knowledge of the African scene. Ormsby-Gore was also Chairman of the East Africa Commission which in 1925 reported on the overall political, economic and social situation in East Africa,[25] a report which inevitably included opinions on educational issues and which echoed the recommendations made by the Advisory Committee in March.[26] Only the previous year and with a more

23 *The Leader of British East Africa*, 14 February 1920.

24 *Ibid.*, 24 September 1921.

25 Cmd. 2387. 26 Cmd. 2374.

predominantly missionary flavour the American-financed Phelps-Stokes Commission had also published its report on African education.[27]

All these reports noted that provision for education had previously been inadequate and that with increasing revenues in the various territories the time had come to devote much more money to African education. The most striking pronouncement appeared in the report of the Advisory Committee which was adopted by the British Government. It stated that while the Government would welcome all voluntary educational efforts which conformed to their policy they would in future reserve to themselves the direction of educational policy and the supervision of all educational institutions. That policy, as now defined, reflected the ideas of indirect rule which Lord Lugard had formulated when he was himself an administrator in Tropical Africa, and it posed the same difficulties in its implementation which were revealed in other spheres. "Education", the report stated, "should be adapted to the mentality, aptitudes, occupations and traditions of the various peoples, conserving as far as possible all sound and healthy elements in the fabric of their social life; adapting them where necessary to changed circumstances and progressive ideas, as an agent of natural growth and evolution."

So traditional Africa was no longer wholly dark, and what was good in indigenous custom was to be used as a foundation upon which to build in the future. This, the committee was wise enough to admit, was not an easy undertaking, since contact with western civilization, and with western education, must tend to weaken tribal authority and the sanctions of existing beliefs. The report gave no clear guidance as to how these difficulties should be overcome. With the hopeful assurance of men who would not have to find the solution in practice the committee insisted upon the importance of religious teaching and moral instruction, stressed once again that such teaching should be related to the conditions of life and daily experience of the pupils, and then emerged triumphantly from the conflict with the proclamation that "with

[27] Thomas Jesse Jones, *Education in East Africa* (London, 1924).

such safeguards, contact with civilization need not be injurious, or the introduction of new religious ideas have a disruptive influence antagonistic to constituted secular authority".

The British, French, Italian and American missionaries who, since the expulsion of the German missionary societies, had borne the brunt of the educational task must have listened ruefully to these comments. Yet they were aware that their resources made it impossible for them to undertake the education of the whole East African population and they could not avoid a feeling of satisfaction that the British Government had now declared their interest in the work. The Advisory Committee had also recommended that grants-in-aid should be made to mission schools which conformed to their policy and reached a prescribed standard, and this could be a valuable aid to hard-pressed missionary finances. Yet the problem remained as to how the missionaries could safeguard their specifically Christian aims while trying to meet the Government's requirements. By its insistence on the value of indigenous customs the Government's policy clearly threatened to thwart the development of a Christian society in spite of the tributes paid to religious instruction.

In the new atmosphere of enthusiasm for African education the missionaries' misgiving tended to be brushed aside. The publication of the new statement of policy provided an opportunity for those who were aware of the importance of education to demonstrate their faith. In Tanganyika the new Governor, Sir Donald Cameron, a disciple of Lugard and a sincere supporter of African advancement, saw the report of the Advisory Committee as his country's Charter of Education. Noting that, due to the lack of educational facilities, all the clerks and artisans and most of the primary school teachers in the territory had been imported from India, Ceylon, Nyasaland and Mauritius, he set himself to remedy the situation at once. He observed, too, that the Government's former reluctance to assist the mission schools had deprived the territory of considerable educational benefits, since to help a mission school would have cost the tax-payers only half as much as to operate a government school.[28]

28 Sir Donald Cameron, *My Tanganyika Service* (London, 1939), pp. 127-8.

As the result of an education conference which sat in Dar-es-Salaam in October 1925 the Government agreed to guide and assist financially the secular educational activities of the missions. A central advisory committee was set up on which Government, missions and prospective employers were all represented and the committee was to be assisted by provincial or district committees.[29] Owing to delays in preparing the details of the scheme grants-in-aid were not paid until 1927, but expenditure on African education rose from £15,754 in the financial year 1924-25[30] to £59,682 in 1927-28[31] with prospects of topping £80,000 in the following year. Efforts were also made to live up to the Charter of Education by providing education for girls, which the Ormsby-Gore Committee had admitted was a matter of the utmost delicacy. Here the mission schools had the advantage for the only African women teachers had been trained by the missionaries and wished to continue to work for the missions.[32]

There is no doubting Cameron's enthusiasm but there is considerable doubt as to whether administrative officers could run happily in double harness with the missionaries. Cameron himself was convinced that wholehearted cooperation was possible and believed sincerely that before he left Tanganyika it had been achieved. But his own reliance upon African tradition was bound to be at variance to some extent with the missionaries' prime aim which was to preach the Gospel of Jesus Christ. In the event, on Cameron's departure the Government's enthusiasm for African education showed a sharp decline. The economic depression which staggered the world in the early 1930s provided a genuine excuse for retrenchment, but more limited support for education was, in any case, more suited to the outlook of Cameron's successors.

The Tanganyika Annual Report for 1934 contained a re-appraisal of the educational needs of the country in the light

[29] Colonial no. 18, *Tanganyika Territory, Annual Report, 1925* (London, 1926), p. 65.

[30] Colonial no. 32, *Tanganyika Territory, Annual Report, 1926* (London, 1928), p. 67.

[31] Colonial no. 39, *Tanganyika Territory, Annual Report, 1928* (London, 1929), p. 19.

[32] *Ibid.*, p. 52.

of returning prosperity. It claimed to be a realistic survey; it was certainly not a bold one. The slump had resulted in serious unemployment among the artisans who had just begun to emerge in small numbers as a result of Cameron's educational programme. There must be no possibility of similar unemployment in the future, stated the report, so the government industrial schools were to be reduced from seven to two. Hitherto, eight government schools and fifteen assisted mission schools had provided slightly more advanced education of a combined general and technical character. In the Government's opinion there were inadequate opportunities of employment for the numbers of pupils who reached this lowly level. Once again the schools were to be cut down so as to retain only sufficient pupils to meet the needs of Tabora school, where they were trained for the clerical service or prepared to go for further education at Makerere College in Uganda. Elementary education for the masses of the people was now to be the Government's main concern.

Had the Government ever shown any intention of making their concern effective the decision to limit the number of Africans educated to a higher level might have been justified to some extent, even though it ran contrary to the policy laid down by the British Government's Advisory Committee to which the Tanganyika Education Department still affirmed its allegiance. In fact little was done by the Government to develop any form of education before the outbreak of the Second World War brought with it more urgent problems. Dogged by memories of the depression and by fears of becoming once again a German dependency the country showed no signs of vigorous development. The missionaries remained the prime agents of education and they pursued their work at all levels as far as their revenue would permit.

Events in Uganda in the inter-war years followed the Tanganyika pattern until 1935 when a new and progressive Governor, Sir Philip Mitchell, dragged the country out of the doldrums in which it appeared to be in danger of stagnating in the timorous thirties. The period during which European public opinion had freely condemned anything beyond the most practical form of education for Africans had been brought to an end in 1923 by the Governor, Sir Geoffrey Archer. "I have serious doubts", he said, "as to whether the Government obligation in the matter of native education is disposed of by paying insignificant sums to assist missionary societies in their educational endeavours, and to giving technical training to a certain number of boys in the government institution at Makerere. A comprehensive and a practical educational policy is required."[33] To achieve his aim Archer called on Eric Hussey, Chief Inspector of Schools in the Sudan, to advise on the appropriate steps to be taken. In the light of Hussey's report and of discussions with the Phelps-Stokes Commission the Government formulated their policy in the first half of 1924. In many ways the policy foreshadowed in a very practical form the hopeful recommendations of the British Government's Advisory Committee of 1925. Makerere College was to provide both the peak, and in many ways the focal point, of the whole scheme. What had begun only a few years earlier as a technical school was to become a training college for Africans offering both literary education and technical training. To make this possible the Government planned to assist existing missionary schools and where necessary to open enough elementary and intermediate schools to provide a regular flow of students for the college. Hussey himself was invited to become Uganda's first Director of Education.

These plans were taken up enthusiastically by Archer's successor, Sir William Gowers, who arrived in Uganda early in 1925. In March an Advisory Council on Native Education was appointed under Hussey's chairmanship. It consisted of representatives of all the missionary societies and the Provincial Commissioner of Buganda. The Provincial Commissioners of the other provinces were added in June, together with an African appointed by the Buganda council, the Lukiiko. The strong missionary representation was appropriate since all elementary education continued for some time to be provided by the missionaries, as too did much of the slightly more advanced education in schools such as King's College, Budo, and the White Fathers' St. Mary's College at Kisubi.

33 *Uganda Herald*, 23 November, 1923.

By these means pupils at the more elementary levels were assured of a soundly based, all-round education. The more practical aspects of the instruction were not immediately appreciated by parents who were anxious to see their children learn English and acquire the sort of academic training which would enable them to gain clerical appointments. This was an old problem for the missionaries and they handled it with tact, refusing to be diverted from their purpose either by the demands of the Africans for a more literary type of education or of those Europeans who still, when the opportunity offered, stressed the need for purely practical training. In 1926 provision was made by both Government and missions for teacher training. A training class for teachers in the intermediate schools was started at Makerere and in 1927 a Government normal school was opened to train elementary teachers. A year later, with the opening of the Kampala Technical School, purely artisan training ceased to be the responsibility of Makerere College where, after a year of general education, students now specialized in medical work, teaching, engineering, agriculture, surveying and, after 1929, clerical and commercial work.

These striking advances did not take place without criticism. At a dinner organized in January 1927 by the Uganda Planters Association and attended by members of the Chamber of Commerce the Chairman of the former body won considerable applause when he said "There are many of us who look upon the money being spent in this country upon education with considerable alarm. The country is not yet ready for such methods of education."[34] Under the driving influence of Gowers, however, such scepticism made little impression, and there were hopeful if guarded suggestions that Makerere might one day become a university. The *Uganda Herald*, never a slavish supporter of government policy, remarked in August, 1929 "It seems only like yesterday when the idea of the Makerere College was dumped upon an astonished, sceptical and somewhat angry public . . . but this 1928 report (of the Education Department) in good measure justifies the policy that then supplemented the mission

[34] *Ibid.*, 28 January, 1927.

schools with an educational institution such as the Makerere College".[35]

The depression and the arrival of a new Governor created the same opportunities for retrenchment and reappraisal as the departure of Cameron had done in Tanganyika, and with the same result. The views of Sir Bernard Bourdillon, who succeeded Gowers in 1932, were clearly set out in his final address to the Legislative Council on 14 August 1935. Given an adequate standard of teaching, he said, it was impossible to have too much elementary education, but it was easy to have too much secondary education. In agricultural countries education had to bear a close relation to the occupation of the people and must definitely be, in the main, of a nature to enable them to pursue that occupation with zest and success.[36] This was the very echo of Tanganyika's policy, but in spite of the Governor's views the missionaries contrived to pursue their own course with their usual determination. Makerere College, too, did not succumb completely to the Government's grass roots policy.

At this stage there came upon the Uganda scene another new Governor, Sir Philip Mitchell, who, during the years he had worked in Tanganyika had remained loyal to the ideals of his mentor, Sir Donald Cameron. After a cautious initial pronouncement which won the approval of even his most conservative hearers Mitchell quickly demonstrated his true colours by asking the Secretary of State to appoint a commission which would advise on the development of Makerere College and of African education generally. From the commission's report[37] emerged the proposal that Makerere should become the Higher College for the whole of East Africa, catering for the Arts, Sciences, Agriculture, Medicine and Education, and that it should be run on the lines of a university college. To underpin this adventurous proposal the commission reiterated the policy first laid down by the Uganda Government in 1924 that primary education should be the responsibility of the missions, augmented by native administration schools, and that the Government should assist existing secondary schools. Thus,

35 *Ibid.*, 16 August 1929.

36 *Ibid.*, 21 August 1935.

37 Colonial no. 142, *Higher Education in East Africa* (London, 1937).

unlike Tanganyika, Uganda put in hand a vigorous programme of development. This was mainly the result of Sir Philip Mitchell's influence, although his efforts depended heavily upon the valuable infra-structure built by the missionaries.

Throughout this period Kenya presented a very different problem. In Uganda and in Tanganyika a handful of Europeans played an important role in the commercial field and were never reluctant to criticize government policy on education or on any other subject. But in Uganda their numbers were very small indeed and they rarely exerted any profound influence upon government policy. Although the Tanganyika Europeans were rather more numerous the mandatory status of the territory made it impossible for the European unofficial community to determine events. In neither country did the newly-appointed Legislative Council make a deep impression upon developments. Policy was a matter for the administration to decide, which in effect meant the decision of the Governor himself. Whatever the views of the British Government in London an enthusiastic Governor with a lively personality could virtually direct the country along lines of his own choosing. A more conservative man could delay progress for the full period of his term of office.

The situation in Kenya differed because the number of unofficial Europeans exceeded that of the other two countries combined. From the first decade of the century they had insisted that their views were taken into account by the country's administrators. Kenya's economy depended heavily upon settler farming and many of the settlers had influential friends in England, so they could not be ignored. In the slump of the early 1920s and in the much more serious depression a decade later the settlers had been badly hit and the country's economy had accordingly suffered much more severely than had that of either Uganda or Tanganyika. Not surprisingly the settlers' views on African education were coloured by their own need for an effective labour force which they believed was synonymous with the well-being of the country as a whole. General education for Africans had little point as long as the country's brain power was supplied by Europeans.

The Kenya Government had appointed an advisory board before the British Advisory Committee reported in 1925, and by 1929 was paying £83,180 towards African and Arab education, a sum which, though small, compared not unfavourably with the provision made by the Governments of Uganda and Tanganyika.[38] Two years later the new Education Ordinance made provision for school area committees on which the local native councils were to be given strong representation. Nevertheless, it was the missionaries who provided practically all the education available to Africans in Kenya while the Government maintained a supervisory role and gave financial assistance. It was this situation which led to an unusual clash between the African population of Kenya and the missionary societies.

In Uganda and Tanganyika African demands for education had increased steadily from the beginning of the century and for the most part had taken the form of a request for further education of the type already being provided by the missionaries and to a lesser extent by the Governments. In Uganda a considerable proportion of the cost of the mission schools was readily provided by Africans either by fees or in the form of voluntary subscriptions to the missionary societies. When the Young Buganda, a group of young men who were the sons of influential African leaders, made a public appeal for funds to help them in an educational venture they were thinking in terms of self-help rather than attempting to assert their independence of missionary and government methods or control, and the same was true of the local government schools set up in Bunyoro.

Among the Kikuyu of Kenya in the 1920s the growing African demand for education changed from a request for more mission schools into a demand for schools specifically controlled by Africans. Here for the first time was the sort of reaction against missionary teaching which had caused some uncoordinated rumblings in India a century earlier and which had aroused such disproportionate fears among the Directors of the East India Company. Yet the Court of Directors may have been more prescient than they realized in their wariness

[38] *Colony and Protectorate of Kenya, Annual Report, 1929* (London, 1930), p. 70.

of the effects of the missionaries' reforming zeal for, although it was against the moral code of the missionaries that the Kikuyu initially reacted, their basic grievance was thoughtless European domination. It was but one of the ironies of the East African scene that the missionaries who had been so prominent in the defence of African interests should have attracted to themselves the whole sense of frutration which had been aroused among the Kikuyu by their contacts with Europeans.

The immediate occasion of the grievance was the missionaries' opposition to female circumcision as practised among the Kikuyu, and not all members of the tribe seized this opportunity to sever their dependence upon the missionaries for their education. Those more active in the emerging Kikuyu political movements, however, saw their chance to acquire the responsibility and status denied them in the political field and in the European dominated social life of Kenya. Out of these aspirations there sprang in 1929 the Independent Schools movement.

The most influential group was the Kikuyu Independent Schools Association which was founded with the object of furthering "the interests of the Kikuyu and its members and to safeguard the homogeneity of such interests relating to their spiritual, economic, social and educational upliftment".[39] In 1934 an unsuccessful attempt was made to reconcile the independence of the Association with a continued relationship with the missions. When this failed the leaders of the Association invited Archbishop Daniel William Alexander of the African Orthodox Church to visit Kenya in order to establish his Church there and to train and ordain Kikuyu clergy. By these means they hoped to maintain their links with the Christian Church while asserting their freedom from European domination. The Archbishop stayed from November 1935 until the middle of 1937 and ordained four men at the end of their training. Shortly afterwards two of the new ministers broke with the African Orthodox Church in order to found the African Independent Pentecostal Church which became

39 *Report and Constitution of the Kikuyu Independent Schools Association* (Nyeri, 1938).

the religious branch of the Kikuyu Independent Schools Association and finally asserted the communal nature of the whole movement.

Unlike their less influential rivals, the Kikuyu Karinga Educational Association, the K.I.S.A. did not cling exclusively to tribal values. From 1936 they accepted the advice of the Director of Education with regard to the best methods of conducting their schools and adopted the syllabuses laid down by the Education Department. But the study of Swahili became optional and elementary teaching was carried on in the Kikuyu language. English was introduced into the schools in standard III and became the medium of instruction from standard IV onwards. Gradually, however, the Association became more deeply involved with the political movement known as the Kikuyu Central Association which was proscribed in 1940. In the post-war years the greater part of the independent schools movement was condemned by the British Administration for the part it played in encouraging anti-Government activities, so underlining the basically nationalist rather than anti-Christian origins of the movement.

In India and in East Africa alike, then, the acceptability of western education depended less upon what was taught than upon the attitude of the teachers or of those who formulated educational policy. The pupils did not blindly fear European interference in their way of life, for they quickly realized that under the new regime interference was inevitable. The majority both of Indians and of Africans accepted missionary education for the material benefits it might bring rather than for its spiritual or moral content, although there were notable exceptions to this attitude. At the same time little alarm was created by the missionaries' open attempts to convert the people any more than by the vigorous prosecution of new educational policies by reforming Governors. Except among some of the more conservative-minded leaders of the Hindu and Muslim population of India and among the most poverty stricken and therefore the most apathetic peoples of both India and East Africa the greatest fear was not of interference but that the people might be neglected by their new rulers. Excuses could be made for well-intentioned if clumsy intervention, but lack of sympathy for the people was quickly resented. The Kikuyu independent schools movement was a foretaste of what might happen even to the good intentions of the missionaries if the latter were too slow to appreciate local aspirations. This may well account for the difference between events in India in the middle of the nineteenth century and those in East Africa a hundred years later. Although the British rulers in India remained wary of the effects of Christian teaching they, like the missionaries, were now striving to introduce western learning for the benefit of the people. In East Africa after the Second World War government educational plans were to take a sudden leap forward when independence became imminent. The missionaries, meanwhile, with their foundations still firmly set upon the theory of a complete education with academic, moral and spiritual content, sometimes found themselves cast in a more conservative role than the leaders of African opinion could wholly appreciate.

# THE INDIAN NATIONAL CONGRESS AND THE MUSLIMS 1885-1896

MUNIR-UD-DIN CHUGHTAI

The Indian National Congress was founded in 1885 on the initiative of A. O. Hume, a retired member of the Indian Civil Service and was supported from the very beginning by a group of Englishmen including Sir William Wedderburn, George Yule and Charles Bradlaugh. In India the Viceroy, Lord Dufferin (1884-88), himself was very favourably disposed towards this organization. In fact it was at his suggestion that this body was given the form of a political organization. Hume's original intention was that it should take up social rather than political questions, the latter being left to the already existing "provincial organizations, like the Indian Association of Calcutta, the Presidency Association of Bombay, and the Mahajana Sabha of Madras".[1] He consulted Lord Dufferin, who, feeling the lack of an organization in India which could perform the function that "Her Majesty's opposition did in England" and could "point out to the Government in what respects the administration was defective and how it could be improved",[2] encouraged it to take a political character.[3] Lord Dufferin's opinion prevailed and

[1] W. C. Bannerjee, *Indian Politics, A Collection of Essays and Addresses* (Madras, 1898), pp. vii-viii; P. Sitaramayya, *The History of the Indian National Congress* (Bombay, 1946), i, 15.

[2] Bannerjee, *Indian Politics*, p. viii.

[3] R. Symonds, *The Making of Pakistan* (London, 1950), p. 39.

the Congress came into being as a political body "with the full approval of the Government".[4]

The introduction of representative government into India was the chief aim of the Congress. The reform of legislative councils became its demand from inception. It urged their expansion and enlargement "by the admission of a considerable proportion of elected members".[5] It suggested that the right to elect members of the Provincial Councils should "be conferred only on those classes and members of the community" who were "prima facie capable of exercising it wisely and independently". It should be given to the members of municipalities, district boards, chambers of commerce and universities, or persons possessing such educational and pecuniary qualifications as might be deemed necessary.[6] With regard to the elected members of the Governor-General's Council the suggestion was that the elected members of the several Provincial Councils should constitute the electoral college.[7] The Congress also demanded that all appointments, excluding the minor ones, should be filled by competitive examinations.[8]

The Muslims regarded these demands as detrimental to their interests.[9] They were lacking in western education and were not able to compete with the Hindus for Government appointments.[10] They were too poor to be considered qualified to become electors in proportion to their numbers if wealth became the basis of the voting qualification.[11] They would not get proper representation in the Legislative Councils if the right to vote was confined to the members of municipalities, district boards, chambers of commerce and universities, as these bodies were dominated by the Hindus. The acceptance

4 P. Griffiths, *The British Impact on India* (London, 1952), p. 280; S. N. Banerjea, *A Nation in Making* (London, 1925), p. 92.

5 See *Report of the First Indian National Congress*, Resolution III, p.1.

6 *Report of the Second Indian Congress*, pp. 41-42; A. Besant, *How India Fought for Freedom* (Bombay, 1915), p. 30; D. Chakrabarty and C. Bhattacharyya, *Congress in Evolution* (Calcutta, 1935), p. 3.

7 *Ibid.*

8 Resolution IV, passed at the first Indian National Congress.

9 Sir Sayyed Ahmad Khan, *The Present State of Indian Politics* (Allahabad, 1888), pp. 2-23.

10 *Ibid.*, pp. 10-11. 11 *Ibid.*, p. 13.

of these demands would not benefit them; they would, rather, be condemned to the perpetual subjection of a religious majority. Therefore, the more the Congress emphasized these demands the more the Muslims opposed them. This development, later intensified by religious and cultural conflicts between the Hindus and the Muslims, prepared the way for the inauguration of a movement for separate electorates for the Muslims.

The first Indian National Congress was attended by 72 delegates.[12] Only two were Muslims. Both came from Bombay, where the Congress met, and neither was a prominent figure in the Muslim community.[13] The reaction of the Muslim community to this Congress was one of quiet watchfulness. It was only on the eve of the second Congress that the Muslim leaders indicated their disapproval and advised their co-religionists to keep aloof. This disapproval came first from Sir Sayyid Ahmad Khan, the founder of the Aligarh Movement, and then from others, including Sayyid Ameer Ali and Nawab Abdul Lateef.

A vocal section of the Indian and British press had made the Congress realize that unless it received considerable support from the Muslims its national character remained untrue. Therefore, the Reception Committee of the second Congress took particular care to ensure enough Muslim representation. At about the time when the Committee was approaching certain Muslim organizations to send delegates to the next Congress Sir Sayyid, in an article in the *Aligarh Institute Gazette*, condemned the Congress movement as "seditious".[14] A. O. Hume realized the harm Sir Sayyid's criticism would do to the Congress and replied in a long letter to the *Statesman*. He was surprised that Sir Sayyid should so utterly disapprove and dislike what the Viceroy looked upon "with so much favour".[15] He said that Sir Sayyid's view that the Congress wanted to establish parliamentary government in India

12 *Report of the First Indian National Congress*, p. 5.

13 These Muslim delegates were Bombay solicitors, Rahimutalla M. Siyani and Abdullah Mehrali Dharamsi. (*Ibid*).

14 See *The Aligarh Institute Gazette*, 23 November 1886.

15 *The Statesman* (Calcutta), 18, 19 and 21 December 1886. For this letter, see also *The Indian Mirror* (Calcutta), 25 December 1886 — Supplement.

was incorrect. All that it asked for was "such a tentative measure of representation as shall ensure a full knowledge by the Government of the wants and wishes of the country".[16] Hume's reply did not, however, appear convincing enough to the Muslim intelligentsia, and even at the second Congress, held in December, 1886 at Calcutta, the number of Muslim delegates remained very small. There were 33 out of a total of 431 delegates, and none was a prominent member of the Muslim community.[17] The two Muslim associations of Calcutta, the Central National Muhammadan Association and the Muhammadan Literary Society kept completely aloof.[18] These associations were approached by the Reception Committee to send delegates but neither agreed, because they did not regard the Congress movement as beneficial for the Muslims. On behalf of the Central National Muhammadan Association, Sayyid Ameer Ali disapproved of the policy and the demands of the Congress.[19] The secretary of the Muhammadan Literary Society, Nawab Abdul Lateef, said that the Muslims did not want to bring about changes which they considered unsuited to the conditions of the India of that day and "the various conflicting interests" therein.[20]

The Hindu press severely criticized these attitudes.[21] Even the *Statesman* disapproved of "Muslim indifference" towards the Congress movement, which it called "great", and thought that the succeeding Muslim generation would be wiser.[22] However, later developments showed that what seemed, in the beginning, mere indifference on the part of the Muslims became, in the succeeding years, direct opposition to the Congress movement.

An open conflict between the Muslims and the Congress, began in 1887. It was Sir Sayyid who proved to be the most formidable opponent of the Congress and led his community

16 *Ibid.*

17 *Report of the Second Indian National Congress*—see the List of Delegates.

18 *Ibid.*, pp. 8-9.

19 *The Statesman*, 19 December 1886.

20 *Ibid.*, 25 December 1886.

21 See the remarks of *The Advocate of India*, quoted in *The Statesman*, 2 January 1887.

22 *The Statesman*, 28 December 1886.

away from it. In the first two years he had not been involved in any open opposition. In 1886 he had founded the Muhammadan Educational Conference[23] but not with a view to opposing the Congress movement. His main object had been that the Muslims should remain absorbed in their social and educational affairs. From the time of the third Congress, however, events took such a turn that Sir Sayyid stepped into the political arena and came out openly against the National Congress. The organizers of that Congress had invited a Bombay Muslim, Badruddin Tyabji, to preside over its deliberations at Madras in the last week of December 1887, and had succeeded in having among their delegates 75 Muslims,[24] including some Muslim students of the M.A.O. College, Aligarh.[25] In proportion to the total number of delegates this number showed a marked improvement on that of the previous year, and indicated the influence the Congress movement could exercise on Muslims in the absence of a clear and definite policy of the Muslim leaders. Moreover the appointment of a Muslim President of the Congress within two years of its birth showed how far the Congress could go to win Muslim support for its demands, which, if accepted, would adversely affect the social and political conditions of the Muslim community.[26] It had also come to light that undue pressure was being used to bring Muslims into the Congress[27] and various inducements were being offered to the more pliable.[28] Sir Sayyid was much alarmed at this situation and henceforth adopted an attitude of open opposition to the Congress' demands and activities. He adumbrated Muslim policy in a public speech delivered in Lucknow on 28 December, 1887 and in a lecture at Meerut in March 1888.

[23] This body was originally called the Muhammadan Educational Congress and retained this name till 1890.

[24] *Report of the Third Indian National Congress.* See Appendix I, List of Delegates, pp. 168-98.

[25] *The Pioneer*, 11 January 1888.

[26] A. H. Hali, *Hayat-i-Jaweed* (Lucknow, 1901), i, 273.

[27] Khan, *The Present State of Indian Politics*, p. 32.

[28] *Ibid.*, pp. 27, 32; *The Pioneer*, 13 July 1888, see Mian Muhammad Shafi's statement.

The Madras Congress started its proceedings on 27 December, 1887. Tyabji, in his presidential address, stressed the representative character of the Congress[29] and said that there was nothing whatever in the position or the relations of different Indian communities — Hindus, Muslims, Parsees or Christians — which should make them stand aloof from one another "in their efforts to obtain those great general reforms, those great general rights which are for the common benefit of all."[30] He maintained that this was the principle on which he and his colleagues had always acted in Bombay and that he had no doubt that the same principle was being practised by his Muslim brethren in other provinces "with few, though perhaps, important exceptions".[31]

The day after Tyabji had pleaded for the aims and objects of the Congress, Sir Sayyid delivered his Lucknow speech.[32] Two and a half months later in his speech at Meerut he warned them that if they joined the Congress nothing but national disaster lay in store for them.[33] Sir Sayyid feared Hindu domination if Congress demands were accepted. He described in clear terms what he thought would be the position of the Muslims if the Congress succeeded in its objects. Speaking of the competitive examinations, he said that the introduction of such a system in India would be unjust because all people in that country did not belong to one nation, nor were they equal with regard to higher English education, an essential requisite for these examinations. If the Congress demand for filling all posts, except a few minor ones, by competitive examinations was accepted, the Government offices in every part of the country would be monopolized by the community which had had a start in English education, and the Muslims would be at the biggest disadvantage.[34]

As to the demand that the people of India should elect a certain proportion of the members of the Imperial and Provincial Legislative Councils, the basis of Sir Sayyid's criticism

29 *Report of the Third Indian National Congress*, p. 72; and Besant, *How India Wrought for Freedom*, p. 37.

30 *Report of the Third Congress*, p. 72. 31 *Ibid.*

32 For the full text of the speech, see Khan, *The Present State of Indian Politics*, pp. 2-24.

33 For the full text of the speech, see *Ibid.*, pp. 30-53. 34 *Ibid.*, pp. 8-11.

was against the view that in a country inhabited by two "different nations"[35] the introduction of an elective system meant domination by the Hindu majority. He said that whatever system of election was adopted, there would be four times as many Hindus as Muslims. This would lead to the control of legislation by the Hindus and the degradation of the Muslim community.[36]

Sir Sayyid advocated that the best way for the Muslims to safeguard their rights was to cultivate friendship with the British and strengthen their rule in India so that it might not pass into the hands of the Bengalis. If they joined the Congress they would reap nothing but loss, because that would place them under the subjection of the Hindus.[37] They should boycott it and should try to improve their education, because only through education would they be able to obtain an honourable position in the Government and acquire wealth in the higher ranks of trade.[38]

It seems important to mention that Sir Sayyid's attitude towards the Congress was not based on any sentiment of hatred or dislike towards the Hindu community. Nor was it indicative of his opposition to the inclusion of Indians in the Imperial and Provincial Councils. Similarly it did not imply his disapproval of appointing Indians to high administrative posts. During the years after the revolt of 1857 his relations with the Hindus had been cordial.[39] His scientific society consisted of a combined Hindu-Muslim membership,[40] with Raja Jaikishandas as its first secretary.[41] His College, established especially for the Muslims, kept its doors open to other communities[42] and out of regard for Hindus prohibited slaughter of cows within its precincts.[43] As for the admission of Indians to the Councils of the Government, he had been its strong supporter. He had advocated the acceptance of this

35 *Ibid.*, p. 37. 36 *Ibid.* 37 *Ibid.*, p. 50. 38 *Ibid.*

39 Hali, *Hayat-i-Jaweed*, i, 272. 40 *Ibid.*, p. 121.

41 H. K. Sherwani, *Studies in Muslim Political Thought and Administration* (Lahore, 1945), p. 224.

42 Mohsinul Mulk (ed.), *Addresses and speeches relating to the Mahomedan Anglo-Oriental College, in Aligarh* (Aligarh, 1898), p. 126.

43 Abdul Haq, 'Sir Sayyid Ahmad Khan', *Quarterly Urdu* (Karachi), April 1950, p. 57.

principle as early as 1858 in his treatise on the Indian revolt.[44] Again, at the time of laying the foundation of the Ghazipore school in 1864, he gratefully approved of the decision of the Government, embodied in the Indian Councils Act of 1861, that Indians should be eligible for appointment to the Viceroy's Council of representatives from every division or district.[45]

It was, in fact, the demand that Indian members of Councils should be appointed by election that became the chief reason for Sir Sayyid's opposition to the nationalist movement. He knew that India was inhabited by people of different religions and cultures who had not yet learnt to keep their political ideas and aspirations free from religious prejudices. In such a country, therefore, the introduction of the principle of election in an unqualified form would only mean representation of the views and interests of a majority based on religion and would adversely affect the smaller community.[46] Sir Sayyid seems to have held these views long before the establishment of the Indian National Congress. He first expressed them on 15 January 1883, while speaking in the Council of the Governor-General on the Central Provinces Local Government Bill.[47] He claimed that it was due to his stand against the introduction of the system of election in an unqualified form that Lord Ripon (Viceroy and Governor-General, 1880-84) agreed to the appointment of one-third of the members of local bodies by nomination.[48]

These views seem to have aroused no controversy at that time. In 1888, however, their effect was different. The Muslims welcomed them, while the Hindus, particularly Bengalis, who seem to have ignored the fact that there was also a Muslim point of view in the Indian political question,[49] condemned them vehemently. The Hindu press subjected Sir Sayyid to severe attacks, describing him as a tool in the

44 G. F. I. Graham, *The Life and Work of Sir Syed Ahmad Khan* (London, 1909), pp. 56-57.

45 *Ibid.*

46 *Proceedings of the Council of the Governor-General of India*, 15 January 1883, Sayyid Ahmad Khan's speech on the Central Provinces Local Self-Government Bill.

47 *Ibid.* 48 Khan, *The Present State of Indian Politics*, p. 22.

49 A. H. Al-biruni, *The Makers of Pakistan and Modern Muslim India* (Lahore 1950), p. 41.

hands of the enemies of the Congress and his views as borrowed from them.[50] On the other hand the Muslim press was all praise for Sir Sayyid. The *Mahomedan Observer*, the *Rafiq-i-Hind* and the *Muslim Herald* all supported his views and spoke with one voice against the Congress movement.[51] The *Muslim Herald* said, "The Sayyid does not mince matters but hits out straight from the shoulder, like the giant he is. In a mawkish time, enslaved by senseless conventions, it is a relief to find one man at least who, avoiding periphrasis, honestly calls a spade a spade .... We proudly accept the Syed as our leader and exponent—the summit and the crown of Islam, a faith that binds together with withers of iron 50,000,000 Indian Musalmans. Sir Sayyid leads the way. His speech sounds the keynote of our policy."[52] The Muslims in almost all parts of India supported Sir Sayyid's views. Resolutions condemning the Congress activities were passed by the Muslims of Allahabad, Lucknow, Meerut, Lahore, Amritsar, Ludhiana, Madras and other important towns.[53] The Central National Muhammadan Association of Bengal, the Muhammadan Literary Society of Calcutta, the Anjuman-i-Islamia of Madras, the Dindigul Anjuman, the Central National Muhammadan Association, Panjab, the Anjuman-i-Himayat-i-Islam, Lahore, the Anjuman-i-Rifah-i-Am, Allahabad, denounced the aims and activities of the Congress, supported Sir Sayyid's Lucknow speech, and expressed full confidence in his leadership.[54]

Sir Sayyid's reasons for opposing the Congress Movement were further explained in a rejoinder to the Hindu attacks.[55]

50 See *The Indian Mirror* (Calcutta), 25 January 1888; also *The Tribune* (Lahore), 21 January and 8 January 1888. For extracts from the editorial comments of *The Bengalee*, *The Indian Spectator*, *The Hindu Patriot* and *The Hindu*, see *The Pioneer*, 2 February 1888.

51 *The Aligarh Institute Gazette*, 21 July 1888.

52 Quoted in *The Pioneer*, 2 February 1888.

53 *The Aligarh Institute Gazette*, 21 July 1888. See also *The Civil & Military Gazette* (Lahore), 19 May 1888. For information about the meeting of the Muslims of Madras, the place where the third Congress met, see *The Times* (London), 11 May 1888.

54 *The Aligarh Institute Gazette*, 21 July 1888; *The Civil & Military Gazette* (Lahore), 19 May 1888.

55 For the full text of the rejoinder, see Khan, *The Present State of Indian Politics*, pp. 25-28.

He was no harbinger of ill-will between his co-religionists and the Hindus. "There is no person," he said, "who desires more than I that friendship and union should exist between the two peoples of India, and that one should help the other. I have often said that India is like a bride whose two eyes are the Hindus and the Muhammadans. Her beauty consists in this — that her two eyes be of equal lustre . . . . But when my Hindu brothers and Bengali friends devise such a course of action as will bring us loss and heap disgrace on our nation, then indeed we can no longer remain friends. Without doubt it is our duty to protect our nation from these attacks of the Hindus and Bengalis by which we believe that she will be injured."[56] The object of the promoters of the Congress, he believed, was that the Government of India should be English in name only, and that the internal rule of the country should be entirely in their own hands.[57] "They do not", he said, "publicly avow that they wish it for themselves; but they very well know that the Muhammadans will be unable to do anything, and so the rule of the country will be monopolised by them"[58]

Sir Sayyid's criticism and the growing support of the Muslim community for his views was a matter of no little concern to the Congress.[59] However, it did not evoke among Congress leaders any desire to consider the Muslim question from the Muslim point of view. Nor did they show any inclination towards taking some practical steps to allay Muslim fear of Hindu domination. To the contrary they continued to claim that the Congress enjoyed the support of a considerable number of Muslims who shared its views. This propaganda enjoyed some success in England. Even men like Sir William Hunter[60]

56 *Ibid.*, pp. 25-26. 57 *Ibid.*, p. 27. 58 *Ibid.*, p. 28.

59 R. P. Masani, *Dadabhai Naoroji*: *The Grand Old Man of India* (London, 1931), p. 302; Dadabhai to Wacha, 9 February 1888; Dadabhai to Malabari, 2 March and 18 April 1888.

60 Hunter was supposed to be an authority on Indian Muslims. He was the author of *The Indian Musalmans* (London, 1872), a book still considered a very important work on the social and economic conditions of Indian Muslims in the Nineteenth Century and their reaction to the new developments.

who were supposed to have a fairly sound knowledge of the Muslim mind in India believed that the Congress was supported by a considerable number of Muslims. Speaking at the annual meeting of the National Indian Association in London,[61] in April 1888, Hunter said that, with the exception of certain parts of Lower Bengal, Muslims from all parts of India attended the Congress sessions and took part in their proceedings.[62] A strong reply to this assertion came from a young Muslim from the Panjab, Mian Muhammad Shafi, who later played an important role in Muslim politics in India and more than once became the president of the All-India Muslim League. On the basis of reports published in newspapers Shafi proved that Hunter's information was incorrect.[63] He admitted that a few Muslims sympathized with the Congress but "their voice was not the voice of Islam". He contended that none of the true representatives of the Muslims had any concern with the Congress.[64] Speaking of those Muslims who attended the Madras Congress session Shafi made the following remarks:

(1) "The majority of them were of that type who, being themselves in a lower status in society, are always ambitious of moving in the higher orbit. When it was represented to them ... that many noblemen and Rajas would attend the sitting of the Congress, and that they would have ample opportunities of making acquaintance with

[61] See "Recent Movements in India", *The Indian Magazine*, April 1888.

[62] Hunter said in the recent Congress session the resolutions "were voted for by 83 Mahomedan delegates". (*Ibid*). In fact, the total number of Muslim delegates to the Congress of December 1887 did not exceed 75 (see the *Report of the Third Indian National Congress*, Appendix I — List of Delegates).

[63] For the full text of Shafi's letter, see *The Pioneer*, 13 July 1888.

[64] Shafi said that the following were the true representatives of the "Muhammadan nation ... in whom all fully trust and take pride" : Sir Sayyid Ahmad Khan, K.C.S.I., of Aligarh; Sayyid Ameer Ali, LL.D., C.S.I.; Sayyid Hussain Khan Bahadur; Raja Ameer Husain Khan Bahadur; Nawab Bahadur Abdul Lateef Khan, C.I.E.; Maulavi Abdul Jabbar of Bengal; Muhammad Ali Bogai; Qazi Sahib Dean Khan Bahadur, C.S.I. of Bombay; Nawab Sir Nawazish Ali Khan Qazilbash, K.C.I.E.; Nawab Abdul Majeed Khan, C.S.I.; and Khan Bahadur Muhammad Barkat Ali Khan of Lahore. (*Ibid*.).

the nobility of the country" they could not resist the temptation to go.

(2) "Then there were those whose eyes can easily be blinded by honeyed words of flattery and adulation and could thus be won over to any side, no matter if it be injurious to their own cause and to that of their community."

(3) "Again the upholders of the Congress . . . induced the Shias to join them because their opponents, the Sunnis, had not done so."[65]

(4) "Then there were those who went out of sheer curiosity, those who were promised notoriety, and those who were under the influence of their Hindu brethren — the clients of Hindu lawyers, the debtors of Hindu bankers, etc., being bound neck and feet to their patrons."

Sir Sayyid decided to take some practical steps to counteract this propaganda. Early in August 1888, he issued an appeal to the Muslims and those Hindus who were opposed to the Congress to join together to counteract the "false impression" that the Congress movement drew support from the whole of the people of India and to make known to the British public that not only Muslims, but also many influential and powerful Hindus, were opposed to it. A few days later he laid the foundation of the Indian Patriotic Association. This Association consisted of both Hindu and Muslim members. Its chief objects were :

(*a*) To publish and circulate pamphlets and other papers for the information of members of Parliament, English journals and the people of Great Britain, in which those mis-statements will be pointed out by which the supporters of the Indian National Congress have wrongly attempted to convince the English people that all the Nations of

[65] This point might appear exaggerated, but contemporary evidence indicates substantial truth in it. Pandit Ajudhia Nath, pleader of the Allahabad High Court, who became the chairman of the Reception Committee of the fourth Congress, delivered a lecture at Lucknow in which, strangely enough, he tried to prove "from the *Koran* that the National Congress was good for India, and denounced all Muhammadans who opposed the Congress as followers of Yazid". (See *The Civil & Military Gazette*, 19 May 1888).

India and the Indian chiefs and rulers agree with the aims and objects of the National Congress;
(*b*) to inform members of Parliament and the newspapers of Great Britain and its people by the same means of the opinions of Muhammadans in general, of the Islamia Anjumans, and those Hindus, and their societies which are opposed to the objects of the National Congress.[66]

Over 40 Anjumans in various parts of the country became affiliated to it.[67] Although the Association was short-lived, mainly because of Sayyid Ahmad Khan's inability to devote proper attention to it, it made a good deal of effective propaganda to disprove the claim of the Congress to represent all sections of the Indian population.

The Congress on its part carried on the campaign to enlist enough Muslim support as it was extremely important to uphold its claim as a national organization. Sir Sayyid's formidable opposition had made its position difficult. To attract greater Muslim attention, therefore, either its demands would have to be modified so that Sir Sayyid would not consider them opposed to Muslim interests, or something would have to be done to weaken his influence on his co-religionists. The Congress leaders and the Hindu press seem to have decided to pursue the latter course. A theory was now developed that a sudden change had occurred in Sir Sayyid's views and that it was due to the influence of Theodore Beck,[68] the British principal of the Aligarh College, and those Englishmen who did not like the activities of the Congress. Lala Lajpat Rai, a well-known Arya Samaj leader who later became a president of the Indian National Congress, in a series of letters to the *Tribune*,[69] severely criticized Sir Sayyid's policy and accused him of going back on what he himself had advocated previously. He said that the

[66] *The Aligarh Institute Gazette*, 28 September 1888.

[67] *Encyclopaedia of Islam*, ii, 483.

[68] See *The Tribune* (Lahore), 21 January 1888. Criticising Sir Sayyid's opposition to the Congress movement the paper tauntingly remarked: "Poor old Syed: Old age and Beckish counsels have been the ruin of you."

[69] For these letters, see *The Tribune* of 27 October, 17 November, 5 and 19 December 1888.

Congress was demanding nothing more than Sir Sayyid had done in his book *The Causes of Indian Revolt* and alleged that he opposed the Congress just to flatter officials.[70]

A close examination reveals that none of these allegations had any foundation. Sir Sayyid had, no doubt, advocated the inclusion of Indians in Legislative Councils on more than one occasion but he had never recommended the introduction of the elective system in India. Nor was there any evidence that official influence or Mr. Beck had affected his views. In fact, when he first openly criticized the Congress, in December 1887, it still enjoyed the support of the Viceroy, Lord Dufferin, and other high officials.[71] If his political views had been influenced by officials, he would have spoken differently and would have advised his co-religionists to co-operate with their Hindu brethren in the Congress movement, because it was patronized by high Government officials in India and was supported by a number of influential people in England. But he did not do so, and contemporary evidence shows that he would not have done so even if it had been the desire of the Viceroy and other British officials. As a result of a correspondence relating to the Congress movement, between Auckland Colvin and A. O. Hume,[72] in which Sir Sayyid was blamed by Hume for having told his friends that one of his "violent speeches" against the Congress had been made at Colvin's suggestion,[73] Sir Sayyid issued a public statement and disclosed that two years before, when Hume wrote to him about the Congress, he "unmistakably stated" that he did not approve of the movement, and that even if Sir Auckland Colvin, Lord Dufferin, the Secretary of State for India and the whole House of Commons had declared in favour of it he would have been "as firmly opposed to it as ever".[74]

70 See *Report of the Fourth Indian National Congress* (1888), pp. 92-93, Lala Lajpat Rai's speech on Resolution I, "Reform of the Legislative Councils"

71 When Sir Sayyid was criticising the Congress Movement in a public meeting at Lucknow, Lord Connemara, Governor of Madras, was entertaining the delegates to the third Congress at a garden party (see Masani, *Dadabhai Naoroji*, p. 303).

72 See *The Pioneer*, 7 November 1888.

73 *Ibid.*

74 For Sir Sayyid's statement, see *The Pioneer*, 10 November 1888.

As for Beck, he had, no doubt, assisted Sir Sayyid a great deal[75] in his opposition to Congress demands and in the representation of the Muslim point of view to the British public, but the assertion that Sir Sayyid's views had undergone a change under his influence shows not only ignorance about the nature of the man himself, but also indicates complete disregard of the events contributing to the development of political institutions in India. Documentary evidence exists to the effect that the views Sir Sayyid expressed about Congress demands were neither new, nor the product of any foreign influence. He had expressed similar views as early as January 1883,[76] nearly eleven months before Beck arrived in India,[77] and almost three years before the birth of the Indian National Congress.

To some extent Sayyid held religious views which brought him into disfavour with more orthodox Muslims. This anti-Sayyid sentiment seems to have been exploited by Congress to secure their support. Out of a total of 1,248 delegates to the Allahabad Congress of 1888, Muslim delegates numbered 222.[78] This sudden increase in their percentage was claimed by one of their spokesmen, Maulavi Hidayat Rasul, to be due mainly to the opposition of the people in the "Aligarh Camp".[79] He assured his fellow-delegates that if his "hostile brethren had not made such a great show of opposition, the Congress would certainly not have been the success that it has been today."[80] He further stressed that Sir Sayyid could have no claim to the leadership of Muslims because he had been declared an infidel.[81]

About the same time the supporters of the Congress persuaded such 'Ulama as were opposed to Sir Sayyid to issue a *Fatwa*. This approved of Muslim participation in the Congress on the grounds that it discussed only such matters as concerned the common good of the people of India as a whole

75 Graham, *Sir Syed Ahmad Khan*, p. 273.

76 See *Proceedings of the Council of the Governor-General of India*, 15 January 1883.

77 Al-biruni, *The Makers of Pakistan*, p. 43.

78 *Report of the Fourth Indian National Congress* (1888). See the List of Delegates.

79 *Ibid.*, p. 129. 80 *Ibid.* 81 *Ibid.*

and did not affect the religious or social interests of any community.[82] On the other hand the *Fatwa* warned the Muslims against following Sir Sayyid in religious as well as temporal matters and declared participation in his Patriotic Association as *haram*[83] and *Kufr*,[84] because it had, among its members, bigoted and anti-Islamic Hindus like the Raja of Benares.[85]

This negative approach to a question which involved the future of a community which had not yet forgotten its past glory and ascendancy over Hindus was no solution. Some genuine and practical effort was necessary to allay Muslim fear of Hindu domination. The Congress, having failed to do this, soon began to lose the sympathy of that section of its Muslim supporters which had joined mainly through hatred of Sir Sayyid but which was not unmindful of the interests of Muslims as a community. When in the Congress session of 1889, the Resolution on the Expansion and Reform of Legislative Councils (which was to become the basis of a bill to be introduced in the House of Commons by Charles Bradlaugh)[86] came up for discussion, Maulavi Hidayet Rasul, who the previous year had ascribed the increased Muslim support to the Congress to the growing opposition of the people in the "Aligarh Camp", proposed that the resolution should provide "that the number of Muhammadan members shall always be equal to that of the Hindus in both the Imperial and Provincial Councils."[87] This led to a heated discussion in the course of which Maulavi Rasul said that he was now convinced that those Muslims who opposed the Congress were justified, and that if the Muslims were not conceded what they had been frequently promised they should not support the Congress movement because that would injure their national cause.[88] He was supported by several Muslim delegates[89] in-

82 S. M. Mian, *'Ulama-i-Haq*, i, 100. 83 Forbidden by the Law of Islam.

84 Blasphemy. 85 M. A. Zuberi, *Sayasat-i-Milliya* (Agra, 1941), p. 31.

86 See *Report of the Fourth Indian National Congress*, pp. 11-12.

87 *Report of the Fifth Indian National Congress* (1889), p. 28.

88 *Ibid.*

89 Sayyid Wahid Ali Rizvi (a delegate from the N-W. Provinces) supporting Maulavi Rasul said: "Taking this Congress as a whole, I can hardly allow it the title of National. . . . It is more a Hindu than Muhammadan Congress". (*Ibid.*, p. 29).

cluding Ali Muhammad Bhimji, a devoted Congress Muslim. The amendment was, however, defeated by an overwhelming majority and no special provision was made in the resolution which the Muslims could regard as guaranteeing their rights.

This development within the Congress seems to have served two important purposes from the Muslim point of view. Firstly, it showed that the Congress stand was not fully acceptable to many Muslims, even within that body, and that they wanted a provision which would safeguard their rights and help to maintain their existence as a community. Secondly, it checked the influence the Congress had recently gained over Muslims. But what was extremely important at that time was to make known to the British Government the feelings of the Muslim community about the bill intended to be introduced in Parliament. With the co-operation and help of Theodore Beck, Sir Sayyid, in April 1890, submitted to the House of Commons through Richard Temple a petition signed by nearly 40,000 Muslim inhabitants of about 70 cities and towns of India. A similar petition was sent to Parliament by the Muhammadan Literary Society of Calcutta.[90]

However, the Indian Councils Act of 1892 provided for an elective element in the Councils and thus partly fulfilled Congress demands. The method for appointment was, in theory, nomination by the Head of the Government, but the Act regulated that some of the seats on each Council were to be filled by representatives of various bodies or interests, such as corporations, municipalities, district boards, associations of land-holders, universities, and chambers of commerce.[91] The system was not strictly a system of election, for the elective bodies could only recommend their representatives to the Head of the Government for nomination. In practice, however, nomination was never refused. The privilege of selecting the members for the Imperial Legislative Council was conferred upon the Legislative Councils of Madras, Bombay, Bengal and the North-Western Provinces and Oudh, and upon the Bengal Chamber of Commerce.[92]

90 *The Pioneer*, 12 May 1890.

91 *India Office Collection. Question of Muhammadan Representation*: "The New Legislative Councils", p. 2.

92 *Ibid.*, p. 7.

The privilege to select and recommend members for the Bengal Legislative Council was bestowed upon the Corporation of Calcutta, the Senate of the University, trade associations and groups of municipalities and corporations. Rules on similar principles were drawn up for Madras, Bombay and the North-Western Provinces and Oudh.[93]

This system opened the door for the election of Indian politicians to the Imperial as well as Provincial Councils. From now on many Congress leaders managed to sit on these Councils. The Muslims, however, did not feel happy about this system as it did not provide them with any safeguards and appeared to increase the influence and prestige of the Hindus who had already surpassed them in education and economic benefits. Recent communal strife had made their situation depressing. Sir Sayyid once again emphasized that where there was "no tangible homogeneity among the voters in point of race, religion, social manners, economic conditions and political traditions, the representative system could never be productive of any good."[94] He fervently hoped that the British Parliament, regardless of party, would remember that India's population consisted of more than one community, each with greatly different economic, moral, social, political, religious and historical traditions; he also hoped that the British public would not be misled by the propaganda of the Congress.[95] The Central National Muhammadan Association reacted to the situation somewhat differently. A deputation of the Association waited on the Viceroy, Lord Lansdowne (1888-94), on 22 January 1894 and presented an address to him in which it pointed out that hitherto the benefit of representation in Councils had been almost exclusively enjoyed by one community and asked that the Muslims be given fair representation on each Council. The Viceroy in his reply assured the deputation that it had, from the first, been Government's "intention to secure them a reasonable number of seats".[96]

93 *Ibid.*, pp.7-9.

94 *The Pioneer*, 29 September 1893.

95 *Ibid.*

96 *Speeches by the Marquis of Lansdowne 1888-1894* (Calcutta, 1895), pp. 375-77.

The assurance proved ineffective in practice, and the number of Muslims on the Councils remained significantly small. Even in the municipal committees and local boards, where the elective principle had been in vogue for many years and members were elected on the basis of a joint electorate, the Muslims could not get proper representation. Calcutta,[97] Allahabad[98] and Poona[99] were a few important instances. This situation did not prevail only in Hindu-majority areas. Even in Muslim-majority areas the well-educated and wealthy Hindus could deprive the Muslims of their proper representation.[100]

The Muslims became more apprehensive of the nationalist movement started by the Congress when from about the middle of the 1890's this organization passed gradually under the influence of the militant Hindu nationalists, who aimed at establishing Hindu *raj* in India through violent means. B. G. Tilak, the founder of militant Hindu nationalism, himself enjoyed a prominent position in the Congress. That a number of other Congress leaders supported his movement became manifest in December 1895. In the last week of that month the annual session of the Congress was held at Poona. Tilak took advantage of this opportunity and organized a large public meeting in honour of Shivaji, the well-known Hindu hero, who had, during the early part of Aurangzib's rule, revolted against Muslim supremacy and treacherously killed

97 In the triennial elections for the Calcutta Municipality held in 1897, of the newly elected members only 6 were Muslims as against 36 Hindus. (See *Statement Exhibiting the Moral and Material Progress of India 1897-98*, p. 6.).

98 In Allahabad the Muslim element was quite large and important, but on account of the preponderance of Hindu electors over Muslims it had become "impossible" for the latter "to secure representation". ("The Representative System in India," *The Pioneer Mail* (Allahabad), 24 December 1896).

99 In the election for the Poona Municipality held in March 1895, the Muslim voters almost completely abstained from voting, because they were so scattered over the city that everywhere they formed an ineffective minority and were not able to elect even one Muslim candidate. (See *The Times of India* (Overland Weekly Edition), 9 March 1895).

100 For the scanty representation of the Muslims in the Montgomery Municipal Committee, see *Report on the Working of Municipalities in the Punjab, 1890-91*, p. 3.

the Muslim General Afzal Khan at a conference.[101] The meeting was addressed by a number of important Congress leaders including that year's president, Babu Surendranath Banerjea. Addressing the meeting Banerjea said:

> My first feeling is one of intense admiration for those gentlemen who have organized this vast, this enthusiastic, this unparalleled demonstration in favour of the Shivaji movement. The reflection which at the present movement at the sight of this imposing demonstration occurs to my mind is this — what may not be expected from the organizers of a movement like this in the cause of national advancement and progress? We are all — I think I may say the members of the National Congress are all — in strict sympathy with this movement, the object of which is to commemorate the memory of the greatest Hindu Hero of modern times and the founder of the mightiest Hindu Empire in these latter days.[102]

Speaking at the same meeting Pandit Madan Mohan Malaviya urged that "the great Shivaji should not be forgotten; his memory should be cherished".[103] Several other prominent Congress Hindus from different parts of India "gave expression to similar sentiments".[104]

The Muslims now decided to devise a definite line of action in the political field to check the onslaught of the movement developing in the name of Indian nationalism but only promoting the interests of the Hindu majority. Sir Sayyid had founded in 1893 the Muhammadan Anglo-Oriental Defence Association to protect the political interests of the Muslims. In December 1896 Sayyid Mahmud[105] and Theodore Beck drew up a scheme on behalf of this Association, dealing with the question of Muslim representation which, in the view of the authors, provided a reasonable basis for political co-

101 For a brief account of the event, see V. A. Smith, *The Oxford History of India* (Oxford, 1961), p. 406.

102 Quoted in R. Gopal, *Lokamanya Tilak* (Bombay, 1956), pp. 103-4.

103 *Ibid.*, p. 104. 104 *Ibid.*

105 Sayyid Mahmud was the son of Sir Sayyid Ahmad Khan who became the first Muslim judge of an Indian High Court.

operation between the Hindus and Muslims.[106] The salient features of the scheme were as follows:

1. *Legislative Councils:* On the Imperial and Provincial Legislative Councils the number of Hindu and Muslim members should be equal.
2. *Municipalities:* (*i*) In towns where the Muslim element approximated "to one-fourth of the community or more, an even balance should be secured by distributing the seats equally between Hindus and Muslims"; (*ii*) In towns where the Muslim population exceeded 15 per cent and fell short of 25 per cent, their representation should be as far as possible proportionate; (*iii*) In towns where Muslims did not exceed 15 per cent of the population there should be at least one Muslim on the municipal committee.
3. *District Boards:* As to the district boards the percentage of Muslim representatives should be fixed as far as possible on the lines and principles suggested with regard to municipalities.

The most important feature of the scheme was the suggestion that Muslim members of the Legislative Councils and local bodies should be elected by Muslims and Hindu members should be elected by Hindus.[107] The authors said that the great majority of electors consisted of Hindus. If their suggestion was not accepted and Hindu electors were asked to elect Muslim members as well, the latter would, in fact, represent the Hindu viewpoint and the Muslims would remain almost as much unrepresented as before. These proposals, said the authors, assumed one cardinal fact: namely that the Muslims were for political purposes a community with separate traditions, interests, political convictions and religion. It was not a question of whether they were right or wrong. The point was that they had "different views,

[106] For the full text of the scheme, see *The Pioneer Mail* and *The Indian Weekly News* (Allahabad), 24 December 1896, pp. 20-21.

[107] "Elementary principles of representation demand that the electors of Muhammadan members should consist of Muhammadans and the electors of the Hindu members of Hindus". (*Ibid.*).

and any rational system of representation should provide for their expression".[108]

The Muslim press welcomed the scheme and assured the Congress that if it agreed to its proposals the Muslims would have no objection to joining that organization as a community. But the Congress did not agree to consider these proposals as a possible basis for Hindu-Muslim co-operation in political matters unless the Muslims first joined the Congress "in the same numbers and with the same enthusiasm as the Hindus".[109] The result was that the Muslims as a community snubbed the Congress.

Although the Mahmud-Beck scheme could not induce the Congress leaders to look at the Indian political question from the point of view of the Muslims, it became in subsequent years the basis of the Muslim political movement which ultimately developed into the movement for a separate Muslim State in India.

108 *Ibid.*

109 *Report of the Twelfth Indian National Congress* (1896), p. 42.

# MISSIONARIES AND THE BEGINNINGS OF THE SECULAR STATE IN INDIA

E. DANIEL POTTS

The first Prime Minister of independent India, Jawaharlal Nehru, a noted defender of the secular state, said in 1951 that the most important aspect of modern democracy, its "cardinal doctrine", was "the separation of the state from religion".[1] As defined by the major authority on the modern secular state, it is "a state which guarantees individual and corporate freedom of religion, deals with the individual as a citizen irrespective of his religion, is not constitutionally connected to a particular religion nor does it seek either to promote or interfere with religion."[2] More specifically, it means the insurance by the state of several points: religious liberty, for all to practise their faith freely, provided that the rights of the individual are fully respected; a common basis for citizenship for the people of the nation, a basis devoid of religious tests for voting, office-holding, and so forth; and the separation of church and state in the strict sense — that is, no state church (such as the Church of England), nor a state religion (such as Islam in Pakistan).

Although the idea of a secular state, *per se*, was generally unknown in the early 19th century, most of the facets which make up its character would have met with the approval of certain Christian missionary groups in India at that time. Not

[1] *The Hindu*, 17 July 1951, 11 April 1950, quoted in Donald Eugene Smith, *India as a Secular State* (Princeton, N.J., 1963), p. 155.

[2] *Ibid.*, p. 4.

only that, it is possible to illustrate that some of these groups actively sought and were instrumental in obtaining governmental recognition of some of these facets, and so laid the cornerstone for those later advocates of the secular state, whose ideas were more mature on this concept. Partly because a small but highly active group of British Baptists were far and away the most important of such groups in the earlier half of the century, partly because they were foremost (though not the first) in these attempts,[2a] this essay will deal primarily with some Baptist contributions to the "cardinal doctrine" of Indian democracy.

It is well known that under the leadership of William Carey[2b] the Baptists began their operations in Bengal late in 1793. Not so well known is the pre-19th century historical background of the secular state in India, and of Baptist ideas on this subject, which are briefly sketched below.

The Hindu belief that all religions are true in the sense that all can lead to spiritual liberation (or salvation) is certainly conducive to the development of religious tolerance; a virtue for which in practice Hinduism, as the religion of the majority of Indians, has not always been noted, just as Christianity has never really achieved the ability to "turn the other cheek". But even so, the freedom to profess divergent religions does not necessarily make the state a secular one, though it helps contribute to this goal. By guaranteeing religious liberty and a common citizenship, if not the separation of church and state, it was that enlightened Muslim, the Emperor Akbar, who unwittingly became the first Indian ruler of importance to attempt to give the state a secular nature, and at a time late in the 16th century when Protestants and Catholics, some of whom appeared at his Court, were busily warring among each other, in the name of religion, in Europe. Akbar unfortunately was succeeded by Emperors who reverted in due course to the more common Muslim practice of aggressively promoting the tenets of that faith, by force if necessary.

[2a] And partly because this collection of essays honours Dr. Cuthbert Collin Davies, himself as a Welsh Baptist, one of their idealogical descendants.

[2b] 1761-1834; founder of the Baptist Missionary Society and famous biblical translator and missionary; resided at Serampore (outside Calcutta) from 1800 until his death.

British traders of the East India Company as early as 1662 set an important precedent for later developments by promulgating an order (in Bombay) providing that there should be "no compulsory conversion, and no interference with native habits;"[3] an imaginative step in view of previous Portuguese and Dutch rulers whose "intolerance, persecution, racial arrogance and forcible conversions . . . left a deplorable legacy for the future of Christianity in India."[4] Over a century later, and after the British had greatly extended the range of their political control, Act No. 37 of 1797 was passed, providing in some detail for the safeguarding of the "civil and religious usages of the natives." These edicts were a good beginning. However, their interpretation often allowed them to be used, for instance, against those who pressed for the abolishment of sati and similar social reforms, so the dissenting missionaries of Serampore, where from 1800 onwards the Baptists had their main base, endeavoured to have them more humanely defined.

At much the same time as Akbar ruled large parts of India, the English Reformation had brought into being radical new sects which did not respect the unity of church and state. The English Baptists[4a] were one of these. In their view the Church was not the religious arm of the state; rather it was a free association of like-minded believers who voluntarily ruled their associations or churches separately from either an ecclesiastical or a secular authority. Religion, they felt, was a personal matter. They were prepared to give the state full respect and obedience as dutiful citizens, while totally excluding it from the policy or government of their individual churches. In return, their churches, as churches, were to be excluded completely from all interference in the affairs of the state. Persecution could not force the Baptists to surrender

[3] Arthur Mayhew, *Christianity and the Government of India* (London, 1929), pp. 30-8.

[4] H. L. Gupta, 'The Christian Missionaries and their Impact on Modern India in the Pre-Mutiny Period,' p.1. Paper delivered at a Seminar on 'Ideas motivating religious and social movements and economic and political changes in the 18th and 19th centuries in India', held at Delhi University in November 1964.

[4a] Their relation with European Anabaptists of the same period is, at best, tenuous, despite frequent references to them as Anabaptists.

these radical beliefs, which were followed in practice when one of their persuasion named Roger Williams founded in 1636 the colony of Rhode Island where, for the first time in modern history, something approximating the contemporary concept of the secular state was brought into being.

The handful of Baptists who came to India from 1793 onwards repudiated therefore the idea of state support or interference with any religion or mission, especially the latter. Besides being theologically opposed to such interference they correctly thought it would be harmful to their evangelical cause to have the peoples of the sub-continent see the Government involved, even as an auxiliary, in such an enterprize. The influence of the state might, as William Carey once told Lord Minto (Governor-General, 1807-13) in an often misunderstood statement, "make Hypocrites but could never make Christians."[5] Or, as it was later expressed by the chronicler of the Serampore Mission, they "desired that the missionary should appear before the people simply as the messenger of divine truth, without any secular inducements."[6] Missionary agitation in favour of the British in India adopting a more impartial religious policy took many forms. Two major ones will be considered.

Before doing so a number of factors which might at first glance suggest gross contradictions in attitudes should be clarified. First, Baptist beliefs did not free the state of its duty to regulate moral affairs when these impinged on the rights of others, and especially when they impinged on the rights of women (as with sati) or children (as with infanticide); neither did they free the Baptists of their duty to urge the Government to take action against such practices. Again, it could be and has been suggested that by accepting a position under the state the missionary who professed to believe in the separation of church and state would be acting counter to his beliefs. In 1801, for instance, Carey accepted the post of "teacher" of Bengali, and later became Professor of both

[5] Journal of Wm. Ward, iv, 11 April 1808, B(aptist) M(issionary) S(ociety), London.

[6] J. C. Marshman, *The Life and Times of Carey, Marshman, and Ward* (London, 1859), ii, 26.

Bengali and Sanskrit, in the College of Fort William. Lord Wellesley (Governor-General, 1798-1805) avowedly appointed him "as a Missionary, or in conjunction with the Mission", and 90 per cent of the salary paid went to support the mission's work.[7] Here Carey meant that his missionary vocation was known to Government, which accepted this continued association while his employer, or rather was prepared to overlook the association. In other words, there was nothing in Baptist ideology to prevent its proponents from accepting posts of honour and profit under the state. There would however be an objection to allowing the state to sponsor Baptists for the set purpose of propagating their beliefs. As much as they wished to see India become a mainly Christian country, they felt that this was for the churches to achieve by attracting the people to what they considered a more satisfactory religious view: Christianity should triumph without assistance or hindrance from the state. Finally, there was nothing which prohibited Baptists from voicing their individual complaints or individual praises regarding the actions or lack thereof of the state in which they resided. For instance, the disapproval expressed by missionary William Moore, who wrote early in 1808 about the supposedly increased dissipation which the papers of Calcutta revealed, with their numerous accounts of "theatrical amusements, Masquerades, Horse-racing, etc. etc.",[8] was simply that of a private individual, who was not acting as a spokesman of a church. And so it should clearly be understood that Baptist contributions to the evolution of the secular state arose naturally out of their basic belief in the separation of church and state.

One of these contributions centred around the policy followed by the East India Company until 1813 of formally excluding Christian missionaries from entry into regions under their *de facto* or *de jure* rule. Together with allied groups, the Baptists argued that the Government was not carrying out its policy of neutrality towards the religions practised in

[7] Carey to John Sutcliffe, Serampore, 13 April 1801, B.M.S.

[8] Wm. Moore to John Sutcliffe, Serampore, 19 April 1808, B.M.S. Often this policy is forgotten by contemporary Baptist leaders in such countries as the United States, United Kingdom, and Australia; they ignore their ideological heritage by speaking out on such matters as spokesmen for "the Baptists".

India by showing prejudice against Christianity. (The debates of 1792-93 were *not* over whether to accede to Charles Grant's and William Wilberforce's pleas to send missionaries and school-masters to India, or whether Government employment of missionaries would violate that policy. They were mainly directed against any attempt by any group to "enlighten" the inhabitants of the land by the introduction of Christian ideas and western education.) Carey's arrival with a colleague in Calcutta in 1793 put the Government to the test. Would it, in practice, deport missionaries who came to India in defiance of John Company's orders, with the avowed and published purpose of "converting the heathen"? The answer at first was no. Carey and other pre-1800 Baptists were all but ignored, even by the officials of the area in which they settled who perfectly understood their "Errand".[9] However, when four additional missionaries, who travelled to India on an American ship and landed in the tiny Danish enclave of Serampore (15 miles north of Calcutta), attempted to join Carey in Malda (north Bengal) early in 1800 they were summarily threatened with arrest if found on British-ruled territory. Later Carey decided to join the newcomers in Serampore, and the Mission of that name, which Wilberforce later declared to be "one of the chief glories" of the British nation,[10] came into being.

Soon Lord Wellesley was convinced sufficiently of the outstanding qualities of the men at Serampore, and especially of Carey, Joshua Marshman,[10a] and William Ward[10b] — the Serampore Trio — to express publicly his "good-will towards the undertaking" and his view that in such hands Christianity "would ultimately prevail" throughout the land. He emphasized that officially he could not and would not "do any thing to help forward" this objective; nor could he permit any other official "*in his official capacity* to do so."[11] This attitude, combined as it was with a refusal to interfere with the objective, was certainly proper. The Government would not interfere

9 Carey to John Sutcliffe, Mudnabati, 10 October 1798, B.M.S.

10 Wilberforce to Ryland, Deanery Wells, 28 September 1819, Letters from Mr. Wilberforce to Dr. Ryland, Bristol Baptist College.

10a 1768-1837; missionary and educator at Serampore, 1799-1837.

10b 1769-1823; missionary and printer at Serampore, 1799-1823.

11 Journal of Wm. Ward, ii, 15 March 1806, B.M.S. (My italics).

with missions anywhere in India, and would not implicate Government in their operations. However, it did so indirectly, by hiring Carey (teachers of Bengali were few and far between) and by subscribing to the Mission's increasingly voluminous publications. In 1804, for example, the Government gave eight hundred pounds for 100 copies of Carey's pioneering Sanskrit grammar.

This policy continued until the outbreak of the Vellore Mutiny in a totally different part of India in June, 1806 frightened the weak men who succeeded Wellesley into taking restrictive action: two missionaries who arrived in Bengal shortly afterwards were immediately ordered to leave the country; and Carey was told that Sir George Barlow (Governor-General, 1805-1807) did not want those remaining to "interfere with the prejudices of the natives" by carrying on their work.[12] Soon, however, these restrictions, which Wilberforce had called a most "shocking Violation of all Religious Liberty",[13] were eased. And an attempt in England to secure the Baptists' recall was thwarted by the Chairman and Deputy-Chairman of the Court of Directors, Edward Parry and Charles Grant. In fact Grant had written to Lord William Bentinck, who because of the outbreak had been relieved of his post as Governor of Madras, that "the English in general resident in India have been as likely to become Hindoos as to compel Indians to profess Christianity."[14] The success of this struggle for the missionaries was, as C. H. Philips has said, "the necessary preliminary to the insertion of a clause in the Charter Act of 1813, which permitted the licensing of missionaries to introduce into India useful knowledge and religious and moral improvements."[15]

Before 1813, however, the issue of a pamphlet in Persian derisive of Islam and its founder from Serampore's press had caused Lord Minto to attempt the press's removal, on the

12 Carey to Andrew Fuller, Calcutta, 26 August 1806, B.M.S.

13 Wilberforce to Ryland, Brighton, 8 August 1807, Letters from Mr. Wilberforce to Dr. Ryland, Bristol Baptist College.

14 Grant to Bentinck, India House, 17 April 1807, Lord Wm. Bentinck — Madras, Bentinck MSS., MS. 218, Nottingham University.

15 C. H. Philips, *The East India Company, 1784-1834* (Manchester, 1940), p. 169.

grounds that the publication of tracts critical of Indian religions marked "a departure from that principle of toleration which the British Legislature has prescribed, which we have uniformly professed and observed, and to which the Faith of Government is invaslably [sic] pledged." The Baptists were ordered to curtail their printing and other operations so as to leave Indians in the "full free and undisturbed exercise of their respective Religions."[16] In other words, the Government felt itself duty-bound to prohibit written criticism of, in this case, Islam. A plea that the pamphlet in question and similar ones were detrimental to public order, though difficult to substantiate, would perhaps have been more acceptable to the historian of the secular state than the Government's claim that these publications printed in non-British territory by a private organization endangered the Government's policy of toleration.[17] The Baptist view was summed up five decades afterwards when John Clark Marshman wrote :

> . . . this is the first instance in which the Government of India brought forward the plea of being bound by a *pledge* to grant the natives the undisturbed exercise of their 'respective religions.' No such pledge was ever . . . granted . . . [and] To assert the existence of . . . [one] . . . and then to maintain that any 'effort directed to the object of converting the natives to Christianity', was a violation . . . was, in fact, to assert that Government had solemnly pledged itself to resist every effort to Christianise the country, — which is simply absurd.[18]

Lord Minto soon relented from this position to the extent of allowing the continued publication of religious works provided, as the missionaries were naturally obliged to agree,

16 G(overnor)-G(eneral) Minto in Coun(cil) to J. Krefting, Ft. William, 1 September 1807; N. B. Edmonstone to Carey, Ft. William, 8 September 1807, Home Misc(ellaneous) Series, dcxc, 26-7 and 55-9, Ind(ia), Off(ice) Lib(rary).

17 Later Minto did say that because the Serampore Press was directed by British subjects who were virtually "under the protection and authority of the British Government" Indians would think that any tracts issued therefrom had official British sanction. He did not enlarge on this. See *Parl(iamentary) Papers H(ouse) of C(ommons)*, 1812-13, viii, 46.

18 *Carey, Marshman, and Ward*, i, 317-8.

they first be submitted to Government censorship. This certainly implicated Government in the Baptists' day-to-day operations. Meanwhile, the Governor-General proudly sought approval from the Court of Directors for his actions, and in an aside asked the Court to discourage more missionaries from coming to India.[19] Instead of receiving approval, Minto, partly due to internal British politics, found himself rebuked. Joined by others, the Prime Minister, Spencer Perceval (who told Wilberforce of "the necessity of setting the face of government against the offensive and abominable project of interdicting the circulation of religious knowledge in India"),[20] secured a despatch, written by Robert Dundas,[21] which correctly told Minto to limit any dealings with the Baptists to private and not official ones, for by using the full authority of the Government in this matter he had exposed it to the "inference of specially sanctioning and countenancing such publications and such conduct as it does not prevent, and thereby making Government in some degree a party to the acts of the Missionaries, and making the Missionaries appear in the character of the agents of Government." In addition to being reminded of the undoubted fact that not one of the Baptists had travelled to India with the permission of the Court, Minto was told to follow the practice of abstaining "from all unnecessary or ostentatious interference with their proceedings."[22]

Having found that the Baptists were hardly the friendless individuals they sometimes claimed to be, Minto became more discrete in his relations with them. In 1810 applications were made to send two missionaries to a frontier station near the Panjab to study the Panjabi and Hindostani languages with the view to producing improved translations of the Bible in those tongues.

19 *Parl. Papers* (*H. of C.*), 1812-13, viii, 46-7.

20 Spencer Perceval to Wilberforce, Downing St., 19 December 1807, quoted in R. & S. Wilberforce (eds.), *Correspondence of William Wilberforce* (London, 1849), ii, 139.

21 Draft letter by Robert Dundas (President of the Board of Control) from Court of Directors to Lord Minto, approved for despatch on 16 August 1808, Correspondence on Missions in India, 1807, Bodleian.

22 *Parl. Papers* (*H. of C.*), 1812-13, viii, 73-4.

Minto refused on the more acceptable grounds that "considerations" rendered it "generally inexpedient that any Europeans . . . not . . . in the public service, should be allowed to settle in any of the frontier districts."[23] This, even by Baptist standards, was justifiable. Moreover, shortly afterwards the two received permission to settle in a less dangerous area. The very asking for and receiving such approval, however, worried at least one of the Trio. William Ward did not like the idea that future movements could be, as this incident implied, entirely subject to Government permission.[24] The Government, he felt, had no business in such matters, and the Baptists had no business acceding to its control, regardless of the possible advantages. One of the agents so sent continually antagonized local officials in Agra by, against the instructions of his superiors, engaging in normal missionary evangelical activities, rather than confining himself to language study. When this became known in Calcutta, Ward's misgivings were realized for the Government professed to feel that peace and calm were endangered and refused further requests from Serampore to send other missionaries into different parts of India. Later, by preaching to *European* soldiers in the garrison at Agra against the advice of the local Commander, the obstreperous Baptist was arrested and sent under guard to Calcutta, where he was immediately set free.[25]

This incident led to still another, and as matters turned out the final, major missionary-Government conflict over the basic issue of whether the Baptists in particular and all missionaries in general should be allowed complete freedom to propagate their doctrines, just as Hindus and Muslims were allowed complete freedom to propagate their doctrines, subject, as always, to *bona fide* public safety precautions. In 1812 two more missionaries, a medical doctor and an engraver, arrived at Serampore, which from late 1807 to 1815 was under British rule. On 5 March, 1813, — at the very time the question of allowing

23 *Circular Letters of the Serampore Mission* (September 1810), iii, 128-9.

24 Ward to Andrew Fuller, n.p., 21 October 1810, B.M.S.

25 Chamberlain to John Williams, Serampore, 12 October 1812, quoted in L. & M. Williams (eds.), *Serampore Letters* (New York & London, 1892), p. 140.

missionaries into India was being debated at Westminster in conjunction with the regular 20-year renewal of the Company's Charter — the new recruits were ordered to return to England.[26] Upon appeal, the order against John Lawson was revoked (mainly because his work upon the first complete metal fount of Chinese type would advance Joshua Marshman's publications in that language, and in turn these were expected to be useful in assisting the Company's trade with China). Dr. William Johns was summarily deported; the only Baptist to be forced to leave India in the history of their mission. Later that same year the possibility of this happening again was all but eliminated. Wilberforce, who with the slave trade legally abolished now felt that the official exclusion of Christianity from India was "by far the greatest of our national sins",[27] actively aided by the Baptists and other Christians in England and using the achievements of the Serampore Mission to lend weight to his arguments, secured in the Charter the well-known clause on the duty of Britain to "promote the interests and happiness" of the Indian people by taking "such measures . . . as may tend to the introduction . . . of useful knowledge, and of religious and moral improvement." Specifically, missionaries were to be officially allowed, upon the payment of a licence fee, to proceed to and reside in India.[28]

Obviously this was not a victory for the Dissenters' desired total separation of church and state. A concurrent clause in the Charter went directly counter to this ideal by creating an Anglican ecclesiastical establishment for India and other parts of the East (including Australia), with a Bishop in Calcutta, and Archdeacons there and at Madras and Bombay. The Baptists were naturally opposed to "every political establishment of religion"[29] and, as was their wont, were sceptical of the claimed practical benefits of such an organization. In 1826 the Secretary of the Baptist Missionary Society, John

26 C. M. Ricketts (Secretary to Government) to Marshman, Calcutta, 7 January 1813, B.M.S.

27 Quoted in R. & S. Wilberforce, *Life of William Wilberforce* (London, 1838), iv, 103.

28 *Parl. Papers* (*H. of C.*), 1812-13, ii, 15.

29 Carey to John Ryland, Calcutta, 16 August 1809, College Street Baptist Church, Northampton.

Dyer, although noting that they were glad the Anglicans were increasing their missionary operations, expressed his group's doubts that more conversions would "follow from investing the religion of a meek and lowly Saviour in the transient decorations of 'pomp and splendour', however adapted these may be to dazzle and attract the thoughtless and unholy."[30] In addition the Baptists feared their own activities might actually be curbed by any Bishop who had the ear of Government. These fears were not realized.

Soon after the passage of the Charter the first licence was given to a missionary to enter India. Interestingly, the Board of Control changed the Court of Directors' wording that the man concerned (Eustace Carey, a nephew of William Carey) would be allowed to proceed to Bengal "in the Character of a Christian Missionary" to read "for the purpose of introducing among the Natives useful knowledge and religious improvement."[31] In a second test case, which again involved a Baptist, the Court, perhaps resenting the more active role seemingly allowed Eustace Carey by the Board, refused a licence. An appeal immediately resulted in the Board overruling the Court, which ceased its formal opposition. Although the Act of 1813 empowered the Court to cancel the licence of a missionary if given just cause, this right was never exercised. The Charter Renewal Act of 1833 eliminated the requirement of a licence altogether and set the stage for the hordes of missionaries from all over the Western world who poured into the sub-continent throughout the remainder of the century and on into the 20th century.

Not only were missionaries after 1813 allowed almost free access to territories under British rule; they were also sometimes actively encouraged to expand their operations in certain directions. In 1813 the Resident of the Molucca Islands (which had been captured from the Dutch) suggested to Lord Moira (later Lord Hastings; Governor-General, 1813-1823) that Serampore might contribute to the spread of "the benefits of true religion" among the inhabitants by extending their

30 John Dyer, *A Letter to the Editor of the Quarterly Review* (London, 1826), p.15.

31 Letter in the Public Dept. from the Court of Directors to the G.-G. in Coun., London, 18 February 1814, Bengal Desp(atches), lxiii, 489, Ind. Off. Lib.

schools into the area. Moira favoured the idea. He told the Court of Directors of his promise to give every assistance to any members of the Mission who might be disposed to go there.[32] This and similar incidents obviously involved the Government in promoting the spread of Christianity. To be absolutely true to their principles the Baptists should have refused to implicate themselves in the operation. Their zeal appears to have exceeded their ideal. Lord Moira further involved Government with the Mission by visiting the Trio's extensive headquarters, schools, and printing plant in 1815; the first Governor-General to do so.[33] William Ward had apparently forgotten his earlier scruples to such an extent that he told the Annual Meeting of the Wesleyan (Methodist) Missionary Society in London in 1821: "The Government of India acts, as far as is prudent, entirely with us; and, in a variety of ways, they are assisting us, and assisting us in the most powerful manner."[34]

Another point on which the Baptists agitated in hope of a more impartial religious policy was the Government connexion with Hindu and Muslim religious activities. They thought the state should not openly associate itself with such activities, just as they thought it should not interfere with missionaries who wanted to come to India to convert these same Hindus and Muslims. It is important to remember that the Dissenters' position was comparatively straightforward — unlike that of those Anglicans who opposed Government connexion with Hinduism or Islam while welcoming complete Government support for their own activities, and most of whom would have had a very difficult time answering the question: "If the religion of the few is to be supported from the revenues of the country, why, on any conceivable principle of neutrality, is not the religion of the many."[35]

32 E. A. Payne, *South-East from Serampore* (London, 1945), p.16; Letter in the Colonial Dept. from Lord Moira to the Court of Directors, Ft. William, 8 January 1814, Bengal Letters Received, lxviii, Ind. Off. Lib.

33 Sophia, the Marchioness of Bute (ed.), *The Private Journal of the Marquess of Hastings*, 2nd edn. (London, 1858), ii, 94.

34 Quoted in the *Missionary Register*, May 1821, p. 179.

35 John Kaye, *Christianity in India* (London, 1859), p. 439.

British withdrawal from all official support of the indigenous religions presented many complications. Attempting to assume fully the responsibilities of the Indian rulers it displaced, the Company's Government sometimes found itself financing and supervising religious festivals and pilgrimages, as well as the internal affairs of temples or mosques. It did not "invariably" provide for the continuance of "all the rights, privileges, and immunities which had been enjoyed under the former Hindu or Muslim" ruler, although it did so often enough to arouse great resentment among missionaries, who could see to their horror that "a Christian government, by restoring public confidence in the administration of the institutions, had greatly promoted the standing and prestige" of the two religions.[36] Concentrated as they were in Bengal Presidency, the Baptists in particular paid far less attention to Government involvement in Madras and Bombay Presidencies, thinking that once the Government in Bengal set a precedent for withdrawal those in the other areas would soon follow suit. In common with allied organizations in Bengal, the Baptists therefore devoted much of their time to opposing strenuously the supposed evils of Britain's connexion with the temple of the God Jagannath,[36a] at Puri near Cuttack. To a lesser extent they deplored the Company's support and management of the temples and festivals at Gaya and Allahabad. By studying the Jagannath campaign, that is the techniques of agitation and the arguments for and against withdrawal, one should be able to see how the success of the agitation contributed to the secular state concept.

In 1803 Lord Wellesley had wisely rejected the suggestion of some of his officials that he should continue the practice of the former Mahratta rulers in that part of newly-conquered Orissa where the Temple of Jagannath was situated of collecting taxes from its pilgrims, and so win the favour and loyalty of the priests to whom some of the tax money would be paid, assuring them of a certain source of income.[37] Not that

[36] Smith, *India as a Secular State*, pp. 72, 75-6.

[36a] Jagannath is a title of the God Krishna, the eighth manifestation of Vishnu. There is also a temple of the God Jagannath near Serampore.

[37] Lt.-Col. George Harcourt and J. Melville to N. B. Edmonstone, Cuttack, 6 December 1803; Wellesley to Col. Campbell, Ft. William, 3 August 1803, Home Misc. Series, xcv, 423-6, 444.

he prohibited the priests from themselves imposing a pilgrim tax. The Government did not interfere either way. However, when Sir George Barlow became Governor-General in 1805 he went against the senior member of his Council, George Udny (a former indigo planter and a close friend and confidant of the Serampore missionaries), and ordered British collection of a tax "for the superintendence and management of the Temple . . . and the payment of its officers." Rejected was Udny's argument, which was also to be the basic missionary argument for half a century, that this step "would operate to sanction, and tend to perpetuate a system of gross idolatry". This Government was neither bound nor morally obliged to do.[38] In England, Udny received the support of Charles Grant and Edward Parry, who in 1808 wrote to the powerful Robert Dundas to beg, without success, his acquiescence to the "Principles that a Christian government . . . [should not] . . . appoint the Priests and direct the worship of a Heathen Temple;"[39] neither of which principles were directly involved in Barlow's orders. It might appear strange to some that it was the Board, the agency of Parliament, and not the hated commercial and 'money-grabbing' Court of Directors, which approved Barlow's order for the collection of a tax which, as shall be shown, proved profitable. Indeed, the Board ordered the Court to omit from a draft despatch to India paragraphs which dealt with the moral wrong of Government interfering with Hindu religious ceremonies or taxing "the Hindoos purely on a religious account."[40]

Three years passed before the first public attacks on this connexion with Jagannath were launched. These came when Claudius Buchanan, a former Anglican Chaplain in Calcutta, published his *Christian Researches in Asia* which among many other things described in horrified terms the temple and its yearly festival; ironically, he was at the same time vigorously promoting the creation of a far grander Church of England hierarchy than that which was established in 1813. During

38 *Parl. Papers* (*H. of C.*), 1812-13, viii, 41.

39 Parry to Dundas, East India House, 23 August 1808, Home Misc. Series, dcccxvi, 289-90.

40 Letter in the Revenue Dept. to the G.-G. in Coun., London, 24 March 1809, Bengal Desp., 1, 117-24.

the Charter Renewal Debates of 1812-13 Buchanan's arguments, which were based on his own observations and on material furnished him by Serampore, were widely quoted against those returned civil servants, such as Charles Buller (former Commissioner at Cuttack), who assured Parliament that interference, if it could be so inaccurately termed, was undertaken merely to guarantee the priests a certain revenue, so that they in turn could "protect and secure" the Company's "native subjects in the due exercise of their religious as well as civil liberties."[41] Not surprisingly, the Charter Renewal Act did not affect the Government's relation with Jagannath in any way. The appeal for change, led in Parliament by Wilberforce, lost its force when the proposals for subsidizing a Church of England establishment in India from general revenues of the Company were put forward. There were some members of Parliament who recognized the ambiguity of refusing finance to the Hindus and Muslims while granting it to a Christian group.

By now the Baptists' recurrent worries about their status in India had been alleviated, leaving them freer to develop some of their particular reasons for opposing the existing official association with temples and festivals. Through their influential quarterly *Friend of India* they maintained in an argument since accepted by most historians that this association had increased the fame of the supported temples and festivals at a time when Hinduism in general was "languishing, its temples falling into decay, and its absurdities sinking into contempt as light pours in upon the Native mind." Even taxation helped, as the tax enhanced "the merit of the journey [to places like Puri] by adding to its difficulty." More importantly, the Baptists declared the tax an oppression on the religious practices of the people for "if a man be so unhappy as to deem a log of wood a god, capable of conveying indescribable benefits . . . we think he has as much right to behold that log free of all expense, as a Christian has to worship the God of the whole earth from sabbath to sabbath."[42] Those

41 *Parl. Papers* (*H. of C.*), 1812-13, viii, 57.

42 "Reflections on the Incidents which occurred this year at the Rut'h Jattra of Jugunnat'h in Orissa," *Friend of India* (Quarterly Series), October 1825, xiii, 270-1.

who opposed any change on the time-won grounds that an insurrection might result were assured that "*Nothing could be more popular among them* [*the Indians*] *than the removal of this unproductive tax on their sacred places.*"[43] These arguments did not have the desired effect. When in 1829 sati was made a criminal offence in Bengal, it was suggested futilely to Lord Bentinck (Governor-General, 1828-35) that pilgrim taxes be abolished.[44] James Peggs, Baptist missionary in Orissa from 1822 to 1825 and a leading proponent of reform, wrote to Bentinck rejoicing "in the abolition of the Suttee, but [declaring] the discontinuance of British connection with Idolatry would save more lives & confer a greater boon upon India than even your Lordship's late popular measure."[45] Earlier Peggs had argued that the tax and Government interference, with the possible exception of necessary police supervision, should cease, because it encouraged "emissaries of idolatry" to wander all over India collecting devotees who might not even survive the trip, and also occasioned the death of many pilgrims who spent money on taxes instead of on food and other vital necessities; and because it was "*inhuman, impolitic, and unchristian.*"[46] In due course this had been followed by, coincidentally or otherwise, a brief but ineffectual parliamentary debate on "Hindoo Superstitions".[47]

Undoubtedly many officials, including Lord Bentinck, were sincere in believing that the *status quo* should be preserved. Their stand was justified in 1831-32 to a Select Committee on the Affairs of the East India Company which investigated the proposals to renew its Charter. In answer to a question on the extent pilgrims taxes identified the British Government "with the superstitious and idolatrous worship at the places where the taxes are levied, and how far the abandonment of such taxes might tend to aggravate the evils that result from

43 *Ibid.*, p. 283.

44 Minute of Bentinck's dated 8 November 1829, Bengal Criminal Judicial Consultations, dccxxxii (pt. 1, 4 December 1829), 28-9, Ind. Off. Lib.

45 Peggs to Bentinck, Coventry, 28 April 1830, Papers Relating to Suttee, 1828-1832, Bentinck MSS. MS. 2611.

46 James Peggs, *India's Cries to British Humanity*, 2nd edn. (London, 1830), pp. 258-9, 262-4.

47 *Hansard* (3rd Series), ii, 1-1356.

the assemblage of large bodies of pilgrims at places, and at periods when their feelings are peculiarly excited", John Stuart Mill wrote that the Government was no more identified with them than they were with "stews, and gaming houses" in England, which were licensed in order to control evils Government could not prevent. He denied that taxes increased the number of pilgrims any more than the abolition of taxes on spirits would lessen the number of alcoholics by making liquor easier to obtain and thereby less desirable than when more costly.[48] Another official spoke of the Government's duty as well as of its right to tax pilgrims: duty because abolishment of the tax would "excite distrust and suspicion in the minds of the natives, rather increase their idolatry, place the pilgrims more under control of the priests, and more liable to their grinding extortions, and render the assemblages of large bodies of pilgrims at such places dangerous to the peace and tranquillity of the country."[49] Others confirmed these opinions. One, however, concluded that "the evil of discontinuing the collection of the taxes in question consists, I conceive, simply in the loss of revenue" as Government would still have to police the festivals.[50] Another thought that it would be foolish to lose the revenue because in any case "every assemblage at a native festival, increases the custom and excise duties, and the brass used for holy vessels and for images pays tribute to our treasury."[51] Still another Company official said that if the pilgrim tax was given up another agency would impose it in a less satisfactory manner, causing "tumult and bloodshed." Ignoring the facts at issue, he continued with the supposition that the next step of these "weak minded zealots" would be "to overthrow all Hindoo temples, and to erect methodist conventicles on their ruins"; and added, forgetting that the missionaries lived in the midst of the people whose institutions were under discussion, that it was "a gratuitous and easy task for pious persons in this country, reposing safe and secure from the danger of revolt and massacre, to declaim loudly against the practices of idolatry, and to

[48] Answers to Circular Letter from T. Hyde Villiers, Esq., on the Revenue Administration of British India, *Parl. Papers* (*H. of C.*), 1831-2, xi, 274.

[49] *Ibid.*, pp. 280-1. [50] *Ibid.*, pp. 312-3. [51] *Ibid.*, p. 324.

deprecate the participation on the part of Government in the profits of these superstitions."[52] Of those officials who answered the question concerned, only two dissented; and both of these did so on other than secular grounds. While undoubtedly quite a few honestly feared that Government withdrawal would lead to tragedy of one kind or another, some of the answers strengthen one's suspicions that the pilgrim tax receipts must have been an important consideration to many. Significantly, all official letters on this subject originate in the Revenue Department of the Home Government. In any case, the figures tell the story: over a 17-year period the Government reaped a net profit of £99,205 from Jagannath; and £445,941 and £159,429 from Gaya and Allahabad respectively over a 16-year period.[53]

Those who opposed Government withdrawal were fighting a losing battle, however. The turning point came soon after, in 1833, when the Board of Control under the Presidency of none other than Charles Grant, Jun. (Lord Glenelg) ordered a now reluctant Court of Directors to have Bentinck disassociate his Government from the management or arrangement of religious festivals, abolish pilgrim taxes, and prohibit servants of the Company from collecting or receiving fines and offerings, or handling any money connected therewith. Costs of any necessary police action were to be drawn from general revenue. Although a small step towards the secular state, it was largely an unconscious one, as the reasons for this reversal did not tally with the supposed official neutrality in religious matters. The communication to Bentinck specified only disassociation from those religious rites which were opposed to the "*precepts and spirit of Christianity*"; contrarily emphasizing that the Home Government was not abandoning its policy of religious toleration, but returning "to that state of real neutrality from which we ought never to have departed."[54]

Meant only as guide-lines for future policy, their implementation was left to the Governor-General's discretion. The Court was required to advise Bentinck of its desire that

52 *Ibid.*, p. 337.

53 Kenneth Ingham, *Reformers in India, 1793-1833* (Cambridge, 1956), p.38.

54 Letter in the Misc. Revenue Dept. to the G.-G. in Coun., London, 20 February 1833, Bengal Desp., cxxi, 1273, Ind. Off. Lib.

he carry out their "views . . . with all prudent and practicable expedition", while exercising "Much caution and many gradations . . . in acting on the conclusions at which we have arrived."[55] The very vagueness of these instructions allowed Bentinck to ignore even a private letter from Grant which expressed his hope that the issue would be dealt with as satisfactorily, and with as little trouble, as sati had been.[56] Disgusted, the Baptists renewed their attack; while the new Bishops of Madras and Bombay (bishoprics having been established in these places by the Charter of 1833) settled into their sees. As usual, the *Friend of India* edited by John Clark Marshman presented best the Baptist position in their continued campaign. Basically, the missionaries "demanded" the cessation of all patronage of religion by Government (defining the difference between toleration and patronage while so doing) because, in addition to arguments previously cited, it compromised "the Christianity of our national character" and impressed "the Hindoos with the belief that we are insincere in matters of religion, and deficient in fixed principles."[57] There was little interest in their demands from non-missionary Europeans, most of whom had a reputation for total unconcern towards either Christianity or fixed principles. The editors of *The Englishman* (Calcutta) expressed the prevailing view. They said in 1837 that Government connexion must continue as long as the British continued to rule over a people, "the great bulk of whom are idolators" — a change from three years earlier, when they had written of the "objectionable" practice of Government implicating itself "in the immediate superstitions of the natives."[58]

Most certainly the Baptists harmed their case by bringing in the issue of Christianity at all. They might not have been receiving direct support from the Government, but most Christians in India were. Nevertheless, this argument impressed some of its audience and was used again the next

[55] *Ibid.*

[56] Grant to Bentinck, London, 13 May 1833. Lord Wm. Bentinck—Bengal, Bentinck MSS. MS. 1060.

[57] *Friend of India*, 31 March 1836. From January 1835 published weekly.

[58] 10 October 1837; 28 June 1834.

year by Charles Lacey of the General Baptist Missionary Society.[58a] Lacey issued a virulent pamphlet entitled *Appeal to the Friends of Religion and Humanity to their Fellow Christians on the Propriety of Dissolving the Connection of the British Indian Government with the Idolatry of India* in which he stated that the matter involved "the sacrifice of conscience of some of the best servants of the Government, and is one of the foulest blots on our divine and blessed faith."[59] Without doubt, continued Baptist agitation was unappreciated by Government. Of particular annoyance would have been statements such as that made in the *Friend* of 29 March, 1838, declaring the "power of public opinion combined upon a holy principle and directed to a sacred end" would eventually force the Court of Directors effectually to order withdrawal from all associations with Indian religions.[60] This is basically what happened later the same year. The Court informed Lord Auckland (Governor-General, 1836-42), of its "anxious desire" that he "should accomplish with as little delay as practicable" that very end.[61] In reluctant compliance Auckland duly noted the immediate surrender of the tax at Allahabad and outlined plans to do the same at Gaya and Jagannath, maintaining at the same time that Britain was duty-bound to "an honest and efficient" policy of "protection to the native religions."[62] He planned no immediate change in Bombay and Madras, and even in Bengal proposed to continue paying Rs. 20,000 annually to Gaya and Rs. 30,000 to Jagannath on these historically inaccurate grounds:

> We took forcible possession of Cuttack; we conciliated submission by binding ourselves to the accustomed maintenance of the temples of the country; and the same principle which would withhold this pledged payment; would, if followed out, pluck its endowment from every religious

[58a] Charles Lacey was a missionary in Orissa from 1823 to 1852. The General Baptists were divided from other British Baptists on obscure theological issues.

[59] (Calcutta, 1838), p. 28.

[60] *Friend of India*, 29 March 1838.

[61] Letter in the Revenue Dept. to the G.-G. in Coun., London, 8 August 1838, India and Bengal Desp., xvii, 361-2, Ind. Off. Lib.

[62] *Parl. Papers* (*H. of C.*), 1840, xxxvii, 205-6.

> institution in the country. We could not, and ought not, to hold India on such terms . . . . Our promise of the allowance 'for the support of the temple' is distinct and unconditional, and I would fulfill it to the letter.[63]

On 20 April, 1840 an act was passed abolishing the tax at Jagannath and transferring the charge of that temple "to a competent Hindu superintendent."[64] Auckland's actions, approved by both missionaries and the Court, clearly represented only a partial relinquishment of Government's association. The Court wrote on 31 March, 1841 of concern because similar progress "on this important subject" had not been made at Madras, asking that the matter be disposed of there by early the following year. A further despatch ordered the Government and its officials to refrain from all unnecessary interference with the religions of India.[65] It provided however that the lands attached to Jagannath were to be retained under the direction of Revenue Officers "in order that protection and justice might be secured to the ryots."[66]

This provision caused further contention with the missionaries, who wanted even that dissolved, together with the abolishment of subsidies paid to Gaya, Jagannath, and other temples. Lord Ellenborough (Governor-General, 1842-44) had adopted Auckland's position. He wrote on 11 April, 1844 that if the remaining subsidy to Jagannath was given up a moderate pilgrim tax, collected and disbursed by the priests, should be substituted. He added that, contrary to missionary forecasts, the effect of the curtailment of the earlier tax had "been to increase the number of pilgrims, and thereby to strengthen the religion taught by the Brahmins."[67] Whether or not true, this did not quieten the missionary agitation. A "Memorial" signed in 1850 by 15 Baptists and 22 of all other denominations desired Government to check the "vice, suffering . . . loss of life" and other evils "by discontinuing altogether a support" which was

[63] *Ibid.*, pp. 206-7. [64] *Ibid.*, p. 223. [65] *Ibid.*, 1841, xvii, 735-6.
[66] *Ibid.*, 1845, xxxiv, 323. [67] *Ibid.*, p. 411.

> so inconsistent with reason, humanity, and religion, and which contributes in no light degree to the misery, temporal and eternal of the people whom providence has entrusted to your charge, and whose welfare your Honourable Court is bound by every means in your power to promote.[68]

Finally, in February, 1856, the Government severed all official association with Jagannath, after providing that the administration of the temple lands be handed over to the priests in compensation for the withdrawn subsidies. The Resolution embodying this proposal was passed after consideration of letters from the Calcutta Missionary Conference and other missionary organizations.[69] But it was not until 1863 that the control of all temples and mosques was transferred to religious organizations representing the specific religions concerned in their management.

Yet another strong advance had been made in the secular state concept by the Government withdrawal from the support, taxation, and management of Indian religious activities. By no means did India become a secular state in 1863, or at any other date, even excluding the Anglican establishment. Government connexions of various sorts with Indian religions continued, as they continue today in independent India.[70] For instance, the Government kept up its practice of subsidizing the educational activities of religious groups, be they indigenous or Christian; a subsidization in which the Baptists shared and which, as it is not commonly understood, long predated the Wood Despatch. Both the end of direct Government association with Indian religions and the obtaining of the free entry of missionaries into India were nevertheless major contributions to the development of a secular state, as it was now considered the duty of the Government, one which ruled over a fantastic melangery of religious groups from Animists to Zoroastrians, to be as neutral towards these as strongly entrenched pressure groups would allow. Neutrality is certainly not the same thing as secularism, but it greatly contributes to its

68 *Ibid.*, 1851, xli, 321-3.

69 *Ibid.*, 1857-8, xlii, 295-6.

70 For examples of these connexions, see Smith, *India as a Secular State, passim.*

growth. The constant, if not always consistent, insistence of Christian missionaries following the lead of the Serampore Trio, allied mainly with English evangelicals, brought about this metamorphosis; just as their efforts brought about or stimulated many reforms in Indian society. This in turn laid the groundwork for what is today, for most practical purposes, a secular state. Its existence is now threatened, as it often has been in the past, by Hindu communal groups and others. One can only hope that the heritage left by those who assisted in its creation may be rich enough to assist in its preservation. The experiment of democracy in one of the few Afro-Asian countries in which this Western concept has survived is vitally sustained by the state's secularism, and could die without this sustenance.

# AURANGZIB AND DARA SHUKOH: CONFLICT OF IDEOLOGIES*

GULAMMOHAMMED REFAI

No other figure of Indian history has been more controversial than Aurangzib, the Emperor of India for almost fifty years (1658-1707). Many historical figures often acquire a legendary existence, obviously by virtue of human imagination and emotion. This is equally true for the Medieval Emperors and for the great men of our own time. Many of them received their share of *scandalum magnatum*. Aurangzib was one of them. Either he has been glorified or criticized, revered or cursed, idealized or stigmatized, venerated as a saint or denigrated as a demon! The Sunni Muslims have showered their praises and panegyrics on him as an ideal Muslim ruler, while the Marathas, the Sikhs, and the Shias have condemned him outright as a puritanical tyrant. One of the Shia writers — probably belonging to an eighteenth century petty Shia state of Northern India — went so far as to compile a devastating pasquinade to which he ingeniously gave the title of "The

*This essay owes its inception to a suggestion by Dr. C. C. Davies. I am grateful for advice from Dr. T. G. P. Spear and would like to thank the relevant Libraries and persons whose material I used. Since writing this I have investigated the rise of Hindu-Muslim communalism as a social force during Aurangzib's reign. It has not been possible to include my findings which I hope to publish elsewhere.

Royal Court Bulletins" ('akhbarat i darbar i mu'alla').[1] On the other hand, the Sunnites have always been very sensitive about any criticism of his reign, for they revere Aurangzib as a saint. Shibli Nu'mani, the celebrated scholar who wrote the monumental work the *Shi'r ul 'Ajam* (The Poetry of Persia), heads the list of the writers who polemically argue in praise of his character and policies. In his popular Urdu work *Aurangzib per ek nazar*, Shibli stoutly defends Aurangzib and says that the European writers have purposefully distorted his acts and misrepresented his policies. Shibli particularly charged Bernier, Elphinstone, and Lane-Poole[2] with gross exaggeration, although agreeing with such of their remarks as were in tune with his acquittal of Aurangzib. In fact most of the European writers have based their verdict on the contemporary travellers' accounts which usually rested on bazaar gossip, hearsay, or at the most on a hasty judgment of an event which was taken at its face value. Therefore, some of the European writers have sometimes misinterpreted if not misrepresented Aurangzib's policies, especially his conquest of Golconda and Bijapur which, although ascribed to his bigotry, was in fact a result of their own misrule and palace conspiracies.[3] Aurangzib hunted the Marathas because they had harboured the rebel Prince Akbar, and ravaged the

[1] Corpus Or. MS. No. 198 C(ambridge) U(niversity) L(ibrary). It was written, according to a note on the fly leaf, by Buland 'Ali Munshi, and because of its misleading title, it was classed among the official documents of Aurangzib by E. G. Browne in his *A Supplementary Handlist of the Muhammadan MSS.* (Cambridge, 1922), p. 247. It is outrageously abusive in places. In the beginning the writer says: ". . . that day His Majesty (Aurangzib) held a private audience. Her Majesty the Queen of the spinning-wheel (*Bibi Charkhajot*) petitioned that His Majesty was so much occupied with the conquest of the Deccan that the ruinous condition of the empire of Hindustan has escaped his notice. His Majesty replied that when he had placed his head into a mortar why should he fear the blows!"

[2] Francois Bernier, *Travels in the Mogul Empire A.D. 1656-1668*, tr. Constable (London, 1914); Mountstuart Elphinstone, *The History of India* (London, 1889); and Stanley Lane-Poole, *Aurangzib* (*Rulers of India Series*) (Oxford, 1892).

[3] Theodore Morison, 'M. Bernier upon the establishment of Trade in India: 1668', *J(ournal of the) R(oyal) A(siatic) S(ociety)*, lxxxvii (Jan. 1933), pp. 16-18. This minute was not included by Bernier in his *Travels*; but written especially for Colbert, the Minister of Louis XIV who was the architect of the French Company.

Mughal territories.[4] The fact is that many of the historians of Aurangzib have placed an undue emphasis on such of his policies as were dictated by political and military exigencies rather than by his intolerance. After analysing the contemporary evidence, including his own letters, in a proper historical perspective, it seems as if the only inexcusable wrong of which he was guilty was the reversal of Akbar's policy of universal toleration (*sulh i kull*). It is very true that Aurangzib erred in common with most of the contemporary rulers of the world.[5] His guilt was that he did not rise above his age although his predecessors, especially Akbar, had demonstrated that a state, even a Muslim state which was basically theocentric, could be capable of incorporating in its constitution the principle of universal toleration in an age when the world was mostly dominated by religious dogmas. He was, therefore, not justified in diametrically counteracting the process of integration which Akbar had initiated with great efforts. This he did not only because he was a puritan, but also because he had rallied reactionary forces to oppose Dara Shukoh, an exponent of toleration.

It is generally asserted that after Akbar there was a gradual return to the pre-Akbar orthodoxy, which finally culminated in the reactionary Aurangzib. This theory seems to be an outcome of an unfulfilled optimism that Akbar's successors should invariably have been like him or better. On the contrary, is it not surprising that his own son, who had to rely on the reactionaries for their support to the succession, did not fall a victim to their reaction and did not reverse his father's policy? The isolated acts of Jahangir and Shah Jahan which were in opposition to Akbar's policy were mostly an outcome of the extemporaneous influence of the Muslim theologians, and not a marked policy of their government.[6]

[4] J. Sarkar, *Short History of Aurangzib* (Calcutta, 1962), pp. 273-279.

[5] S. R. Sharma, *The Religious Policy of the Mughal Emperors* (London, 1962), p.177.

[6] Abdul-Hamid Lahori, the author of the *Padshah-nama* (*Bib. Ind. Sers.*) (Calcutta, 1867, pp.57-58) writes that when Shah Jahan was in Gujarat, Punjab, some local theologians and priests petitioned that some of the Muslim women had been converted by the Hindus and had been married to them, and the Hindus had also turned the mosques into houses. Shah Jahan appointed an officer to investigate the charges, and ordered that if they were proved, the Muslim women should be restored to their Muslim families and the mosques to the priests.

But in general, Jahangir and Shah Jahan followed, even if intermittently, the basic policy of Akbar.[7] There is no convincing evidence to the general assertion that Shah Jahan's reign was a prelude to what happened under Aurangzib.[8] On the other hand there is strong evidence indicating that during the last years of Shah Jahan's reign his policy, obviously under the influence of the syncretic Crown Prince Dara Shukoh and Princess Jahanara who were his constant companions, was becoming increasingly liberal. It was this liberalism that gave rise to a reactionary group under Aurangzib. When Prince Aurangzib was Viceroy of Gujarat (1645-47), he had desecrated at Ahmedabad the Jain temple of Chintaman (which had been built at great expense by the Jain plutocrat Shantidas) and had converted it into a mosque which he called the *Quwat i Islam* mosque.[9] But when Shah Jahan was informed, he disapproved of Aurangzib's action and restored to Shantidas his temple granting him a *farman* to this effect in 1648. On this *farman* Shah Jahan is said to have written briefly about the speedy restoration of the temple.[10] Shah Jahan had also granted a similar *farman* to a politically less influential person Goswami Tikayat of Gokul, in the sixth ilahi year of his reign. This Hindu priest was given the village of Jatipura for his use and for the maintenance of his *Thakordwara* temple, tax free.[11] A comparison of the lists of the Hindu officers under Jahangir and Shah Jahan reveals that under the former there were only six Hindu *mansabdars* (commanders) above the rank of 3,000 horse, while under the latter there were fourteen; highest among them were the Imperial finance minister and several provincial finance ministers, and four of them were the commanders of 5,000

[7] Cf. Sharma, *Religious Policy*, pp. 95-96. [8] *Ibid.*, p. 95.

[9] Thevenot, trans. S. N. Sen, *Indian Travels of Thevenot and Careri* (New Delhi, 1949), pp.13-14; *The Mirat-i-Ahmadi* (*Gaekwad's Or. Sers.*) (Baroda, 1928), i, 220. Mandelslo has given a vivid account of this temple. See Harris's *Travels* (London, 1764), i, 757-58. Shantidas (d.1659) was an eminent jeweller; for his life, see *Rajsagarsuri Ras* (1666) in Jin Vijayji's (ed.) *Jain Aitihasik Gurjara Kavya Sanchhaya* (Bhavnagar, 1926), pp. 22-23.

[10] M.S. Commissariat, 'Imperial Mughal Farmans in Gujarat', *Journal of the Bombay University*, vol. IX, pt. I (July 1940), plates IX and XXII, pp. 39-41.

[11] K. M. Jhaveri, *Imperial Farmans, 1577-1805* (Bombay, 1928), nos. VI-VIII.

horse. The highest noble of the Mughal Empire was a Hindu, Maharaja Jaswant Singh, who was a commander of 6,000. Every decade of Shah Jahan's reign shows a slight increase in the percentage of the Hindu *mansabdars*. From 18.5 at the end of the tenth year the percentage rose to 21.5 at the end of the thirty-first year.[12]

In fact, Shah Jahan's reign witnessed a major Hindu revival, social, political, and cultural, to which he undoubtedly contributed by patronizing many Hindu scholars, poets, and astronomers; chief amongst these were Sundar Das, Chintamani (the Hindi poets), Kavindracarya, Jagannath, and Vedangaraja (Sanskrit scholars). Shah Jahan's reign is remarkable for its production of classical Sanskrit writings, some of which are still considered as standard authorities on Hindu Law and Jurisprudence.[13] The Brahmans enjoyed freedom to teach religion and philosophy to Muslim students who came to Banaras from all over India. After his accession Aurangzib discontinued this privilege.[14]

Despite the fact that Shah Jahan was aware of Dara's weaknesses, he chose him to be his successor; presumably because of Dara's liberalism.

Akbar's principle of universal toleration (*sulh i kull*) was based on social justice. The time of Shah Jahan witnessed a class of Muslim thinkers who interpreted the very principles of Islam as advocating universal toleration, and asserted that Islam never approved of compulsion in religion. When Prince Aurangzib converted the *Chintaman* temple of Ahmedabad, as stated, Mulla Abu'l Hakīm, the chief of the *'ulema* (theologians), gave a ruling that as the Islamic Law forbade the construction of a mosque on another's property, the Prince's act was a breach of that law.[15] Amongst those who were

[12] Sharma, *Religious Policy*, pp. 82-85: '... under Shah Jahan the Hindus counted among them the mightiest subject and the highest public servant ....' (p. 85).

[13] *Ibid.*, p. 94.

[14] *Maasir i 'Alamgiri*, ed. Ahmad Ali (*Bib. Ind.*) (Calcutta, 1870), p.81.

[15] S. M. Ikram, *Muslim Civilization in India* (New York, 1964), p.185. 'There is no compulsion in religion', Mohamed Ali's *Koran*, ch. II, sec. xxxiv, 256. Cf. Dara, *Majma-ul-Bahrain* (The Mingling of the Two Oceans) ed. M. Mahfuz-ul-Haq (*Bib. Ind.*), p. 80; see also K. Qanungo, *Dara Shukoh* (Calcutta, 1952), pp. 92-93, 252-68.

trying to interpret Islam and the traditions of the Prophet in a rational way, Hakim Nuruddin Shirazi was in the fore. An encyclopaedist of Shah Jahan's reign, he was to Dara what Abu'l Fazl and Fayzi, his uncles, were to Akbar. His scholarly encyclopaedia, the *Mu'alajat i Dara Shukohi*, which spreads into three folio volumes and extends through not less than 3,338 pages, is full of his rational explanations for the acts of the Prophet. But he goes too far, echoing the liberalism which was gaining ground. He boldly dismissed as absurd the Muslim belief that a celestial angel registers the actions of man in a volume which would be presented to him on the Day of Judgment. He even goes one step further, and maintains that the *viva voce* revelation of the Qur'an by the angel Gabriel to the Prophet was against natural truth and human experience, for an angel is incorporeal and that which is incorporeal cannot speak.[16] The fact that such a heretic, who had repudiated the very essence of the belief in the Day of Judgment and the oral revelation of the Qur'an to the Prophet, enjoyed royal patronage emphasizes the increasing liberalism of his reign towards its end. And it was against this liberalism that Aurangzib rose in revolt. For this, we have his own testimony in his letter which is quoted below. The letter was written after Aurangzib had imprisoned Shah Jahan in the Agra Fort, probably in June 1658.

> I have repeatedly written to Your Majesty that my intention in proceeding to Akbarabad [Agra] was not a rebellion or revolt against a Muslim King. The world knows that I never entertained such an ignoble idea which is contrary to the Law of Islam. The only reason was that during your illness Your Majesty had lost control of the government, and the eldest Prince [Dara Shukoh], who wore no colour of Muslim religion, had become very powerful by assuming the powers of the government. He had also raised the standards of heresy and infidelity in the country. His expulsion, therefore, had become essential from the point of view of wisdom, Islamic Law and commonsense. Hence I considered it best for the sake of dignity to proceed to those parts [Agra]. I had to

[16] David Price, "Extracts from the Mualijati Dara Shekohi", *JRAS*, iii (1935), p. 53. Nuruddin compiled this work during 1642-46 and dedicated it to Dara.

fight first with the perfidious infidels who were desecrating and demolishing the mosques and converting them into the temples. The second battle I had with that wicked infidel [Dara]. But as I had a noble aim, I won and was successful in every battle despite a small army, and was preserved from any harm. But Your Majesty had declared me to be guilty, disregarding with extreme prejudice the interests of the religion [Islam] and the state. And Your Majesty were looking for an opportunity to restore the faithless Prince [Dara] [in order] to turn the illuminated face [of the world] into [dark] infidelity. In such a situation weak rule would have ruined the country. Therefore, I was compelled to take up the responsibility of this grave task in the hope that I will be rewarded with God's grace.[17]

Even Aurangzib's contemporaries felt that he had changed Shah Jahan's liberal policy. In a remarkably conscientious letter written in January, 1672 from Surat, Streynsham Master, a factor at Surat and Ahmedabad during 1656-72 and later a governor of Fort St. George (Madras) during 1677-80, said:

> . . . During the Reignes of JANGEER and SHAH-JEHAUN, the HINDOOES were not at all molested in the exercise of their Religion, but were in favour and preferred to the great and Meane offices of the Kingdome soe well as the Moors. But this Mogull [Aurangzib] who attained the crowne by Hypocrisy and pretence of a great zelot hath proceeded otherwise with them . . . the Mahumetans have allsoe since this Kings time been more zealous in their profession of their owne Religion than formerly . . . .[18]

Dara was not so able a general as Aurangzib; but it seems as if his ability to rule in peace has been grossly understated by the historians of Aurangzib and modern writers alike, who tend to base their valuation on the writings of Rashid Khan, the

[17] 'Ruqa'at i 'Inayat Khani', ff. 27b-28a, Pote MS. No. 194, King's College, Cambridge. This MS. contains a collection of letters written by or to the Timurid Emperors of India from the time of Humayun to that of Bahadur Shah. It was compiled by 'Inayat Khan, the secretary of Aurangzib. Evidently the letter quoted above was taken by this author from the 'Adab i 'Alamgiri' of Qabil Khan, the first secretary of Aurangzib.

[18] Henry Yule, *The Diary of William Hedges* (*Hakluyt Society Series*) (London, 1888), ii, 309.

author of the *Lata'if ul Akhbar*, and an eye witness to the siege of Qandahar by Dara. He seems to have felt slighted that during the reign of Shah Jahan he had not received any promotion in the civil service:

> I am not one of the special favourites aware of secrets, nor a grandee of the inner circle. Neither am I a clerk in [Government] service, nor am employed on the diplomatic missions, or in the news-writing department, that I might tell a lie and live on falsehood.[19]

Furthermore, he was in the service of Mahabat Khan, the Mughal general, who was not on good terms with Dara during the siege. On the contrary, Dara's own letters show him to be a very courteous and generous person. He was always obliging and considerate towards the Rajputs, and especially towards Maharaja Jaswant Singh and Mirza Raja Jay Singh, the premier nobles of Shah Jahan's court. In one of his letters, preserved in the Jaipur archives, he writes to Jay Singh that he holds the Rajputs in special favour. But despite this, Jay Singh seems to have borne him a grudge. Dara's failure was due more to the apathy and indifference of the Rajputs, whom he had helped in their need, rather than to his own weaknesses.[20] This is also borne out by a very unexpected source, a letter of Prince Akbar written during his rebellion. He asserts that characteristically Aurangzib had used flattery and generous promises to discourage Jaswant Singh from going over to Dara's side; and had even overlooked Jaswant's unworthy and inexcusable conduct at the battle of Khajwa (against Shuja').[21] Had the Rajputs rallied round Dara, Indian history would have been different.

19 Qanungo, *Dara Shukoh*, p. 294.

20 K. Qanungo, 'Prince Muhammed Dara Shikoh and Misra Rajah Jai Singh Kachhwah', *Indian History Records Commission Proceedings*, vol. IX (Dec. 1926), pp. 86-95.

21 Appendix to MS. "*Ramz u isharaha i 'Alamgiri*" (MS. Oo 6.37, C.U.L.). This MS. was copied by Budh Mal Ram for Raja Ayamal, the *diwan* of Mirza Raja Jay Singh Savai, in A.H. 1152/A.D. 1738. Jadunath Sarkar has translated this letter (from MS. No. 71 of the Royal Asiatic Society's Library, London) in his *Studies in Mughal India* (Calcutta and Cambridge, 1919), pp. 98-106. As Sarkar has remarked, Akbar had written this letter under the influence of Durga Das, the son of Jaswant's minister Askaran. This is why Akbar puts the blame on Dara Shukoh's enmity with the Rajputs and at the same time acknowledges that Jaswant was not faithful to Dara.

In other respects Dara was certainly superior to Aurangzib; in particular his intellectual and cultural attainments were far ahead. And there was a basic difference between his great-grandfather Akbar's achievement and his own. Akbar evolved his spiritual convictions about universal toleration *after* he had acquired the political power, with which he imposed himself as a founder of his creed upon his people; Dara became a syncretic leader of his people and as a result lost his political power. Akbar had the power to compel obedience to his ideas; Dara had none and could not bring even a moral pressure to bear on the people. Dara was capable of reading, understanding, and compiling a book; Akbar was not. Dara's political and social aim was manifestly nobler than that of Akbar, for he did not aim at founding a *new* religion and thus did not introduce schism into the religion as Akbar had done through his *Din i Ilahi*. Rather he strove to mingle the two great religions of India by showing them the similarities which were inherent in their very principles. He justly asserted that Hinduism and Islam had grossly misunderstood each other for centuries by overlooking that both of them believed in one Supreme God. He was particularly eager to demonstrate to the Muslims that Truth was not a monopoly of only one religion, and that the Hindus did not refute monotheism.[22] Although unsuccessful his well conceived philosophies attracted around him many intellectuals like Nuruddin Shirazi, Baba Lal, Mulla Shah Badakhshi, Shaikh Muhibbullah Allahabadi, Shah Dil-ruba, Shaikh Muhsin Fani and Sarmad (the mystic).[23] Indeed, he was the fountain-head of an intellectual, cultural and social movement, which died with him.

In his political career, we find no crime for which he could be condemned to death. It seems as if Aurangzib was so jealous that he always imagined the worst from Dara, although there is no evidence that Dara had ever planned to do away with him. Hamiduddin Khan 'Nimcha' tells in his *Ahkam i 'Alamgiri* how in 1644 when Dara was conducting Shah Jahan and his brothers to an underground room of his newly-constructed mansion on the bank of the Jumna at Agra, Aurangzib sat

[22] Dara's Preface to 'Sirr i Akbar', ff. 2a-2b, Pote MS. No. 217, King's College. See also Mahfuz-ul-Haq (ed.), *Majma-ul-Bahrain*, pp. 5, 11.

[23] Qanungo, *Dara Shukoh*, pp. 241-68.

down at the door and despite the requests of his father did not get up but remained seated until noon when he went away to his own house without taking the customary leave of the Emperor. Shah Jahan was angry and debarred him from the royal audience for seven months. Through his sister Jahanara, Aurangzib offered the explanation that as the room had only one entrance he had feared that Dara might shut the door and kill his father and brothers.[24] There is no evidence to support this accusation. Shah Jahan had stayed in Dara's house from 20th July to 8th August, 1644 without harm.[25] When his father fell ill and was in a coma, Dara had in fact tended him with every devotion and affection, and had conducted the affairs of the State in the name of his father, although he had a good excuse to usurp the insignia of royalty, unlike Aurangzib who appropriated the sceptre while his father was alive and in good health. Although he was officially nominated as his heir by Shah Jahan, who asked all his courtiers to obey his son as their sovereign, Dara continued to issue orders in his father's name.[26] Aurangzib also charged Dara with an unjust attack on Shuja', especially by an inferior Prince Sulaiman Shukoh. He also considered Dara guilty of planning to destroy his brothers.[27] These charges are baseless for Dara sent an army under Sulaiman Shukoh only *after* Shuja' had crowned himself King and advanced with an army towards Bihar. Sulaiman Shukoh happened to be the only Prince available for the command.

The second charge is also very weak, and when closely examined, we have to admit that the rebellion was stirred up

[24] J. Sarkar (tr.), *Anecdotes of Aurangzib* (Calcutta, 1912), pp. 36-37.

[25] *Ibid.*, p. 38.

[26] J. Sarkar, *Aurangzib*, 2nd rev. ed. (London, 1930), 280-81.

[27] 'Zafarnama i 'Alamgiri', of 'Aqil Khan Razi, ff. 23b-24a. MS. Oo.6.37, C.U.L. This work is usually entitled the *Waqi'at i 'Alamgiri*, and it was lithographed by M. A. Chugtai (Lahore, 1936). Razi, a governor of Delhi under Aurangzib and an eye witness to these events, has quoted many of the letters of Shah Jahan, Aurangzib and Jahanara. He is considered the best authority for the wars of succession as he wrote this work without Aurangzib's knowledge and therefore his testimony is most reliable. See Rieu's *Catalogue of the Persian MSS. in the British Museum* (London, 1879), Add. 26, 234. Rieu had ascribed this work to Mir Khan, subadar of Kabul (pp. 265-66), but later he accepted Razi as the real author.

*first* by Shuja' and Murad, and it was *after* their rash proceedings that Dara sent armies to contain their advance; and after all, they were rebels and they had acted against their ruler. Murad had killed his innocent minister 'Ali Naqi and attacked and looted Surat, the flourishing Mughal port of Gujarat, while Shuja' had overrun Bihar.[28]

The third charge Aurangzib brings against Dara is that the latter had tried maliciously to victimize him by recalling the Mughal generals who were engaged under him in the conquest of Bijapur and Gulbarga, and that Dara had had a tacit understanding with the King of Bijapur to undermine the success of Aurangzib against the latter.[29] Both in the case of Golconda and Bijapur, Dara had intervened in response to their appeal for peace, and asked Shah Jahan to pardon them.[30] When peace was established, there was no need for the armies to remain in the Deccan. They were needed in the north because of the emergency caused by the illness of Shah Jahan.

The fourth charge was that Dara transferred the fief of Berar, which was included under Aurangzib's viceroyalty, to Murad without any cause.[31] As already stated, Murad had crowned himself and was acting rashly by extorting money from the people of Surat and Ahmedabad; it was therefore essential to remove him from that province to a place where he could be restrained by Aurangzib. At any rate, this act was motivated by fear of Murad rather than by enmity of Aurangzib.[32]

[28] Sarkar, *Aurangzib*, 283-84, 294-95, 302-5 and 466-67. Shuja' crowned himself immediately after Shah Jahan's illness. Murad had killed 'Ali Naqi in October, sacked Surat in November, and made himself King in December. Shah Jahan despatched two armies on 18th and 24th December, 1657, and asked the commanders to spare the lives of his sons. Sarkar has not emphasized this point in his history.

[29] 'Zafarnama', ff. 23b-24a.

[30] Muhammad Salih Kambuh in *'Amal i Salih* and Waris quoted by Qanungo, *Dara Shukoh*, pp.139-44. Aurangzib and Sa'dullah Khan represented the military party in the court, always advising Shah Jahan to annex these kingdoms, while Dara and Jahanara restrained him from doing so. See Sarkar, *Aurangzib*, 233.

[31] 'Zafarnama', ff. 24b-25a.

[32] Sadiq, the editor of the 'Adab i 'Alamgiri', who was a partisan of Aurangzib, himself acknowledges that it was because of the cruel acts such as the murder of the innocent 'Ali Naqi by Murad that obliged Shah Jahan to confer the viceroyalty of Gujarat on Qasim Khan. 'Adab i 'Alamgiri' f.316a, Or. MS. dd. 5.3, Christ's College, Cambridge. This MS. is dated 22 Ramadan in the 14th year of Muhammad Shah, who was crowned in 1719. It is entitled not Adab but 'Munsha'at i Aurangzib'.

His fifth charge against Dara was that the latter imprisoned his agent 'Isa Beg and confiscated his property without any provocation.[33] Aurangzib's historians have distorted the facts, for it appears as if 'Isa Beg was imprisoned only after he had written reports of the usurpation of the royal authority by Dara. It was in his letter dated the 10th October, 1657 that he had written this news to Aurangzib.[34] The claim that Shah Jahan had released the agent when he came to know of his innocence is an example of their distortion. 'Aqil Khan, although he was Aurangzib's man, says that when Murad avoided Jaswant's army and went towards Mandu (in order to join Aurangzib), the nobles who were secretly intriguing with Aurangzib went to Dara and told him that as Murad had fled from the royal army his rebellion was presumably at an end. Hence it would be sound policy to send 'Isa Beg to Aurangzib to inform him of the improved health of Shah Jahan; this would remove from Aurangzib's mind any doubt or evil intention and restrain him from taking any dangerous step. Dara was naive enough to believe this advice to be sincere and well-intentioned. He, therefore, *requested Shah Jahan accordingly and the latter*, *in response to his solicitation, sent 'Isa Beg to Aurangzib with a farman which was full of kindness*. 'Aqil Khan had quoted this *farman* in which Shah Jahan said that he had personally instructed 'Isa Beg to set at rest all Aurangzib's doubts about his (Shah Jahan's) health, and to discourage him from taking any evil step. 'Aqil Khan describes 'Isa Beg as a traitor who, against the orders of his sovereign, encouraged and provoked Aurangzib to rebellion by saying that the capital was without any experienced generals.[35]

The last charge of Aurangzib against Dara was that he was an apostate, a heretic, and a polytheist (*kafir wa-mulhid*). This charge has already been refuted by many modern historians. In all his works there is not a shred of evidence to show that he had renounced his religion and embraced another. He was

[33] *Ibid.*, f. 316b. Sadiq, who had extracted this account from the *'Amal i Salih* and the *'Alamgir-nama*, says that Shah Jahan arrested 'Isa Beg on the instigation of Dara and, after finding him innocent, released him, gave him a robe of honour, and sent him back to Aurangzib.

[34] Sarkar, *Aurangzib*, 328.

[35] 'Zafarnama', ff. 15a-16a.

without doubt a great sufi, a student of comparative religion, and a scholar of outstanding merit. Many great sufis and saints of Islam held more paradoxical views than those which Dara preached. But the fact is that he was a syncretist who wanted to blend the incongruous tenets of Hinduism and Islam in order to bring them together at an intellectual level so that the layman might follow suit. As already stated, he essentially differed from Akbar in his approach to this task. He aimed at the very basis of the differences between the Hindu and the Islamic systems, hoping thereby to eliminate the main barrier which had separated the two for centuries. It could therefore safely be asserted that a revival of Akbarism was in process which was more vigorous, more virulent, and more voluntary. Dara as the nucleus of his revival was the target of the reactionaries, led by Aurangzib, who opposed this trend as an apostasy from Islam. To wipe out this revival it was essential to eliminate the pivotal personality. The death of Dara, therefore, was the death of the revival. Had it been allowed to survive and flourish the history of India, for the last two and a half centuries, might not have been a mere record of fratricide and fanaticism.

The guilt of Aurangzib is that he let loose the forces of reaction when they were in the process of being dismantled. He killed a liberal movement, which might have changed the fate of India, in its very infancy. At that time India required a syncretist ruler, not a parochial and puritanical bureaucrat. After all, what benefit had the people of India received from the so called just and efficient rule of Aurangzib? History judges a ruler not from how he ruled his *passions* but from how he ruled his *people*. Aurangzib, consciously or unconsciously, created a chronic vendetta amongst the Hindus and the Muslims. He not only antagonized the Hindus but also fostered and fanned fanaticism amongst the Muslims.[36] He broadened the breach between them in such a way that it survived two hundred and fifty years, and it still widens because

[36] There is a MS. in the C.U.L. (MS. Add.215, ff. $6^b$-$7^b$) entitled 'Awsaf-nama-i-'Alamgiri', a panegyric in mixed prose and verse written by Allah-yar Uzbek of Balkh who was a court poet of Aurangzib. The fanaticism with which he writes is a good example of how much Aurangzib had excited such feelings amongst the Muslims.

of an ever-lingering historical experience of his reign. The myth surrounding the personality of Aurangzib may have added colour to his cult, and his misadventures may have been magnified by biased historians, but the basis on which he had won his throne was itself parochial. Thereafter his every move, every measure, and every motive had more or less a tint of puritanism. His military measures may have some political justification, but the way in which he conducted them left a chronic bitterness amongst the vanquished. His iconoclastic zeal created a similar reaction amongst the Hindus who retaliated by destroying many mosques; obviously fanaticism fanned a reciprocal fanaticism.[37] Thus the murder of Dara and deposition of Shah Jahan was more than a political crime; it was an end of an era — an era of universal toleration, and cultural and social cohesion.[38] His own subjects did not approve the way he usurped the throne, and did not forget it for a long time.[39]

The reactionary forces which Aurangzib had set in motion were so potent that Shah 'Alam Bahadur Shah, his successor, tried to repair the breach, but it was too late.[40] In the sectarian literature of the Sikhs, Jats, Rajputs, Bohras, Khojas, Momnas, Mahdavis, Shias, Satnamis and the Marathas, he is still remembered as a persecutor and a tyrant, worthy of hate. Thus by his persecution of these communities he strengthened their sectarian organization and accelerated their social configuration, thereby activating the centrifugal forces in

37 Sharma, *Religious Policy*, pp. 135-36.

38 'Dara as Emperor might have played the part of a lesser Akbar; the Hindu element might have become supreme in India; and a united kingdom dominated by Rajput chiefs, might have offered a stubborn resistance to the encroachments of the English traders.' Lane-Poole, *Aurangzib*, p. 42.

39 In the Factory Records there is an interesting reference to this. In 1668 Sir George Oxinden, the President of the English Factory at Surat, assured the Governor of Surat, Zainul-'abedin Khan, that Governor Gary of Bombay would not attack the Mughal junks, but the Khan replied that nothing was improbable when a son (Aurangzib) could imprison his own father (Shah Jahan). G. W. Forrest (ed.), *Selections from the Bombay State Papers* (*Home Series*) (Bombay, 1887), i, 215. Manucci has also mentioned such instances.

40 Dr. Percival Spear, in his admirable work, *A History of India* (Penguin Books, 1965), pp.55-60, has treated Aurangzib and Shah 'Alam in a broader perspective.

Indian society. What happened during the following centuries was but a tragic epilogue to what had gone on previously. The prelude may not have been too damaging but the sequel was disastrous. His guilt in changing the history of India from secularism to communalism, and from cohesion to disintegration is immeasurable in its implication and significance. His history is a good example of how a prejudiced but energetic ruler can change the course of a nation's history. Thus in Aurangzib and Dara Shukoh India had not only the choice of an emperor but the choice of an ideology; the selection of one meant the extermination of the other.

# FAMINE IN INDIA: SIR ANTONY MACDONNELL AND A POLICY REVOLUTION IN 1902

MARTIN GILBERT

The stability of Indian finance depended upon Land Revenue, the largest item of government income.[1] The efficient nature of British rule ensured that there were few failures in collecting it, even if at times coercion had to be used, or arrears of revenue received two or three years after they were due. The 1891 Census showed that 131 million Indians tilled their own land, 18 million were agricultural labourers and 18 million received rent from land: making a total of over 60 per cent of the population.[2]

The amount of revenue collected from any individual holding (in the case of ryotwari tenures), or from a landlord (in the case of zemindari tenures) varied according to the assessment, except in the permanently settled areas of Bengal. But even in Bengal, although the government demand was fixed, the landlord had few restrictions on the amount he collected from his tenants. Elsewhere the assessment was generally revised every thirty years: it averaged 50 per cent

[1] In the Indian Budget of 1901-02 revenue from land exceeded 18 million rupees, the next largest items being 6 million rupees from the salt tax and nearly 5 million from Government sales of opium. The largest item of expenditure was the Army, 14-3/4 million rupees and the cost of administration and government, nearly 10 million.

[2] See *Statement Exhibiting the Moral and Material Progress and Condition of India.* Prepared by Francis Drake (London, 1903), p. 136.

of the annual value of the crops, and made no deductions for special hardship or capital expenditure.

The fluctuating rate of assessment caused constant and at times bitter controversy among the British civil servants. Those who considered that the general level of assessment was low saw, in its moderation, an important justification of British rule.

Sir John Strachey, for ten years Finance Member of the Viceroy's Council, thought that the revenue assessments were

> almost everywhere moderate; and they have been made with an earnest and scrupulous desire to strengthen and preserve the rights of private property . . . . The demand of the State, which was originally light, has become far lighter... pressure goes on diminishing as the country increases in prosperity . . . . There is certainly no reason . . . why they [the ryots] should not bear their share of any necessary fresh taxation . . . . Land in India yields two-fifths of the entire revenues of State . . . . India is fortunate in deriving so large a proportion of her Public revenues from such a source. It spares her the necessity of heavy taxation. . . .[3]

Those who considered that the assessment was generally too high, and who disliked the free hand given to landlords, saw, in the revenue demand, a draining away of rural wealth, which could only result in hardship, and in the inability of the ryot to meet famine conditions. The landowner, impoverished by the "rent" or "tax" he had paid, could not survive a severe drought. He had no surplus to see him through a year of crop failure. In famine conditions the added burden of a heavy assessment could lead only to violence, exhaustion, or death.

When a young District Officer, James Dunlop Smith, in his first official diary, wrote that "even where the outturn from the soil is just enough to sustain the cultivator and his family he is evidently comfortable", he was rebuked by his superior officer with the humane advice: "To be comfortable the

[3] Speech to the Legislative Council, Calcutta, on 27 December 1877. Strachey left India in 1880, and with his brother Richard published in 1882 *The Finances and Public Works of India*, in which he confirmed and elaborated these opinions.

agriculturist must have something more than 'just enough' to support him and his family".[4] Later, as a resettlement officer responsible for revising assessments, Dunlop Smith showed that this rebuke had fallen upon fertile soil.

John Lawrence, who saw the effects of famine as a District Officer in 1838, considered the revenue administration "thoroughly vicious . . . the assessment of the land tax was fixed at a ruinous rate. One hundred and thirty-six horsemen were retained in Panipat for the collection of revenue, while twenty-two were considered sufficient for the duties of police!"[5] Later when he was Chief Commissioner of the Punjab he told his Settlement Officer at Jalandhar: "Mind you assess low. If you don't, I shall be your enemy for life, and indeed, what is worse, you will be your own. Let nothing tempt you to assess high."[6] And between 1864 and 1869, when Viceroy, Lawrence continued to assert these Liberal principles.

The famine of 1877 was widespread and terrible, and aroused the conscience of England. The Famine Commission set up to enquire into its causes could not avoid the question of high assessments. Although many Revenue Officials denied the connection between high assessment and famine, the problem was too serious to be brushed aside. Lawrence, in retirement, told a friend :

> I think you were quite right in your remarks as to putting the agriculturists generally in such a position as to care for themselves, and so provide means of scarcity and distress . . . the best means . . . is to fix a maximum of assessment on the land beyond which the Government demand should not rise.[7]

But when Sir Richard Temple was asked by the Famine Commission whether a reduction of Land Revenue would not

[4] James Dunlop Smith, Diary, November 1883, Dunlop Smith Papers. I am grateful to Mrs. Nora Dunlop and Miss Janet Dunlop Smith for permission to see and quote from their father's papers.

[5] Sir Charles Aitchison, *Lord Lawrence* (Oxford, 1892), p. 32.

[6] R. Bosworth Smith, *Lord Lawrence* (London, 1883), i, 229.

[7] Lord Lawrence to Dr. George Smith, 17 January 1878, Dunlop Smith Papers.

protect the ryot against famine, he deprecated reduction. "There would not . . . be any use in that" he told the Commission, "because the assessment is so moderate as to impose no check on agricultural industry".[8] Others disagreed: James Caird, a member of the Commission, thought the assessment "bears very lightly on the good soils and heavily on the inferior,"[9] and that in many districts the majority of holdings were inferior.

Caird found it difficult to discover where the truth lay. He was an expert on English and Irish land tenure: Indian problems were new to him. He had learned from a friend at Simla that the view was growing in Government circles that there ought to be "a more elastic system of revenue better suited to a varying climate".[10] But he found little evidence of such views in the Provinces.

Some officials justified strictness on account of native laziness. It was not a question of reducing the ryot to poverty, they explained, but of forcing him to work at all. Temple told the Famine Commissioners that in the opinion of many administrators "the obligation to pay has a stimulating effect on the apathetic native character."[11] When Caird opposed this view, he was rebuked by Lord Lytton (Viceroy, 1876-1880), and Sir John Strachey, who explained that a system which allowed the possibility of revenue reductions "would destroy every stimulus to thrift and independence."[12] Lord Northbrook (Viceroy, 1872-1876) told Caird in 1879 that he thought the land-holders too improvident to profit from a relaxation of revenue;[13] but he came to accept Caird's viewpoint and wrote to Lord Ripon (Viceroy, 1880-1884) in 1881:

8 *Famine Commission of 1880, Select Evidence*, question 71.

9 James Caird to Sir Louis Mallet, 25 May 1878, Temple Papers, 86/17. I am grateful to the Ind(ia) Off(ice) Lib(rary) for making available, in the pleasant surroundings of the Old India Office, the papers of Sir Richard Temple, James Caird, Lord Elgin and Lord George Hamilton.

10 Caird Papers, Home Misc(ellaneous) Series, 5 October 1878, Ind. Off. Lib.

11 *Famine Commission of 1880, Select Evidence*, question 71.

12 Government of India, Department of Revenue and Agriculture, *Reply to J. Caird.*

13 Northbrook to Caird, 16 September 1879, Caird Papers, Home Misc. Series, Ind. Off. Lib.

> I have always had my suspicions that the Land Revenue has been over-assessed, and always treated with great suspicion the opinion of Sir John Strachey, who was all for screwing up the land revenue.[14]

But the Famine Commission of 1880 rejected the view that there was a connection between assessment and famine. Caird alone dissented. At the time few believed his criticisms to be valid. Yet writing of Gurgaon in 1908, the *Imperial Gazetteer* could assert firmly that "in conjunction with a new and excessive assessment of land revenue and an unsympathetic revenue administration" famine had "sadly crippled the district for some time".[15] Between 1880 and 1908 a revolution took place in official thinking, and low assessments, advocated in vain by Caird, found an effective champion in a Conservative Viceroy, Lord Curzon. Strachey's hostility to leniency sprang from economic, not humanitarian considerations. It was difficult to balance the Indian budget in "normal" times. When war threatened, either in Asia or Europe, all the resources of the State were geared to economy. Expense had to be limited in order to finance the British Army. As Dunlop Smith wrote during the Anglo-Russian crisis of 1885:

> Here we are with only a threatened war pouring out money which can bring no return. G of I have issued a strong circular calling on Local Govts for Retrenchment. I cannot tell you what that means for a poor province like the Punjab. H. Ex. has responded nobly and although for the last three years he has been working under great financial pressure he has promised 14 lakhs . . . this means that the Province will be thrown back for two or three years. And each time Russia moves in the Herat direction this will be repeated. Well India can't afford that.[16]

Caird thought that in most areas the revenue could be reduced, and that in this way the danger of famine would be

14 B. Mallet, *Northbrook*, *A Memoir* (London, 1908), quoting Northbrook to Ripon, 7 September 1881.

15 *Imperial Gazetteer* (1908 edition), entry Gurgaon, Punjab.

16 Dunlop Smith to his mother, 10 May 1885, Dunlop Smith Papers.

essened. The rains might fail; but the ryot would have better means to deal with distress. Economic difficulties, however, continued to prevent the Government from considering a reduction of land revenue. Being the major item of income, it bore the major expenditure upon its back — the Army, training for imperial wars; the administration and communications.

Assessments continued to rise. Between 1872-83 re-assessment in Gurgaon increased the land revenue by 17 per cent, and forthe five years following the famine of 1877 no reduction was allowed. "By that time", according to the *Imperial Gazetteer* "pestilence and famine had stamped upon the people an impress of poverty which years of prosperity could hardly remove".[17]

In 1885 the re-assessment of six districts in the Punjab had to be considered. Aitchison, the Lieutenant-Governor, had been a pupil and intimate friend of Lawrence, who had known the "painful experience of crushing land assessments". The "Strachey" tradition, dear to economists and utilitarians, was thus confronted by an equally stubborn, equally uncompromising "Lawrence" tradition.

Aitchison was opposed to a simultaneous re-assessment of the six districts, and in a letter to the Government of India he insisted upon "extreme leniency in the new assessments". But the Government of India, unwilling to seek new sources of revenue, turned down Aitchison's recommendations, and insisted upon simultaneous re-assessment, and a general raising of the revenue demand.[18]

Dunlop Smith, who had been Aitchison's private secretary, explained later to Lord Minto, that in 1885

> The Government of India thus deliberately reversed the established policy of working gradually round the province with settlements going on in only five districts out of 31. They risked the alienation of the cultivating classes, they forced their settlement officers to work with untrained esta-

[17] *Imperial Gazetteer* (1908 edition), entry Gurgaon, Punjab.

[18] Note on Land Assessment in the Punjab by Dunlop Smith, dated 30 June 1907, Minto Papers. I am grateful to the National Library of Scotland for affording me access to Lord Minto's Papers.

blishments, and they gave the superior revenue authorities more than they could effectively supervise.

Dunlop Smith was indignant, not only because the Lawrence tradition had seemingly been reversed, but because he himself was re-settlement officer in one of the six districts — Sialkot, from 1888 to 1895. Despite his own protests, Sialkot was re-assessed at 20 per cent more than previously, and it was suggested that a further assessment should be made, not after thirty, but after ten years.[19]

Hearing of this, Aitchison wrote :

> It is indeed very very serious, and the most depressing thing to me is the lightheartedness with which the Government of India seems to act about it . . . . A ten year settlement . . . is not only a retrograde but an insane measure!
>
> The adoption of a 10 years' arrangement must produce a great sense of insecurity as indication of an unsound revenue policy. It must be very alarming to the people to be told they are liable to have a system of short term assessment imposed on them. Who under such circumstances will invest their capital in the improvement of the land, if they think that in a year or two the Government is to put its hand on a share of the profits. If the Government want stable and certain revenue, they should lengthen rather than shorten the settlement in the advanced districts of the Punjab and encourage the people to develop and improve their agricultural methods. And of course when to the short term is added the enormous enhancement of the demand, the situation becomes very serious . . . .
>
> Now all this is forgotten under a King that knew not Joseph. It is very deplorable. If there is any part of India where everything depends on the contentment of the peasantry, it is the Punjab. One can only pray and hope that the eyes of those who have the ultimate control may be opened before it is too late.[20]

19 The Revenue demand fixed in 1847 was 1,502,679 rupees. In 1856 it was reduced by 20 per cent to 1,183,781 rupees. In 1866 it was raised by 5 per cent to 1,243,225 rupees and in 1895 it was raised again, by 20 per cent, to 1,500,140 rupees.

20 Sir Charles Aitchison to Dunlop Smith, 11 Aug. 1893, Dunlop Smith Papers.

Increased revenue demands were made throughout British India between 1880 and 1890. It was a decade free from famine; though not from scarcity. The raising of revenue was in almost all cases harmful: a deterrent to increased cultivation, and a stimulus to rural indebtedness.

Aitchison, when retired, published his views in 1892, in his biography of Lawrence:

> The increase of assessment has risen from the subordinate to the prime place in Settlement work. Indeed it is now an accepted principle that no revision is made unless a large increase of revenue is expected to result.
>
> Now there are many more mouths to feed . . . with facilities of communication and increase of purchaseable commodities the standard of living among the peasantry has rapidly risen. Expenses of cultivation have largely increased. The rates of tax on the best soils also have been enhanced, while the extension of cultivation has naturally been for the most part in land of poorer quality.
>
> In these days when money is sorely needed to meet on every hand the growing demand for improvement, not to speak of the military sieve into which so much of it is poured, there is a strong temptation to force up the assessments. It is a dangerous policy. The mischief of over assessment is insidious. The millions of India are as yet voiceless . . . they suffer in silence, and their sorrows reach the ear of authority only when the mischief is done — when the wells get out of gear, when the Cultivation grows slovenly . . . when men begin to leave their ancestral homes, when perhaps the seeds of revolution have been sown.
>
> Capital must be accumulated to provide the improvements. For this a margin of profit must always be left to the landowner. A system of assessment which periodically dips into every increase requires to be carefully supervised at all times. *One injudicious turn of the screw* may do mischief to a District which cannot be repaired in one or two generations.[21]

[21] Aitchison, *Lord Lawrence*, p. 231.

The vernacular press took up the cause of the cultivator. Its motive was mixed. The raised assessment made life more difficult for the ryot; it also gave the ambitious town politician a stick with which to beat the administration. Yet under autocratic rule, criticism from outside antagonizes more often than it influences, and in the 1880's violence in the vernacular press only strengthened government conservatism.

The Bengali *Dhumketu* published, in 1887, an article headed "Why do we starve?":[22]

> The times are critical for us. The cultivator is starving; and starve he must. As soon as he gathers in his harvest, he is called upon to pay all current rent and all arrear rent.... He is now a beggar.... We give rice and get wine in return. ... Anyhow it is you that take away everything, and we that part with everything. You have no qualities by which you can draw people nearer to you in love and affection.

Some administrators realized the need for those very qualities, and sought native friendship as well as respect. To them the decade of rising assessments seemed harsh and dangerous. Among these energetic and humane officials was Antony MacDonnell. While Acting-Governor of Bengal he criticized the policy of the Governor, Charles Elliot, and sought to reverse it. Elliot had insisted on swift re-assessments. To cut down the inevitable bureaucratic delays, he made the settlement officers directly responsible to him through the Director of Land Records — a man almost as young as the settlement officers themselves. The Board of Revenue was by-passed. So too were the experience and caution of the Board. The result was injustice.

MacDonnell saw what was wrong, and asked Lord Lansdowne (Viceroy, 1888-1894) to intervene. MacDonnell told Lansdowne that Elliot's method of re-assessment was "very dangerous"; and explained how one settlement officer "had

[22] *Dhumketu*, 27 May 1887 ; MacDonnell Papers, c. 355. I am grateful to the Bodleian Library for access to these papers, and to the Hon. Anne MacDonnell for permission to see and to quote from the records of her father's administration in India, and for discussing various aspects of his policies with me.

recently decided to enhance rent in the cases of 4,164 ryots". These enhancements, wrote MacDonnell, "were totally wrong and illegal". The Director of Land Records was a young man, unaided by the Revenue officials. The illegality of the enhancements "had entirely escaped the notice—or was beyond the knowledge of the Director".[23]

Lansdowne agreed that all was not well. "I fancy" he wrote to MacDonnell, "Elliot increased his difficulties greatly . . . by his habit of acting hurriedly through men possessing his special confidence, and setting aside those whom, in the natural course of business, he should have consulted."[24]

Yet MacDonnell realized it was not enough to criticize the excess zeal of a single official. Tenants must be protected from zemindari extortions. He urged the Government to carry out, irrespective of criticism, the Cadastral Survey of Bengal, to clarify land tenure rights, which would enable the tenancy laws to be asserted in favour of the ryot.[25]

MacDonnell, working in the Permanently Settled area, saw that even the liberality of the Permanent Settlement was not as genuine as it seemed. The zemindar was, of course, protected from any rise in assessment — and had been since 1793 — but the ryot had no protection. He could be deprived of his capital; and in time of drought had nothing to fall back on, except the liberality of the zemindar, which was not always assured, or possible.

MacDonnell wrote a minute for Lansdowne, in which he explained the need for legislation to protect the ryot from poverty. The zemindar would have to accept a diminution of power, for the Government should not allow the privileges of a few to affect, adversely, the health and prosperity of many. Lansdowne replied to MacDonnell's plea :

> I had no idea of the extent to which our action favoured the Zemindar at the expense of the ryots. Your Minute makes it perfectly clear that the former have, from the

[23] Sir Antony MacDonnell to Lord Lansdowne, 8 August 1893, MacDonnell Papers, d. 235.

[24] Lord Lansdowne to Sir Antony MacDonnell, 14 August 1893, *ibid.*, d. 236.

[25] *Ibid.*

> first, been the spoilt children. We began by converting them from officials into landlords . . . we allowed them to acquire an enormous increase of revenue under the Permanent Settlement, and have, from time to time, strengthened their legal position as against their tenants. Per contra, the obligations which it was intended to impose upon them have remained unfulfilled, owing, it seems to me, to culpable negligence on our part. It is high time that the other side had its turn.[26]

MacDonnell intended the "other side" to have its turn. But Lansdowne left India before any general principle of revenue assessment was reached. The Cadastral Survey of Bengal continued. It clarified territorial rights, and enabled the existing tenancy legislation of 1885 to be enforced in favour of the ryot. But changes in most of Bengal were within the framework of the Permanent Settlement. Elsewhere the burden of heavy assessments remained. The ryot had insufficient surplus to build up capital, and when the rains failed he had no assets to fall back on.

When Lord Elgin succeeded Lansdowne as Viceroy in 1894, MacDonnell sought Elgin's help in righting what he considered to be the assessment inequalities outside the area of Permanent Settlement, in the North-Western Provinces, where he had become Lieutenant-Governor.

MacDonnell instituted an enquiry into the economic situation in Bundelkhand as a result of which he was convinced, as he told Elgin, that "something more than mere famine relief would be needed to get the Bundelkhand districts on their legs again". The answer lay in the assessment, which MacDonnell thought too high. "I hope" he wrote to Elgin "we may thus be able to see our way to some permanent improvement".[27] But Elgin had other worries. Civil disturbance spread through India. There were rumours of widespread social discontent. These were urgent and immediate problems. Land Revenue inequalities were a less visible, if ultimately more vital problem. Elgin neglected them.

26 Lord Lansdowne to Sir Antony MacDonnell, 10 October 1893, *ibid.*, d. 236.

27 Sir Antony MacDonnell to Lord Elgin, 26 December 1896, Elgin Papers, MSS. Eur. F. 84/69, no. 308, Ind. Off. Lib.

One class of zemindar had been as much in need of assistance as most zemindars were in need of rebuke. These were the landlords who, though benefiting through the employment of ryots, were nevertheless hard hit by scarcity or famine and unable to pay their full assessment. In most cases they were forced to surrender, to the government or the money-lender, some portion of their lands. MacDonnell had urged legislation that would enable these zemindars to entail part of their estates. When he had asked Lansdowne to put forward proposals to this effect to the Secretary of State they had been rejected in London. MacDonnell asked Elgin to press them once more, and knowing that Elgin's fear was rebellion, explained that loyalty and revenue were connected. "The Hindu landlords" wrote MacDonnell to Elgin, "are by far the most powerful influence for good or evil in the [NW] Provinces. Some of them are in debt and I look with great regret on the postponement of the legislation which would enable us to deal with the question of indebtedness in a way which while being fair to creditors would retain the old families in their ancestral lands". Entailment was needed; but the MacDonnell-Lansdowne proposals were rejected. "I shall not soon cease to lament the unfortunate times which have prevented you from giving effect to them".[28]

Another pressure upon the ryot concerned land mortgaged during famine. Famine mortgages could not be redeemed. MacDonnell saw a clear need for legislation to facilitate redemption. Yet Elgin, while expressing interest took no action. Despite MacDonnell's remonstrances, he was unwilling to take issue with the economy-dominated Secretary of State, who, far from the parched fields and impoverished peasantry, could gauge neither the extremity of distress nor the simplicity of the remedy.

When a later Secretary of State remonstrated with a Viceroy's private secretary that "The Viceroy should always remember the British public", the Private Secretary replied that

> All that could be seen out of the windows of the India office was the British Public walking about in a peaceful

[28] Sir Antony MacDonnell to Lord Elgin, 16 July 1897, MacDonnell Papers c. 353.

> green park. But the Viceroy is in the midst of the Indian Public; he is responsible for law and order and for tranquillising the minds of a very heterogeneous and jumpy public.[29]

It was also, when famine struck, a starving public. Lord Northbrook told the Indian Currency Committee in 1898 that the "real safety of India depended on the land revenue being easy".[30] But committees, though taking volumes of evidence, could take no action. They deliberated long, but without results. What use were committees and commissions, asked an irate M.P. in the House of Commons. One was always sitting and one was sitting then. "It has lasted nearly as long as the walls of Troy or the trial of Warren Hastings".[31]

The famine of 1896 aroused the alarm of those men who felt that the Government ought to do something to mitigate the extent of rural distress. In 1898 a missionary, John Murdoch, wrote to the Secretary of State, Lord George Hamilton, deprecating the severity of assessment and collection. "There is a temptation" he wrote, "to get in as much as possible to earn the reputation of being a 'crack collector'." Collection should be less rigid, the assessment less severe, and agricultural improvement taken more seriously.[32]

There seemed no need to answer Murdoch's criticisms for, as a missionary, however strongly he might feel about the injustices of Land Revenue, his aim was not to disrupt the Government or make political capital. Bengali publicists were not so easy to ignore. One in particular found that he could pose as a distressed victim in the salons of English liberalism. The Home Government was alarmed and passed on its anxiety to the Government of India. The Bengali was Romesh Chunder Dutt. In 1900 he decided to raise the question of land revenue and famine in as challenging a way

[29] Dunlop Smith to Lord Minto, 13 June 1908, Minto Papers. Lord Morley was the Secretary of State and Lord Minto the Viceroy.

[30] *Indian Currency Committee, 1898*, Evidence of Lord Northbrook.

[31] *Hansard* (*H. of C.*) (4th Series), 1106, 3 April 1900; the M.P. was John Maclean.

[32] J. Murdoch, *Letter to Lord George Hamilton*, 31 January 1898, Madras.

as possible. In his widely publicized letters to Lord Curzon he claimed that high assessments were the cause of famine.

MacDonnell believed that assessments, when high, aggravated famine conditions. But they were not the cause. Dutt overstated his case, and in doing so, weakened it. But he spoke with sufficient force for the Government of India to feel obliged to answer him. With Curzon Viceroy, there was no doubt the answer would be as forthright and devastating as possible.

Dutt saw Curzon on January 10, 1900. Curzon wrote of him: "He is an amiable and I daresay an accomplished man but he has the incurable vice of the Bengali, namely, the faculty of rolling out yards and yards of frothy declamation about subjects which he has imperfectly considered, or which he does not fully understand".[33] It was an unfair judgement. Dutt had carefully considered the subject of land revenue, but his understanding had been marred by his enthusiasm. Over-anxious to expose the Government of India to ridicule and censure, he destroyed a strong case by exaggeration and inaccuracy. Paternal rule did not take kindly to such strident criticism. It could not afford a battle of wits, and disliked exposing either its arguments or convictions before a public that would do its best to see them in as bad a light as possible.

Hamilton asked Sir Charles Bernard, a distinguished Indian Civil Servant, to examine Dutt's facts and figures. "He shows me conclusively that Dutt did not understand what he was talking about, and that not only his conclusions, but his whole statement of fact on which the conclusions were based, are erroneous".[34] A month later Sir W. Wedderburn put down a motion in the House of Commons on famine. Hamilton asked Bernard to examine Dutt's arguments once more. "And from Bernard's statement Romesh Dutt is ludicrously wrong in all his assertions of fact". Dutt's arguments were dismissed; Dutt himself maligned.

Hamilton wrote about Dutt to Curzon: "An unreliable, shifty fellow. He wrote me an effusive letter thanking me

[33] Lord Curzon to Lord George Hamilton, 10 January 1900, Hamilton Papers, Ind. Off. Lib.

[34] Lord George Hamilton to Lord Curzon, 1 February 1900, *ibid.*

. . . he then makes a violent attack on me, ascribing to me the ignorance of the proverbial schoolboy for the statement I made".[35]

While searching for facts to disprove Dutt, Bernard had discovered facts that disquieted him. "Bernard has a sort of uneasy consciousness" Hamilton told Curzon, "that our assessments in certain parts of India are too high; and he further proves that the tendency in recent years has been to enhance the assessments, and to endeavour to curtail the period of settlement".[36] Hamilton was also uneasy about these discoveries. "I believe in low assessments" he told Curzon.[37] He hoped that Curzon would examine assessment rates after the famine that was then raging; and that where adjustments in favour of the ryots were needed, they would be made.

In the House of Commons Wedderburn demanded an inquiry "to ascertain the causes which impair the cultivators' power to resist the attacks of famine and plague". He was defeated by 155 votes to 72. "We hold these people in the hollow of our hand", he said. "Cannot something be done to strengthen the weak knees of the ryot, and put him in a better position to resist when the bad time comes?"[38] During the debate Samuel Smith had quoted both Caird and Dutt to make his point that the "root of the problem" was land assessment.

While examining Dutt's criticisms, Bernard had discovered that the Lieutenant-Governor of the Central Provinces, Sir Edward Buck, had insisted on the highest possible assessment. Bernard told Hamilton that "in certain cases his instructions were too literally obeyed".[39] Hamilton passed

[35] Lord George Hamilton to Lord Curzon, 27 April 1900, *ibid.*

[36] One wonders whether Bernard's political opinions — he was a Liberal — were known to these two Conservative administrators. They were certainly well enough known to be commented on in the *Dictionary of National Biography* (Second Supplement, 1912, p. 150).

[37] Lord George Hamilton to Lord Curzon, 1 February 1900, Hamilton Papers, Ind. Off. Lib.

[38] *Hansard* (*H. of C.*), 3 April 1900.

[39] Lord George Hamilton to Lord Curzon, 18 April 1900, Hamilton Papers Ind. Off. Lib.

on these doubts to Curzon. In certain cases, he wrote, assessments "have been unduly screwed up". When the Government of India were "hard up", Buck "undoubtedly instigated his subordinates to re-assess up to the full value".[40]

Hamilton was puzzled by the discrepancy between the nature of the grievance, and the men who put that grievance forward. "I have a sort of hankering after the Dutt-ian views . . . but I believe his character as a man of accuracy is gone". Many critics used Caird's examples : "Caird", Hamilton told Curzon, "was very dissatisfied with the system of land revenue . . . . But the Indian officers laugh at his views as if they had been founded on a complete ignorance and misapprehension of the scope and objects of Indian agriculture".[41] A more credible advocate of low assessments was needed, someone with administrative experience and sound judgement.

Curzon realized that something was seriously wrong, and was determined to see where famine responsibility lay. He agreed to discuss the matter with Vaughan Nash, the correspondent of the *Manchester Guardian* who was an outspoken critic of the Government of India. Nash told Curzon that the majority of his revenue officials "appeared to know little or nothing of the actual circumstances, holdings, assessments, fortunes or identity of the people in the district to which they belonged". Nash pointed out the difference between the outlook of officers in Bombay and the Punjab: the latter, he said, were much less severe. Curzon told Hamilton: "all that I have myself heard confirms both statements".[42] Hamilton, understandably, doubted Nash's credentials. Curzon was less scornful, replying: "Although he writes in the modern impressionist style, and lays on his colours rather thickly, I cannot truthfully impute to him gross exaggerations."[43]

Curzon saw the danger of high assessments, but needed more than a journalist ally before he could take decisive action. He needed someone with expert knowledge to advise

40 Lord George Hamilton to Lord Curzon, 27 April 1900, *ibid.*

41 Lord George Hamilton to Lord Curzon, 30 May 1900, *ibid.*

42 Lord Curzon to Lord George Hamilton, 9 May 1900, *ibid.*

43 Lord Curzon to Lord George Hamilton, 18 July 1900, *ibid.*

him. MacDonnell had long sought a Viceroy willing to take drastic action. The opportunity was at hand. Curzon knew of MacDonnell's deep concern over assessment; and when he appointed a Famine Commission he chose MacDonnell as its Chairman.

MacDonnell's liberality in questions of assessment was well known. Alone of Provincial Governors he had taken a personal interest in all re-assessment. *The Pioneer* described his policy as "a new departure". He had not been content with

> a merely general guidance or policy, but had scrutinized all the assessments in detail, and satisfied himself that the assessment of individual villages were fair and such as could be reasonably demanded . . . . A lieutenant Governor is more likely to take moderate views than an impersonal controlling revenue authority which has not final and real control.[44]

MacDonnell saw the danger of judging the rate of assessment by examining the total figures of a district. Aggregates and averages gave no clue as to extremities of assessment: individual villages were lost in the total amount. He was determined to remove this anomaly by legislation.

MacDonnell, as Chairman of the Famine Commission, inquired into high assessments. Government critics, not knowing his terms of reference, continued their activities. In December 1900 a memorial urging an "equitable" limitation of land tax was signed by Dutt, Wedderburn, Puckle, Reynolds and Garth.[45] In February 1901 a resolution, moved by Dutt, was passed at the National Liberal Federation Conference, claiming that as a result of high land tax "the people could save nothing; and every year of drought was a year of famine".[46]

Curzon consulted MacDonnell and the other Provincial Governors about the reply he should give to Dutt. MacDonnell

44 *The Pioneer* (Allahabad), 22 April 1900.

45 Memorial of 20 December 1900, quoted in R. C. Dutt, *Indian Famines* (London, 1901).

46 Resolution of 27 February 1901, quoted in *ibid*. Dutt was the delegate for Lewisham at the Conference.

made it clear that the danger of high assessments would have to be admitted, despite the political risk. It was also clear that legislation was needed to avoid the danger of high assessments in future.

Curzon asked the Provincial Governors for advice on land revenue policy, and MacDonnell at once provided a comprehensive and radical review of the whole question, explaining the urgency of the legislation that was being prepared and urging upon Curzon the need for a firm Government commitment to a Liberal policy:

> I have sent the Legislative Department of the Government of India the revised Tenancy Bill and the revised Land Revenue Bill . . . . I accept the Land Revenue Bill in its entırety — Your Excellency will remember that I am deeply interested in the success of these measures — (you are good enough to speak of the Commissioner's Report as the crown of my work in India: but I myself attach even more importance to these Bills!) I therefore venture to hope that you will have precedence given to them in the Departments at Simla . . . . I am of opinion that the 50 per cent should be introduced at the first convenient opportunity in those temporarily settled Provinces in which it does not operate.
>
> Furthermore I think that the practice I have introduced in the N.W.P. and Oudh of regarding the pitch of the enhancement as of as great consequence as the share of the assets taken, should be generally observed — The Revenue payer looks more (and the people look more) to the increase of his burden than to the percentage of assets taken. If his Revenue is increased from Rs. 1,000 to Rs. 2,000 it is no consolation for him to know that while the Rs. 1,000 was 50 per cent of the then assets, the Rs. 2,000 is only 47 per cent of existing assets. I think that in all further re-settlements *if they involve an increase of the Revenue incidence per acre*, the Settlement officer should avoid placing on the Revenue-payer any great, and he should particularly avoid placing on him any sudden, substantial increase of his burden. If the enhancement of Revenue was 25 per cent (I had written 20 per cent and am tempted to let it stand) it should always be made

progressive, unless indeed the actual amount is small. Even an enhancement of 15 per cent will sometimes call for gradual enforcement in the interests of the tax-payer.

In settlements of the Zemindari class the all-important matter is to secure a fair determination of the assets. There should never be an assessment on prospective assets, the assets should be 'in being': *in esse* not *in posse* — we have in recent years made great advances in the recognition of this cardinal principle: to its neglect is to be attributed most of the ill-success which has attended settlements in the past. A settlement in prospective assets only succeeds when the seasons immediately following the settlement are good — followed by bad seasons such a settlement usually breaks down.

I have within the last five years reviewed the settlements of over 30,000 estates: and I have never found the principles at fault, though I have had very often to moderate their application.

To sum up: The main points to be attended to are these: not to assess on prospective assets: not to assess on unstable rents: to allow for improvements: to be specially careful and lenient when cultivation is precarious: to allow for short collections: to be tender with village communities and with shareholders when they are numerous . . . we may, without intending it, very easily place on the ryots a heavier burden than they can bear: and (that) this danger has not been altogether avoided in Bombay. The success of the ryotian system hinges far more on the efficiency and honesty of the Land Revenue Staff.[47]

In a Minute for his successor MacDonnell summarized his views on Land Revenue:

I strongly advocate leniency and avoidance of heavy and, above all, sudden enhancements of land revenue. There can be no doubt that many districts, both in Oudh and the North-West, have seriously suffered by over-assessment in the past. Therefore I consider that in future assessments

47 Sir Antony MacDonnell to Lord Curzon, 17 June 1901, MacDonnell Papers, c. 354.

> there should be greater consideration towards the proprietors, but also in the interests of the cultivators . . . .
>
> A high assessment means high following rents, and increased pressure on the cultivators. A moderate assessment means moderate rent enhancements. We cannot logically object to rack rents unless we ourselves moderate our revenue enhancements.
>
> If further taxation is necessary, it ought to be raised from other sources than the Land.[48]

The legislation which MacDonnell had sought was enacted, and in all provinces the rights of tenants were strengthened.[49] These changes were not mere defensive measures to avert local discontent. They were the reflection of a new attitude of mind. In its Resolution of 1902 the Government of India confirmed the principles for which MacDonnell had argued and put them forward as guide-lines for future policy. These "liberal principles", as the Resolution described them, were to be based upon the need for "greater elasticity in the revenue collection, facilitating its adjustment to the variations of the seasons and the circumstances of the people". As a specific measure of wide and indeed revolutionary application, it advocated "for future guidance" the measure which had been the essence of MacDonnell's demands, "a more general resort to reduction of assessments in cases of local deterioration".[50] This Resolution, issued with the full weight of Curzon's authority, set an official seal upon a movement that had been long and vigorously fostered, but had lacked a political champion.

After 1902 the relative importance of the Land Revenue in the Indian Budget declined steadily, and both British and Indian attention turned away from agricultural to political problems, in particular those of Indian representation in government. But MacDonnell's persistence and Curzon's energy had combined to halt and remedy a serious deficiency in the Land Revenue administration of British India.

48 Minute . . . for my successor's information, by Sir Antony MacDonnell, October 1901, c. 355, *ibid.*

49 See, for example, the United Provinces Tenancy Act of 1901.

50 *Resolution of the Government of India*, issued as Command Paper No. 1089 of 1902.

# THE DECLINE OF THE MARQUESS OF HASTINGS

RICHARD JOHN BINGLE

The administration of Francis Rawdon-Hastings, second Earl of Moira, first Marquess of Hastings (1754-1826), as Governor-General and Commander-in-Chief in India from 1813 to 1823, has long been recognized as a landmark in the development of British power in India.[1] His military successes in the Nepal War (1814-16) and against the Pindaris and Marathas (1817-18) established British paramountcy beyond all question; he has been hailed as the man who completed Wellesley's work in India.[2] These successes, however, were the fruit of the early years of Hastings's administration, and his later years were marked by constant quarrels with the Bengal Council, with the Court of Directors of the East India Company, and by the failure to check the financial operations of William Palmer and Company in Hyderabad. It is usual for historians to refer only in general terms to Hastings's failure in relation to the Palmer Company and then to discuss in detail his other achievements.[3] In my view this failure was something more than a momentary lapse; it is indicative of a general decline in administrative ability and concentration which affected Hastings during his later years.

1 Cf. H. H. Wilson, *The History of British India from 1805 to 1835* (3 vols., London, 1845-46), iii, 587-88.

2 M.S. Mehta, *Lord Hastings and the Indian States* (Bombay, 1930), pp. 261-262.

3 V. A. Smith, *The Oxford History of India*, 1st ed. (Oxford, 1919), p. 646; ed. P. Spear, 3rd ed. (Oxford, 1958), p. 585.

The aim of this essay is to indicate three factors which operated with particular force during the latter part of Hastings's administration, and tended to distract him from his duties; these factors are his physical decline, personal financial worries, and the series of disputes with the Court of Directors. Of these the most serious is the deterioration in health. Hastings was 58 years old when he arrived in India in 1813;[4] he had had an active military career in the American War of Independence, and had followed this with a career of thirty years in English politics. At a time when other men might have considered retirement he was forced to adapt to an Indian climate, and cope with a strenuous administrative routine. The Marquess managed to survive the transition, but the effort of doing so, coupled with the long tours (1814-15, 1817-18) undertaken in connection with two major military campaigns, weakened him considerably. It is not surprising that, towards the end of his administration, there were signs of physical and mental exhaustion. The second factor has never been discussed in detail, and yet while he was in India the precarious structure of his finances almost collapsed under the weight of his enormous debts. Thirdly, an examination of Hastings's private letters has revealed his personal opinions about the disputes with the Court of Directors, and how much the task of self-justification distracted him from fulfilling adequately his Indian administrative duties.

## *Physical Decline*

Hastings arrived in Calcutta in October 1813, and at that time appeared to be in very good health. One eye-witness of the new Governor-General's arrival gave a fulsome description of his appearance:

> Tall and majestic, the Marquis of Hastings makes a lasting impression on every beholding eye. In his firm step we hear fortitude; in his friendly smile we see benevolence; and his bright eye conveys to feeling the flash of valour.[5]

[4] Hastings arrived in Calcutta on 4 Oct. 1813 and left on 1 Jan. 1823.

[5] R. G. Wallace, *Forty Years in the World* (London, 1825), i, 148-9.

Soon afterwards he established the exhausting daily routine maintained without variation throughout his administration. [6] He rose at 4.00 a.m., and looked "cursorily over the Packets which are brought in at that hour, in order to see if there be anything requiring instantaneous measures";[7] by 5.00 a.m. he was out riding (on a horse in Calcutta, on an elephant at Barrackpur, the Governor-General's country residence), while his wife Lady Loudoun[8] and their children rode in a carriage. The eleven hours between 6.00 a.m. and 5.00 p.m. were needed to "work unremittingly",[9] interrupted only by a formal breakfast at 8.00 a.m., and by tiffin at 1.00 p.m. At sunset he and Lady Loudoun went riding again, and dinner followed at 7.30 p.m.; then Hastings proceeded "to take Coffee while walking about the room and talking over points of business with different People",[10] before retiring to bed. Friday, Saturday and Sunday of each week were spent in Calcutta, in order to attend Council meetings, and the rest of the week at Barrackpur,[11] where he could work without interruption, attended only by the Secretaries.[12] This exacting routine was made more onerous by the number of official functions, dinners, reviews and audiences.[13] It was necessary therefore to accustom himself at one time both to a hot climate, and a heavier burden of administrative and social duties than he had ever experienced before.

The burden of these multifarious duties began to show itself in eye-strain after six months.[14] There are repeated

6 Moira to Sir C. Hastings, 30 Oct. 1813, 8 May 1822, Hastings Papers, Huntington Library, California (Ind(ia) Off(ice) Lib(rary) microfilms, Reel 782). Extracts printed by permission of the Huntington Library.

7 Moira to Sir C. Hastings, 31 July 1821, Hastings Papers.

8 Flora Mure Campbell, Countess of Loudoun in her own right (1780-1840).

9 Moira to Sir C. Hastings, 31 July 1821, Hastings Papers.

10 Moira to Sir C. Hastings, 8 May 1822, *ibid.*

11 Moira to Sir C. Hastings, 28 Dec. 1813, *ibid.*

12 Moira to Sir C. Hastings, 6 Dec. 1813, *ibid.*

13 Wallace, *Forty Years*, i, 150-1.

14 Moira to W. F. Elphinstone, 14 April 1814, Elphinstone Collection, MSS., Eur. F.89, Box 2A, Ind. Off. Lib.

references to this in his correspondence,[15] until in 1818 he reported with a touch of vanity,

> I am fighting off Spectacles as long as I can, but possibly you may find a trouble in deciphering this letter sufficient to make you think I push the struggle too far.[16]

At the same time Hastings was beginning to complain about over-work. In the middle of the campaign against the Marathas and Pindaris, in January 1818, he stated: "My present toil is too much for me or for any man. Still, I hope to hold out to the Close of the Campaign."[17] This may be considered an over-exaggeration, but on the other hand, there can be little doubt that, at the successful conclusion of the war the Marquess was feeling very tired, for he wrote, "The Campaign has set me desperately forward in Age";[18] when he recalled the campaign some eighteen months later, he could not resist remarking on the "Mental Toil"[19] which had been involved.

From the middle of 1818 Hastings became increasingly conscious of the onset of old age, which he refers to as "my Night Cap".[20] By May 1819, he was complaining that he had "grown old and somewhat clumsy"[21] although still only 64; an attack of fever in the following August further reduced his strength,[22] and led him to counsel his son to "reflect frequently on the precariousness of Human Existence".[23] The hot weather of 1820 brought on attacks of fever and boils,[24] and complaints about his work:

15 Moira to Sir C. Hastings, 20 Dec. 1816, Hastings Papers; Hastings to his son George, Earl of Rawdon, 24 July 1817, *ibid.*

16 Hastings to W. P. Elphinstone, 23 June 1818, Elphinstone Collection.

17 Hastings to Sir C. Hastings, 4 Jan. 1818, Hastings Papers.

18 Hastings to Sir C. Hastings, 22 June 1818, *ibid.*

19 Hastings to W. F. Elphinstone, 22 March 1820, Elphinstone Collection.

20 Hastings to Sir C. Hastings, 22 Sept. 1818 and 21 Sept. 1822, Hastings Papers.

21 Hastings to Sir C. Hastings, 4 May 1819, *ibid.*

22 Hastings to Earl of Rawdon, 17 Aug. 1819, *ibid.*

23 Hastings to Earl of Rawdon, 21 Sept. 1819, *ibid.*

24 Hastings to Col. James Young, 16 May 1820, B(ritish) M(useum) Add(itional) MSS., 38517, ff. 152-153.

> I ask myself sometimes what the Devil pretension I have to be acting a part at my time of life: And the next moment in comes a Bundle of Despatches from the Upper Country, summoning all my activity and decision.[25]

When the cooler weather did not bring an improvement in health he was forced to leave Calcutta for the Rajmahal Hills in the hope that the change of air would, as he wrote, "patch me up for a while".[26] An anxiety to remain in touch with the Council and Secretariat in Calcutta is revealed by the fact that he deliberately chose the river-trip, in preference to the usual voyage round the Bay of Bengal, because during the former it was still possible to receive papers from Calcutta.[27] The holiday lasted from the end of November 1820 until the middle of January 1821, and apparently had the desired effect, because his son, the Earl of Rawdon, was told that "I find myself much better in health",[28] and more able to withstand "the heaviest and hottest weather ever known in India"[29] without illness.

This improvement in health did not mean that the topic was now omitted from his letters; instead it was coupled with references to his anxiety to leave India. In July 1821 he wrote, "I am weary and feverishly solicitous to get away";[30] and complained impatiently a few months later, "Not a hint of my emancipation has yet reached me".[31] In fact his resignation was not received by the Court of Directors until December 1821, and then there were doubts whether it could be accepted, because it had not been made in the prescribed legal form, that is, to the Chief Secretary of the Bengal Government.[32] Nevertheless when Hastings heard the news of its acceptance he was jubilant :

25 Hastings to Sir C. Hastings, 29 Aug. 1820, Hastings Papers.

26 Hastings to Sir C. Hastings, 6 Nov. 1820, *ibid.*

27 *Ibid.* 28 Hastings to Earl of Rawdon, 16 Jan, 1821, *ibid.*

29 Hastings to Earl of Rawdon, 31 July 1821, *ibid.*

30 Hastings to Sir C. Hastings, 15 July 1821, *ibid.*

31 Hastings to Sir C. Hastings, 14 Oct. 1821, *ibid.*

32 C. H. Philips, *The East India Company 1784-1834* (Manchester, 1940); cf. W. F. Elphinstone to J. Adam, 5 Dec. 1821, Adam Collection, MSS. Eur. F.109, Box J, Ind. Off. Lib. John Adam (1779-1825), Member of the Bengal Council 1819-25, Acting Governor-General 1823.

> Never did a Slave in Morocco receive the annunciation of his Liberation from Chains with more joy than your few lines to Adam excited in me.[33]

Thereafter he was more concerned with his impending departure than with his health: "As School Boys cut notches on the approach of the Holidays, I begin to reckon days till the period I have fixed for my embarkation."[34] Such rejoicing, however, could not conceal the fact that his health was failing rapidly. In September 1822 he complained of boils and "violently painful spasms",[35] and a few weeks later noted sadly :

> Within these last few months I have found great change in myself. It is obvious decadence, and I think it will have rapid progress. I have worked myself to the extent of my strength; and once a Machine so strained gives way it is from the snapping of some Spring the want of which soon produces entire stoppage.[36]

This chronicle of illnesses may suggest a preoccupation with health. To some extent this was natural in India, where diseases like cholera could bring death within a few hours, as Hastings himself had seen in 1817.[37] On the other hand, the Marquess was clearly in good health at the beginning of his administration and in very poor health at its end ten years later. Irritating minor illnesses, possibly psychosomatic in origin, had weakened him so much that he had a feeling of "obvious decadence" on departure. The heavy burden of administration, at once the cause and the accelerator of the decline, did not lessen while in office, and this suggests that during the latter years spent in India he was unable to exercise "the constant vigilance of the Superintending Authority"[38] considered essential.

33 Hastings to W. F. Elphinstone, 7 May 1822, Elphinstone Collection.

34 Hastings to Sir C. Hastings, 21 Sept. 1822, Hastings Papers.

35 *Ibid.*

36 Hastings to Sir C. Hastings, 11 Oct. 1822, *ibid.*

37 Hastings to Earl of Rawdon, 28 Nov. 1817, *ibid.*

38 Hastings to W. F. Elphinstone, 19 Aug. 1821, Elphinstone Collection.

### *Financial Worries*

A second personal factor, which caused considerable worry during his Governor-Generalship, was the poor state of his finances. This was no new feature in Hastings's affairs, but like his health his financial situation deteriorated while in India, and reached a critical stage during the later years of his administration.

The origins of this embarrassment lay in a "liberality bordering on profusion",[39] in generosity to French *émigrés* in England,[40] and probably also in large loans to his friend the Prince of Wales, which were never repaid.[41] After failing to form a government during the ministerial negotiations of May and June 1812,[42] Hastings was forced to cut down expenses; leaving his large country-seat (Donington Park, Leicestershire) with the intention of taking a smaller house in Essex or Monmouthshire where one could live more cheaply.[43] It was well known in political circles that this financial pinch forced the Marquess to accept the two posts of Governor-General and Commander-in-Chief in India, in the expectation of receiving the salaries of both positions.[44] The salary of Commander-in-Chief was disallowed almost immediately, to his intense disgust,[45] and he was forced to live on the salary of a Governor-General, which was £30,000 *per annum*. Before going to India, Hastings had to borrow £10,000 to buy an outfit and pay for the passage, and immediately after arrival a further £2,000 had to be borrowed to buy essential items to furnish Government House, Calcutta. Three years later neither of these debts had been repaid.[46]

39 Lord Holland, *Memoirs of the Whig Party during my Time*, ed. by his son Henry Edward, Lord Holland (London, 1852-54), i, 227.

40 J. Ross-of-Bladensburg, *The Marquess of Hastings* (*Rulers of India Series*) (Oxford, 1893), p. 40.

41 A. Aspinall (ed.), *The Letters of King George IV, 1812-1830* (Cambridge, 1938), i, 129 n.

42 M. Roberts, *The Whig Party 1807-1812* (London, 1939), pp. 382-418.

43 Moira to Col. J. McMahon, 31 Aug. 1812, *Letters of George IV*, No. 140.

44 R. Thornton to Col. J. McMahon, 11 Nov. 1812, *Letters of George IV*, No. 189.

45 Moira to Col. J. McMahon, 11 April 1813, *Letters of George IV*, No. 267.

46 William Adam to Hastings, 24 Jan. 1817 (copy), Adam Collection, Box E.

Nevertheless, the Governor-General did make a genuine effort to save money from his salary to pay off some of these debts; at the end of 1816 he was sending home £12,500 for this purpose, and complaining bitterly how expensive life was in the sub-continent.[47] Unfortunately, this thrift was not enough to make any impression on the enormous amount owing; this stood at £943,575 in August 1817.[48] All sources of income, including private estates, profits from a colliery, an income as Constable of the Tower of London and as Colonel of the 27th Regiment, were mortgaged,[49] and the remittances from India provided the only trickle of money to pay off the most pressing demands. By January 1819 the total sum outstanding had risen to £978,640,[50] indicating beyond all doubt the impossibility of keeping pace with the mounting burden of interest. When Hastings heard the news, he was "thunderstruck" and wrote repeatedly and at length to his agent, Edward Mammatt, to order an investigation of the accounts of John Evans (Hastings's London solicitor) and one John Ridge, whom he suspected of conspiring to defraud him.[51]

Fortunately some relief came through a personal grant of £60,000 by the Court of Proprietors of the East India Company in recognition of his successes in the War against Nepal; this money was used to secure land which had been intended for sale.[52] At the same time, however, news came that some of his major assets, estates received by the will of an uncle, Francis, tenth Earl of Huntingdon (died 1789), were threatened with alienation. This was a very nasty shock, and if the claim had been made good, ruin would have resulted. The background to these claims can be stated in a few words. The earldom of Huntingdon had lain dormant since the

47 Hastings to William Adam, 9 Nov. 1816, *ibid.*

48 Edward Mammatt, "State of Accounts of the Creditors of the Marquis of Hastings . . ." 22 Aug. 1817, DE/41/1/205, L(eicestershire) R(ecord) O(ffice).

49 Edward Mammatt, "Sketch of the Income and Property of the Marquis and Marchioness of Hastings and Appropriation thereof", 31 Jan. 1819, L.R.O.

50 Edward Mammatt, "State of Accounts of the Creditors of the Marquis of Hastings . . ." 20 Jan. 1819, L.R.O.

51 Hastings to Edward Mammatt, 7 Sept. 1819, 19 Sept. 1819 and 18 Jan. 1820, L.R.O.

52 Hastings to Sir W. Keppel, 20 June 1820, Adam Collection.

death of the tenth Earl, who had no legitimate heir.[53] Several claims to the earldom had been made, but none was successful until 1818, when Hans Francis Hastings was able to prove his descent from the second Earl (died 1561). This claim was made through the efforts of Henry Nugent Bell, an Irish genealogist, and was allowed in October 1818. Hans Francis Hastings was summoned to the House of Lords as eleventh Earl of Huntingdon in January 1819.[54] The new Earl naturally enough laid claim to the Huntingdon estates, particularly those at Donington and Ashby de la Zouch in Leicestershire, and notice of these claims reached the Governor-General in September 1819. Hastings reacted sharply, and sent long statements of doubts about the new Earl's title, and of his own right to the disputed estates, to all his Trustees and Agents in England. To his Trustee William Adam, Hastings wrote ordering that a prosecution for trespass be brought against the new Earl, and setting out in detail his claim to the Donington and Ashby estates.[55] To Edward Mammatt, his agent at Donington,[56] he wrote suggesting again that the Earl's trespass, which had taken place at Donington, should be punished severely by a bill in Chancery.[57] To John Evans, his London solicitor, he wrote detailing the reasons why the original grant of the Huntingdon estates was not open to any claim by the new Earl.[58] These letters indicate the intensity of Hastings's anxiety and indignation. His next letter to Adam (August 1820) expresses his sense of relief that his friends were looking after his interests.[59]

At this stage the claim to the estates had almost evaporated, but Bell revived it by publishing a fulsome account of his genealogical searches which had secured the peerage for the new Lord Huntingdon. In addition, the book renewed the

[53] Hastings's correspondent, General Sir Charles Hastings, Bt. (1752-1823), was the son of Lord Huntingdon by a French *danseuse*; see F. Bickley (ed.), *Historical Manuscripts Commission, Hastings III*, pp. xii-xiii.

[54] H. N. Bell, *The Huntingdon Peerage* (London, 1820), pp. 318-373.

[55] Hastings to William Adam, 1 Sept. 1819 (copy), Hastings Papers.

[56] Bell, *Huntingdon Peerage*, pp. 381-390.

[57] Hastings to Edward Mammatt, 25 July 1819, L.R.O.

[58] Hastings to John Evans, 7 Sept. 1819 (copy), Hastings Papers.

[59] Hastings to William Adam, 21 Aug. 1820, Adam Collection.

claim to the Huntingdon estates, and insinuated that Hastings deliberately obstructed Huntingdon's claim to the peerage.[60] Hastings himself was extremely worried on two points: firstly, that the claims to the estates were moving his creditors to press for payment;[61] and secondly, because, as he put it, "my Family, and the Friends who feel for me, write to me in absolute Anguish about the unchecked course of these Slanders".[62] Adam again reassured him, pointing out that the course of legal action proposed was fraught with many dangers and was likely to fail if Hastings was not present in England to defend his rights,[63] and further that Bell's book was merely "a very low vulgar effort of the Man to puff himself."[64]

Adam's assessment of the situation seems to have been correct, for the claims to the Huntingdon estates were not pressed, and Hastings had no reason to refer to them again in his correspondence. Nevertheless, the claims had aroused considerable worry and he had had to spend a good deal of valuable time examining them, writing long letters refuting them, and urging representatives in England to take action on his behalf. The real importance of the episode was that it forced the Marquess to see how precarious his financial situation was, and in June 1820 he acknowledged the weakness of his position:

> There are otherwise many obligations upon me of which I have an honest sense and which I labor to discharge according to that conception of them. Bound to the Oar by them, I must repress my personal disposition if the point be left to me.[65]

By the end of 1821, when Hastings's resignation had been presented to the Court of Directors, it had become clear that his financial advisers were pressing him to stay longer in India.

60 Bell, *Huntingdon Peerage*, pp. 189, 192-3 and 289-98.

61 Hastings to Sir W. Keppel, 20 June 1820, Adam Collection.

62 Hastings to William Adam, 28 Sept. 1820, *ibid.*

63 William Adam to Hastings, 8 Mar. 1821 (copy), *ibid.*

64 William Adam to Hastings, 27 Mar. 1821 (copy), *ibid.*

65 Hastings to W. F. Elphinstone, 10 June 1820, Elphinstone Collection.

The Earl of Harrowby wrote in these terms to Earl Bathurst: "His men of business, however, declare that he [Hastings] must stay two or three years longer".[66] The decision to resign in defiance of this advice was made possible by a contingent decision to live quietly on the Continent,[67] on an income estimated by Adam to be about £5,000 *per annum*,[68] thus leaving the income of the English estates to pay off his debts.

It is impossible to estimate the exact extent to which these financial worries were a factor in his decline. In general terms it can be stated that between 1819 and 1821, with the beginning of a decline in health, Hastings was forced to devote an inordinate amount of time in correspondence with financial advisers on two important personal questions. Firstly, despite the large remittances from his salary,[69] the total of the English debts had increased, and much time had to be spent in analysing the accounts sent out by Mammatt, and suggesting measures to be taken to repair the situation. Secondly, the threat of the claim of the new Earl of Huntingdon to a large portion of his capital had had to be dispelled. That these crises passed without serious personal damage did not restore the strength sacrificed in worrying over them. At the end of an Indian administration which had been undertaken for financial reasons, Hastings had to admit wearily, "we have not been making Money and never should".[70] In fact he again had to go into exile as a sop to his creditors. All hope of a quiet retirement in England had gone.

## *Disputes with the Court of Directors*

It is not possible here to present a complete survey of Hastings's relations with his employers, the Court of Directors of the East India Company. Much of the emphasis will lie

66 Earl of Harrowby (to Earl Bathurst), 22 Dec. 1821, *Historical Manuscripts Commission, Bathurst*, p. 526.

67 Hastings to W. F. Elphinstone, 17 Mar. and 7 May 1822, Elphinstone Collection.

68 William Adam to Hastings, 18 Apr. 1823 (draft), Adam Collection.

69 £94,000 between November 1813 and October 1819 "Remittances to England" in Lady Loudoun's handwriting, L.R.O.

70 Hastings to W. F. Elphinstone, 17 Mar. 1822, Elphinstone Collection.

on the later years, when mistrust of the Court animated his correspondence, and convinced him that he could count on little support from the Court.[71]

Initially relations with the Court, although not good, were not so strained as to excite much comment in his correspondence. Above all, he had been able to carry the Nepal War to a successful conclusion without interference. Hastings believed that his next task was to extirpate the Pindaris (gangs of free-booters who ravaged Central India) and conclude a series of subsidiary alliances with Indian States. For this project he could count on the backing of many members of the Bengal Civil Service,[72] but not on the Council;[73] perhaps because it ran counter to the declared policy of the Court of Directors.[74] Hastings expressed his policy in a Minute of 1 December 1815,[75] but this did not gain from the Court the desired permission to act.[76] Four months later, however, the Pindaris raided the Guntur Circar, and in December 1816 they devastated Ganjam and Cuttack. This latter raid forced the Bengal Council to agree to a campaign against the Pindaris,[77] and when news of the earlier raid reached the Court in September 1816, they modified their previous orders, and gave Hastings permission to conduct military operations against the invaders.[78] By the time these orders reached Calcutta Hastings, acting with the support of his Council, had already begun preparations for the campaign.

At this stage, therefore, Hastings's attitude towards the Court may be said to consist of mild exasperation at their vacillation over the policy to be pursued towards the Pindaris, together with a desire to formulate policy on his own understanding of local conditions:

71 In this section my debt to Prof. C. H. Philips for his work on *The East India Company* will be obvious.

72 Particularly C. T. Metcalfe, C. M. Ricketts, M. Elphinstone, R. Strachey and H. Russell.

73 Moira to W. F. Elphinstone, 11 Aug. 1816, Elphinstone Collection.

74 Philips, *East India Company*, pp. 213-215.

75 Minute of the Governor-General, 1 Dec. 1815, Bengal Secret Consultations, 15 June 1816, No. 1, India Office Records.

76 Philips, *East India Company*, pp. 215-216.

77 Moira to W. F. Elphinstone, 30 Dec. 1816, Elphinstone Collection.

78 Philips, *East India Company*, p. 216.

> A person on the spot must have the means of deciding more accurately on Local Interests than you who must form your projects on the representation of circumstances which may be wholly altered before your Orders reach India.[79]

It was on this ground, a common stand of colonial administrators, that he defended himself when charged with keeping the negotiations with Nagpur secret from the Court until a subsidiary alliance had been concluded in May 1816.[80] As the preparations for the campaign against the Pindaris became more complex, there was little time to complain about the Directors. During the actual campaign, which developed into the final war against the Marathas (November 1817-March 1818), Hastings was too much occupied with military matters to reflect on the Court's actions, except to stress that no thought of personal glory had been allowed to divert him from pursuing "the line which I thought the true one for the interest of my Employers".[81] After the successful conclusion of the campaign Hastings expressed the hope that the Court would realize that "our fortunate resolution of destroying the Pindarries caused the premature explosion of the deepest and most extensive Conspiracy ever formed in India against the British Power".[82]

One reason for the relatively cordial relations with the Court at this period may have been his continued private correspondence with each successive Chairman of the Court, with the sole exception of Charles Grant (Chairman 1815-16) on account of his "professed hostility".[83] A few letters to Robert Thornton (Chairman 1813-14) and a long series to William Fullarton Elphinstone (Chairman 1814-15) are in the Elphinstone Collection in the India Office Library,[84] and the letters to the latter refer among others to Thomas Reid (Chairman 1816-17) and John Bebb (Chairman 1817-18);[85]

79 Moira to W. F. Elphinstone, 19 Jan. 1816, Elphinstone Collection.

80 Hastings to W. F. Elphinstone, 6 June 1817, *ibid.*

81 Hastings to W. F. Elphinstone, 3 Feb. 1818, *ibid.*

82 Hastings to Sir C. Hastings, 22 Sept. 1818, Hastings Papers.

83 Moira to W. F. Elphinstone, 3 July 1816, Elphinstone Collection.

84 MSS. Eur. F. 89, Box 2A, *ibid.*

85 Moira to W. F. Elphinstone 26 Oct. 1816 *ibid.*

a small collection of letters to James Pattison (Chairman 1818-19) and Campbell Marjoribanks (Chairman 1819-20) is in the India Office Records.[86] Hastings valued this correspondence because, as he once remarked, "there are many points affecting serious Interests which can be but imperfectly explained, if touched upon at all, in Official Statements".[87] Little official notice appears to have been taken of this correspondence until 1818, when the Governor-General carelessly referred to a private letter in his official correspondence. Thereupon George Canning, the President of the Board of Control, protested, and the Court ordered that the correspondence should cease.[88] In this abrupt termination of an exchange which Hastings appreciated may lie the origin of the intense hatred which he later developed towards Canning.

From 1819 onwards the tone of comments about the Court of Directors became noticeably sharper; the mild irritation about their "want of confidence"[89] had been replaced by violent anger, excited by their criticism of his military policy:

> I therefore avow to you that never again can I have the slightest reliance on the Court, but must hold an attitude of cautious preparation against the insidious attack I ought to expect.[90]

He urged them to replace him with "the dirtiest spirited reptile you can find", but warned them to be careful whom they chose, for "even the most groveling of Men may be made splenetic by insult".[91] This threat of resignation was repeated shortly afterwards. However Hastings had been somewhat perplexed to learn from his wife that "the Directors were in the highest good humour with me".[92] In both of

86 "A Collection of Private Letters from the Marquess of Hastings 1818-1819", Political Library, India Office Records.

87 Moira to W. F. Elphinstone, 26 Oct. 1816, Elphinstone Collection.

88 Philips, *East India Company,* pp. 220-221.

89 Moira to W. F. Elphinstone, 30 Dec. 1816, Elphinstone Collection.

90 Hastings to W. F. Elphinstone, 10 Mar. 1819, *ibid.*

91 *Ibid.*

92 Hastings to W. F. Elphinstone, 16 May 1819, Elphinstone Collection.

these letters Hastings complained bitterly that neither the Court of Directors, nor the Board of Control, nor any individual connected with them had expressed satisfaction at the results of the Maratha War, although "from the King's Government I received warm congratulation".[93] Hastings's perplexity about the Court's attitude towards him increased after Lady Loudoun's return to India in June 1819 (she had accompanied their children to England in January 1816), for she informed him that the Court was "well contented" with his services, and proposed to reward them with "splendid munificence". He was forced to remark "you Directors are the most incomprehensible folks I ever met", and concluded "let Byegones be Byegones, and try the benefit of reciprocal Confidence".[94]

Convinced by his wife that the Court was not inimical to him, his indignation evaporated, and comparative peace reigned from the middle of 1819 until the end of 1820. Two matters continued to nag his mind. The first was that the Court could not, or would not appreciate the scale of his achievements in India: W. F. Elphinstone was told "as yet, the slightest conception of what has been effected for the Company is not apparent in the Court".[95] The second idea was that, as a result of this lack of appreciation, the Court wished to dismiss him. He implored Elphinstone to give him "as early an intimation of their purpose as you can feel justified in imparting, because my arrangements must be consonantly fashioned".[96] At the same time gratitude to the Company was expressed for their grant of £60,000. But his dearest wish, an advancement in the peerage to a dukedom (to parallel the marquisate which he had received for his success in the Nepal War) never came.[97] Even in expressing gratitude, and he was particularly grateful to Elphinstone who he thought was mainly responsible for the grant, Hastings could not avoid a note of sarcasm:

93 *Ibid.*

94 Hastings to W. F. Elphinstone, 15 July 1819, Elphinstone Collection.

95 Hastings to W. F. Elphinstone, 21 Sept. 1819, *ibid.*

96 *Ibid.*

97 Philips, *East India Company*, pp. 222-223.

> I wonder whether it has ever occurred to you that a little courtesy encourages a profitable zeal, at the same time that it is not unsuited to the Character of Gentlemen.[98]

A mixture of self-justification and apology is apparent in many of Hastings's private letters during the uneasy peace in 1820. He justifies his previous anger on the ground that the tone of the Court's official despatches was unnecessarily harsh and admits to "an unfeigned self-condemnation for having groundlessly imputed to the Court an unworthy disposition respecting me",[99] but claims nevertheless that he was never disrespectful to the Court for "disrespect towards the Court would be dishonorable in me".[100] At no stage during this peaceful interlude did Hastings acknowledge that there was some justification for the Court's cautious attitude, considering the vast extent of his military conquests, the expenses which such conquests involved, and the burden, in finance and manpower, of administering the new territories. Only on one occasion did Hastings acknowledge that the tone of his official correspondence had made Elphinstone's support "more laborious".[101] Although reconciled to "staying here a little longer"[102] he had grown tired of administration, and complained to another correspondent:

> This situation of mine, demanding explanation in minute detail (to folks at Home) of almost every procedure, is too laborious to have its Duties fulfilled adequately. The simple discharge of them, without the Burthen of subsequent exposition, would sufficiently tax the industry and the strength of most Individuals.[103]

The easier path of explaining his position in private letters to the Chairman had been denied him, and he felt he no longer had the strength to fulfil all his duties.

98 Hastings to W. F. Elphinstone, 27 Oct. 1819, Elphinstone Collection.
99 Hastings to W. F. Elphinstone, 20 Aug. 1820, *ibid.*
100 Hastings to W. F. Elphinstone, 10 June 1820, *ibid.*
101 Hastings to W. F. Elphinstone, 22 Mar. 1820, *ibid.*
102 Hastings to W. F. Elphinstone, 20 Aug. 1820, *ibid.*
103 Hastings to Sir C. Hastings, 29 Aug. 1820, Hastings Papers.

The peace which had lasted almost eighteen months was shattered abruptly in 1821. Until that time it had been possible to lay the blame for the tone of the Court's despatches on the "vulgar flippancy of a Secretary"[104] who had "raked every Sewer in search of Materials"[105] to criticize him. Early in 1821, however, he heard from a friend in England who his real enemies (supposedly) were. He wrote to Elphinstone:

> I have had the most unquestionable information that Mr. Canning has been moving every Engine to get himself nominated to the Government of India . . . . I understand that Mr. Robinson seconds Mr. Canning zealously.[106]

At the same time Hastings wrote angrily to Canning, complaining that "latterly there has not been a single measure of mine which has not been captiously misconstrued" and deduced that "one solution alone presents itself; that you are anxious to get rid of me".[107] In fact Hastings had completely misunderstood the situation. When Canning had resigned from the Board of Control in 1820, the Directors had favoured his nomination as the Governor-General's successor, but Canning did not want to go to India while there was any hope of political office in England, and certainly not before the incumbent had submitted his resignation.[108] Canning disposed of the charges in a letter which was milder than Hastings deserved. To the charge of wilful misconstruction Canning replied that he had "on more occasions than I ever troubled your Lordship with specifying, softened and conciliated growing misunderstandings between your Lordship and your Employers."[109] And to the charge of engineering Hastings's removal, although he believed his nomination

104 Hastings to W. F. Elphinstone, 10 Mar. 1819, Elphinstone Collection.

105 Hastings to W. F. Elphinstone, 22 Mar. 1820, *ibid.*

106 Hastings to W. F. Elphinstone, 4 Feb. 1821, *ibid.* George Abercromby Robinson (Baronet 1823) was Chairman of the Court of Directors 1820-21.

107 Hastings to G. Canning, 2 Feb. 1821 (copy), B. M. Add. MS. 38411, f.29v.

108 Philips, *East India Company*, pp. 228-229.

109 G. Canning to Hastings, 20 Aug. 1821 (copy). B. M. Add. MSS, 38411, f.54.

would be "not unacceptable to the Court of Directors", he felt he had to state that

> never for a moment has such an appointment been entertained by any one of them, Director or Minister, any more than by myself, except on the contingency (whether more or less near) of your Lordship's spontaneous, unsuggested retirement.[110]

Hastings mentioned two matters on which the Court had directly countermanded his orders: the Court had refused to allow him to solicit from the Nizam a gift of £200,000 for "public works" in Calcutta (which were in fact for the building of a Cathedral and Bishop's Palace — strange objects of charity for a Muslim ruler), and had ordered withdrawal of the Licence granted by the Bengal Council in 1816 to William Palmer and Company of Hyderabad to lend money to the Nizam. Hastings was peculiarly sensitive about both projects: the Cathedral scheme because he seems to have wanted credit for providing Calcutta with a Cathedral, and about the Palmer Company because his protege, Sir William Rumbold, was a partner in that Company. Canning could not accept the contention that the Nizam had a large personal fortune, and therefore could afford the gift, while his State had no public funds, and so needed the loans. Canning commented:

> There seemed to me something peculiarly exceptionable in receiving a "boon" from the Nizam on the one hand, while on the other hand a British House of Agency was obtaining Assignments of Revenue for loans advanced to his Government.[111]

While this altercation was still in progress, Hastings had already made up his mind to resign. A form of resignation was probably sent to England by Lt.-Col. C. J. Doyle, his

[110] G. Canning to Hastings, 20 Aug. 1821 (copy), B.M. Add. MSS. 38411, f.62.

[111] G. Canning to Hastings, 20 Aug. 1821 (copy), B.M. Add. MSS. 38411, f.57v.

Military Secretary who left Calcutta in February 1821,[112] and was handed to an old friend and agent Sir John Doyle (possibly a relation of Col. Doyle). As we have noted earlier, this resignation was presented to the Court in December 1821, but its irregular form prevented it being accepted until the following March, when Canning finally agreed to succeed the Governor-General.[113] From February 1821, therefore, Hastings considered that he had submitted his resignation, for in August he wrote "I have to look daily for the annunciation that my Relations with the Company are dissolved". Hastings now had the absurd idea that Canning was the real enemy firmly fixed in his mind, and accused Canning of "courting the Directors and endeavouring to sow dissension between them and me".[114] Thus he found it possible to acquit the Court of deliberate animosity towards him :

> I have a thorough belief in the fair and honorable disposition of the Court generally to me; but the Court cannot help itself against the President of the Board of Control. The injurious nature of a Power which is to be exercised by an Individual under the name of others, he standing clear of Responsibility, has been seriously exhibited to me.[115]

Seeing Canning as his successor, the Marquess wrote that he would leave him "an easier Game than that which I had on my hands at the outset".[116] Canning was not the right type of man for the post of Governor-General, in Hastings's opinion; he would find "the business here (tho' he will not have that of the Army) far beyond his imagination".[117] The Bengal Civil Service would become lethargic, and "unfavourable preconceptions and those opinions spread rapidly among the Natives who are keenly vigilant in endeavouring to gather from the Europeans their notions of Public Men."[118] These

112 Hastings to Earl of Rawdon, 4 Feb. 1821, Hastings Papers.

113 Philips, *East India Company*, pp. 229-230.

114 Hastings to W. F. Elphinstone, 19 Aug. 1821, Elphinstone Collection.

115 Hastings to W. F. Elphinstone, 21 Feb. 1821, *ibid.*

116 Hastings to W. F. Elphinstone, 16 Jan. 1822, *ibid.*

117 Hastings to W. F. Elphinstone, 19 Aug. 1821, *ibid.*

118 Hastings to W. F. Elphinstone, 12 Dec. 1821, *ibid.*

were rather malicious predictions, and Elphinstone probably did not receive much comfort from Hastings's repeated promise that "to the last moment, every exertion shall be made by me to promote your Concerns".[119]

The transference of much of Hastings's animosity from the Court to Canning did not entirely restore harmonious relations between them. Hastings was still irritated by the Court's criticisms of his policies. He found two scape-goats. The first was George Robinson, whom he saw as Canning's ally, and of whom he wrote: "It is my private belief that the irritating Passages have been inserted by the Pen or Dictation of Mr. Robinson." The second scape-goat reflects a return to his earlier theory that a malevolent clerk at the East India House was responsible for drafting the letters, for as Hastings wrote "a low Man has ever much gratification in insulting a Superior when he can do it with impunity".[120] This position Hastings maintained even after departing India. On the voyage home he wrote of "the belief I have entertained that the general instructions of the Court have been always studiously warped and perverted by some Clerk entrusted with the composition of the Letter".[121] The improved standing of the Court had been to a certain extent due to the thanks which he had received just prior to departure. He recognized this as "very handsome" and "as a reward for no ordinary toil".[122] As a result he made a small gesture of reconciliation in dedicating the report of his administration[123] not to the Court of Proprietors, as he had originally intended (and probably as some acknowledgement for the grant of £60,000 made in 1819), but to the Court of Directors.[124]

There were three main crises in Hastings's relationship with the Court of Directors; in 1816, 1819, and 1821-22: his reaction during the first had been only a mild irritation

119 Hastings to W. F. Elphinstone, 4 Aug. 1822, *ibid.*

20 Hastings to W. F. Elphinstone, 26 Nov. 1821, *ibid.*

121 Hastings to W. F. Elphinstone, 21 Mar. 1823, *ibid.*

122 Hastings to Sir C. Hastings, 11 Oct. 1822, Hastings Papers.

123 Lord Hastings, *Summary of the Administration of the Indian Government rom October 1813 to January 1823* (London, 1824).

124 Hastings to W. F. Elphinstone, 21 Mar. 1823, Elphinstone Collection.

at the Court's vacillations over the policy to be pursued towards the Pindaris; during the second, this grew into anger in belief that the Court had failed to recognize his military achievements (without any understanding of the Court's worries over the problems entailed by these successes) and had assailed him with captious criticism. During the final crisis, this anger was deflected to some extent from the Court to Canning and the anonymous clerk, but he remained on his guard until he had received the Court's thanks for his work in India.

### *Conclusion*

These three factors distracted the Governor-General from his main task of administration in India. The constant one was a decline in health, which meant that he had less energy to devote to his tasks, and was becoming too tired to take a clear view of the problems of policy involved. This had become apparent to some people in India by 1820, for an anonymous observer writing on the transaction of business in the Bengal Council noted that Hastings sometimes fell asleep in Council, and other members of Council gave instructions to the Secretaries contrary to his previously expressed opinions.[125] This physical impairment was aggravated by constant worry about finances and uncertainty about the Directors' attitude towards him, as flagging energy was directed away from affairs in India. In fact the Court's strictures, particularly about the Palmer Company, were aimed at saving Hastings from the dire consequences of his own partiality towards that Company. But Hastings had passed the stage when he could receive advice from the Court, and he felt isolated and without backing from the Court, or the Bengal Council. In this situation he supported his friends in the Palmer Company, and so forfeited all chance of the Court's recognition of his earlier successes, and what was more important, all chance of another grant from the Company which would have paid off some of his many debts.

125 "Marquis of Hastings's methods of conducting business in Council", Bodleian, MSS. Eng. Misc. c. 326, ff.148-150.

# INDIA AND THE EAST INDIES, 1807-13

AMITA DAS

In the wars between France and England in the 18th and 19th centuries, the colonial possessions of the two countries were always pawns in the game. During the wars of 1793-1814 the European war was carried into Asia, Africa and America. In 1793 the English drove the French out of the Indian mainland, but not from the Indian sea. The French footholds in the Indian Ocean were suitable for just the sort of operation the French aimed against the English after the short-lived peace of Amiens in 1802; namely, the destruction of England's commercial prosperity. While Napoleon's grand projects for an invasion of India never materialized, the French were extremely successful in their attacks on English commerce from their outposts in the east. The French privateers operating from the islands of Bourbon and Mauritius during 1803-1810 were so successful in their exploits as to become a serious threat to the prosperity of the Indian trade, despite the apparent naval superiority of Britain after Trafalgar. With the annexation of Holland by Napoleon in 1806, the Dutch East Indies also became a potential source of trouble to the English in India, for if the French privateers established themselves in the East Indies the security of the East India Company's China trade was likely to be seriously threatened. In 1810 the Company's Government in India under Governor-General Minto (1807-1812) decided to tackle the problem, and add to England's colonial territories in the bargain. The conquest of the French Islands and the Dutch East Indies together with the conquests in South America and the West Indies extended the British Empire. According to some historians Britain's chief motive was to secure a monopoly of tropical products to offset Napoleon's attempt to exclude all British products from the Continent.[1] This explanation is however not borne out by facts. The security of the Empire appears to have been the chief concern of British statesmen both in England and in India. By the terms of the peace settlement of 1815 England retained only those recent conquests which were strategically valuable to her and which secured her the control of the Mediterranean and the routes to India, China, and the West Indies. As a matter of fact, it was not the need for more sugar and cloves but the need for greater security of British trade and territories in India that caused Minto to fit out the expeditions against the French Islands and the Dutch East Indies during 1810-11.

Until the end of the 17th century the Dutch East Indies, with its capital at Batavia, included all the Dutch Colonies in the east. In the 18th century, however, the Cape, Ceylon, and the Dutch settlements in India enjoyed a considerable degree of independence from the Batavian Government. The Dutch East Indies in the 19th century consisted of a group of islands, including Borneo, the Celebes, Sumatra, Java, and the Moluccas (or Spice Islands) — Amboyna, Banda, Ceram, Ternate and others. To the Dutch, the most important were Java and the Moluccas, to which they confined the cultivation of coffee, sugar, and spices. They had established numerous fortified posts on the islands to enforce the prohibition of the cultivation of spices outside the allocated areas and to exclude all other European merchants from the eastern islands. The Dutch East Indies commanded the passage to China. Through either the Straits of Malacca or those of Sunda all the trade of the English to China had to pass. For the security of this trade the English established posts on the two Straits: the fortified settlement of Bencoolen, founded in 1685 and officially known as Fort Marlborough, on the west coast of Sumatra, and the tiny island

[1] *Cambridge History of the British Empire* (Cambridge, 1929-59), ii, 105.

of Pulu Penang purchased in 1786 from the Sultan of Kedah and renamed Prince of Wales Island, in the Malacca Straits. In 1800, the English acquired a foothold in the Malay Peninsula which was named Province Wellesley. In view of the strategic value of Penang and the facilities it appeared to offer for shipbuilding, it was created a fourth presidency of the Company's Government in 1805.

When in 1795 the new Dutch Republic through its alliance with France became involved in the war with Britain, the Dutch colonies had to choose between the Stadtholder and the Republic. The Government at Batavia refused to carry out the orders of the Prince of Orange to surrender Java to the English, although Malacca and the Moluccas surrendered in 1795. In 1795-96, Trincomalee and the other Dutch holdings in Ceylon were occupied by the English. The total extinction of Dutch power in the East Indies by the capture of Java was considered desirable by Henry Dundas, then the Secretary of State for War. Orders were sent to the Governor-General of India, Lord Wellesley (1798-1805), to that effect, and parallel orders were received by Admiral Rainier of the India Station from the Admiralty. Rainier decided to blockade Batavia as a preliminary measure while preparations were being made by the Government of India for the military expedition. Though the naval operations against Batavia were eminently successful, sickness and mortality among the troops and seamen forced the British squardon to withdraw in November 1800. In the meantime Wellesley decided to send an expedition under Col. Arthur Wellesley to conquer the French Islands, as in his opinion "neither the local position, actual state, genius, and character of the people, or peculiar resources of either Batavia, or Manilla," rendered their conquest as important as that of L'lle de France.[2] Admiral Rainier, however, refused to cooperate on the pretext that he could not without the orders of the Admiralty. The clash of authority between the naval Commander-in-Chief and the Governor-General was chronic during the war years. The Admirals of the East India Station considered themselves

[2] R. M. Martin, *The Despatches, Minutes and Correspondence of the Marquess Wellesley* (London, 1836-37), ii, 755. Wellesley was in charge of the civil and military government of Mysore, 1799-1802.

under the distinct authority of the Admiralty, and not bound to comply with the orders or suggestions of the Company's Government. (Minto met with the same kind of opposition from Rear-Admiral Drury and Commodore Broughton.) As it happened, no expeditions were to be undertaken by Wellesley, either against Mauritius or Batavia. On the orders of the Home Government, the troops assembled at Trincomalee and Point de Galle were despatched under Major-General Baird to Egypt, with Arthur Wellesley as second-in-command. Wellesley expressed a hope that should the army return to India after a short and successful campaign, the projected expeditions against the French Islands and even Batavia might be revived.[3] Rainier gave orders for the raising of the blockade of Batavia and rallied his ships at Trincomalee for service in the Red Sea.

For the following ten years the Dutch East Indies enjoyed immunity from British attack. At the Peace of Amiens, March 1802, the British restored all the occupied Dutch territories, except Ceylon, to Holland. The Dutch Ambassador in England, Herr Schimmelpennick, was told that as long as French influence was absent from Java the English had no desire to occupy it. The Dutch Government in Batavia was so weak and moribund that no alarm was felt from that direction. Consequently, as a measure of economy, the British greatly reduced their fortified settlements in the East Indies. In November 1805, the British post at Balambangan, an island a few miles north of Borneo, was abandoned, and the evacuation of Malacca was considered by Sir George Barlow's government. Although Malacca was retained, its fortifications were destroyed and the garrison withdrawn. Only a small civil population remained. Penang and Bencoolen badly needed reinforcements, which the government of Bengal declared its inability to provide. The entire burden of protecting British trade and settlements in the East Indies devolved on the Navy. Java, on the other hand, received reinforcements from Europe after 1803. The Batavian Government still felt that so long as it refrained from actual hostilities against the British, the latter would not attack. In

[3] *Ibid.*, pp. 436-52 and 584-7.

November 1806, the British attacked and destroyed the Dutch ships at Batavia as a result of which the Dutch navy was reduced to the few ships which were then in the harbour of Gressie.

On 28 January 1807 Rear-Admiral Sir Edward Pellew of the East India Station sent a lengthy memorandum to Sir George Barlow, the Acting Governor-General of India (1805-7), on the necessity of conquering Java as the best means of guaranteeing the security of the China trade. This was probably prompted by the establishment of French sovereignty over Holland in the person of King Louis Bonaparte in 1806, which placed the Dutch colonies under stricter French control and direction. Under such circumstances the China trade and the Company's ships employed in that trade were liable to be greatly harassed by the French operating from Java. The surrounding waters with its numerous islands and unchartered seas made pursuit difficult, and consequently highly advantageous to piracy. Pellew wrote,

> an active force even of frigates only employed in that quarter, would give serious uneasiness to our commerce in the China Seas, from the facility with which they might elude our pursuit, receiving shelter in the numerous Islands of those Seas, with the convenient resort of the Ports of Java and the Philippines.[4]

Pellew recommended that the Dutch should be dispossessed of Batavia before the French could effectively establish their authority and before any hostile operations against the Company's trade should actually commence from Java. He wanted to dispense with the burden of providing strong convoys for the China trade. He had collected information about the weak state of Batavia, the aversion of the old Dutch colonists towards the French, and the Javanese insurrections in the subordinate settlements. In his opinion a force of a thousand British soldiers and an equal number of sepoys could capture Batavia without a regular siege. The unhealthiness of the city could be avoided by stationing the main

4 Sir E. Pellew to G. Barlow, 28 January 1807, Madras Roads, Minto Papers, 180, National Library of Scotland, as listed in 1962.

body of the garrison, after the conquest, outside the city and frequently changing the garrison in the citadel. But Pellew probably realized that he was being too sanguine in his expectations. He therefore added the alternative proposal that at least the two remaining Dutch ships, the *Pluto* and the *Revolutie*, and the batteries at Gressie should be destroyed.

Barlow rejected Pellew's proposal for an attack on Batavia and questioned the French danger. Conditions in Europe, according to Barlow, would not permit Bonaparte to send a naval force to the east, and even if such an attempt was made, the Home Government could be trusted to counteract it. The more practical objections arose from the Indian Government's financial and political interests in India. Barlow repeated the same arguments which he had used in declining to undertake an expedition against the French Islands: he had no wish to increase the expenditure of his government unless he was forced to do so by "extreme necessity and emergency." Moreover, he felt that the internal security and tranquillity of the Company's territories in India would be exposed to "local agitation", if large numbers of British troops were absent for a long period of time;[5] perhaps with the Vellore Mutiny in mind. As it was, he felt their number was inadequate though he was willing to cooperate in limited operations against Gressie. But before any action was taken Barlow went out of office.

Shortly after his arrival at Calcutta in August 1807, Barlow's successor, Governor-General Minto, reconsidered Pellew's proposition. He concurred entirely with Barlow, now senior member of the Council, and decided that the operation against Gressie should be carried out immediately by Pellew, with the assistance of 500 British troops and artillery, to be fitted out from Fort St. George. But Gressie was not to be permanently occupied. Pellew had recommended its occupation, which he declared would facilitate future operations against Batavia and the Spice Islands. In Minto's opinion, however, the expense of such an undertaking, the lack of adequate numbers of British troops in India, the hazards of

[5] Barlow and Council to Pellew, Fort William, 14 February 1807, *ibid*; Barlow-in-Coun. to Pellew, 16 February, 1807, Adm(iralty Records) 1/179, Public Record Office.

multiplying the objects of defence without an increase in naval force, the state of the Company's finances, and the positive terms of the orders of the Court of Directors against any extensive system of offensive measure against the French and the Dutch in the eastern islands compelled him to limit the object of the naval expedition to the destruction of Dutch ships and the establishment on Java.[6]

Minto has been criticized for delaying the attack on Batavia in 1807, and thereby for giving the Dutch Governor-General time to improve its defences, necessitating a larger expedition at a greater expense in 1811. This criticism however has been based on an imperfect understanding of the obstacles which stood in the way of undertaking any expedition from India, either against the French Islands or Java, in 1807-8. In 1807, Minto's main anxiety was for the security of the north-west frontier. The number of troops in India was, as has been said, inadequate. Moreover, Mauritius was the centre of French naval activities in the Indian seas. If an expedition could have been fitted out from India in 1807-8, it would in all probability have been directed against Mauritius. Minto was anxious to avoid measures which involved large expenditure. He was afraid that the slightest relaxation of the system of rigid economy pursued by the Bengal Government would create an immediate speculation on the money market and drive up the interest on the Company's public debt from 8 to 10 per cent. The financial consideration was not the only one which restrained Minto from adopting "plans . . . which although useful and desirable in themselves, are however not absolutely and obviously necessary."[7] When Minto's friends, the Grenvillites, were in office, plans for the extirpation of all European enemies of England from their military and commercial posts east of the Cape had been favoured. But the new ministers, particularly Lord Castlereagh, the Secretary of State for War and Colonies, were known to be opposed to such schemes. When Castlereagh was President of the Board of Control (1804-6) orders had been given prohibiting expeditions against Batavia or any other place in the eastern seas, and these orders still

[6] Minto and Coun. to Pellew, Ft. William, 4 October 1807, Adm. 1/179.

[7] Minto to Pellew, 6 October 1807, Minto Papers, 159.

stood. Above all, the attention of the Indian Government was focussed on the western part of India. Minto wrote to Pellew that although no actual invasion of British territories by a French army was yet to be feared, it was necessary to keep a watchful eye on their activities between Mauritius, the western coast of India, and the Persian Gulf. He regretted that the military operations against Java could not be immediately undertaken, for he realized its potential to the enemy as a military and naval base. "The impossibility", Minto wrote, "of embarking in these important designs is the more to be regretted as a very moderate effort could hardly at the present moment fail of success; and at a future period the difficulty may be much greater."[8] It is interesting to note that at this time Minto believed that operations against Java should not only be authorized but also in a great measure be carried out by the Home Government. He wrote to Pellew as well as to Robert Dundas, President of the Board of Control, that the Government of India was not only financially and militarily incompetent to undertake such a large-scale operation on its own, but that he also felt "the want of due authority to engage in such an enterprize, and our incompetence to adjust many points of the highest political importance which it must involve."[9] For instance, in whose name was the conquest to be made or posts to be occupied by troops and settlements to be held — Crown or Company? Who was to bear the expense or, if shared, in what proportion? These and several other questions could only be decided by the Home authorities, after due consultation between His Majesty's Government and the Court of Directors. And yet in 1811 Minto went ahead with the operation and settled the political arrangements without waiting for sanction from the Home authorities. In fact, even in 1807, Minto had written to Robert Dundas that if the resources of the Government and the circumstances had permitted, he would not have allowed any "formal incompetence" to stand in the way.

8 *Ibid.*

9 G(overnor) G(eneral)-in-Coun. to the Secret C(ommi)ttee, Ft. William, 26 October 1807, *ibid.*, 193; Ben(gal) Sec(ret) Letters, vol. 10, Ind(ia) Off(ice) Lib(rary); Minto to Pellew, 6 October 1807, and Minto to Robert Dundas, November 1807, Minto Papers, 159.

In the year Minto had arrived in India, French control over the Batavian Republic was more directly established and every Dutch settlement in the East Indies became the equivalent to a French post, where French frigates could shelter and from where attacks against the British might be directed. On the orders of the Emperor, Louis Bonaparte had appointed Marshal Herman Willem Daendels, a Dutch Jacobin and a General in the French Army, as the Governor-General of Java. As early as 1797 Daendels had suggested an attack on the British territories in India from Java.[10] His appointment therefore held significance. He arrived a year later with orders to improve the defences, military strength and finances of the colony. Daendels was as active a promoter of French interests in the Dutch East Indies as General Decaen in Mauritius. Under the mismanagement and corruption of his immediate predecessors Dutch power and authority had declined. The interruption of trade with Europe caused by the British blockade had greatly affected the colony's prosperity. The Batavian Government sold coffee and spices to neutral traders, American, Danish, and Arab, who came to buy and ship the products at their own risk. With the passing of the American Embargo Acts in 1807-8 and the stringency of the blockade, the two million guilders in the Treasury were soon exhausted, and the value of paper money severely depreciated. Daendels had to resort to the sale of government lands to stabilize finances.

Immediately after Daendels's arrival hostilities commenced with the rulers of Cheribon, Mataram, and Bantam, as a consequence of which Dutch authority was once more firmly established. To improve the military strength of Batavia the Javanese regiments were increased by conscription, mainly from the island of Madura, though lack of adequate numbers of European officers resulted in poor discipline. Roads, forts, and coastal batteries were under construction. A highway from Bantam in the west to Pasuruan in the east linked the ports of the northern coast and enabled the Dutch to concentrate troops at any point within one-tenth of the time that would have been needed before. But the roads were

10 H. E. Egerton, *Sir Stamford Raffles* (London, 1900), p. 34.

constructed by forced peasant labour and cost a large number of lives, thus alienating the Javanese. At Bantam he started building a series of forts, again by forced labour, which caused a local revolt. The garrison and the residential quarters of the Governor-General were removed from Batavia to the healthier district of Weltevreeden. A strong fort at Meester Cornelis was to be the main point of concentration in case of an English invasion. Though Daendels introduced many badly needed administrative and judicial reforms, he succeeded in alienating the Dutch inhabitants as much as the Javanese. General Janssens, his successor, reported that both natives and Europeans longed for the arrival of the British, "not from any detestable Anglomania but to escape a terror that desolated all the world."[11]

Minto was very much aware of Daendels's activities. In October 1808 he wrote to Dundas:

> Java is becoming every day more interesting. There has been a change of men and the greatest exertions are now making to strengthen the Dutch, that is to say the French possessions in that Island. We might yet deprive the Enemy of this settlement without great effort; but a little more time will increase the difficulty extremely. Nothing can be undertaken from hence without orders, at the same time I confess I do not feel quite easy in letting one of those seasons for an important service pass, which do not return.[12]

Reports poured into Calcutta from the Governments of Penang, Malacca, and Bencoolen about the latest moves of the enemy in the east. The English commandant at Malacca stated that Java could be taken by a body of 3000 to 5000 men, and that perhaps a lesser force might be sufficient if the disaffected chiefs could be persuaded to join in. The Dutch force was estimated at about a thousand Europeans and about ten thousand native troops shared among Batavia,

[11] J. S. Furnivall, *Netherlands India* (Cambridge, 1939), p. 67.

[12] Minto to R. Dundas, Ft. William, 2 October 1808, Minto Papers, 160.

Samarang, and Gressie.[13] Although the vigilance of the British Navy in Europe largely precluded the possibility, Minto suspected that the French had "a future design of augmenting . . . and rendering it [Java] a centre of operations against our own Establishments to the Eastward and probably in China."[14] In January 1809 therefore Minto placed before the Secret Committee his view that it would be a prudent policy to undertake an expedition against the Dutch East Indies, a measure which would become indispensably necessary and at the same time more arduous if the French were allowed to strengthen and consolidate their position.

The Resident at Bencoolen had expressed his anxiety that the enemy might attack the ill-defended English settlements and destroy the spice-cultivations.[15] His fears were realized in October 1809, when the French corvette *Creole* attacked and destroyed the settlement at Tappanooly, on the west coast of Sumatra. The losses of the Company were estimated at nearly six thousand Spanish dollars, exclusive of the military stores taken.[16] The plunder of Tappanooly showed that the Navy could not be depended upon alone to protect the settlements. And yet the naval force employed by Rear-Admiral Drury on the west coast of Sumatra during these months was considerable. The *Blanche*, *Rattlesnake*, *Sir Francis Drake*, *Dionede*, and the *Sylvia* were in that area, and the *Belliquieu* off Acheen Head. Drury complained to Minto that unless the settlements were capable of making some resistance, they must expect to suffer from such depredations.[17] Tappanooly was immediately recovered and reinforcements hurried to Bencoolen. Minto sought Drury's

[13] R. Parry to Minto, Ft. Marlborough, 17 March 1809, Consultations of 20 May 1809, No. 44, Ben(gal) Sec(ret and Separate) Cons(ultations) 213, Ind. Off. Lib.

[14] G. G.-in-Coun. to the Secret Cttee, Ft. William, 10 January 1809, Ben. Sec. Letters, vol. 11.

[15] R. Parry to Edmonstone, 25 June 1809, Fac(tory) Rec(ords), Java 12, Ind. Off. Lib.

[16] Parry to Edmonstone, 31 October 1809 and 7 November 1809; and John Prince to Parry, 27 October 1809, *ibid.*

[17] Drury to Minto, Bombay, 3 December 1809, *ibid.*

cooperation in measures adopted against Mauritius. In the meantime, the blockade of the Dutch ports went on.

In June 1809 Colonel de la Houssaye, a French aide-de-camp to Daendels, was seized by the British on board a native prow off Sumatra. The Colonel stated that he was travelling for reasons of health, but one or two false statements and the large amount of cash in his pockets created suspicion. The Resident at Bencoolen sent him as a prisoner to Penang. His papers were seized and letters from the Government of Batavia to the King of Ava and to various persons at Calcutta and other parts of India were found, showing that Houssaye was on a special mission from Daendels to the King of Acheen in Sumatra, and to the Burmese Government to promote connexions inimical to the British.[18]

The incident prompted the Government of Bengal to investigate the political climate in the East Indies and Burma more closely. An agent, David Campbell, was despatched to Acheen to detect any French intrigues in that quarter, to propose to the King the exclusion of all Europeans other than the British, and also to ascertain the possibilities of setting up a British settlement there.[19] The King denied any connexion with the French or the Dutch hostile to British interests, and explained that his uncle in an attempt to usurp the throne had applied to Batavia for aid, and that Houssaye's mission probably had some reference to it. The King requested aid to consolidate his position and offered a grant of territory for the use of a Resident.[20]

Meanwhile, in July 1809, Captain John Canning had been sent to Burma with letters from Minto to the Viceroy of Pegu and the King of Ava. Canning was to explain to the King of Burma the nature of the British blockade of the French Islands, and also to find out the extent of French

18 Parry to Macalister-in-Coun., 15 June 1809 and 20 June 1809; and letters and enclosures from Prince of Wales Island; and Lumsden and Colebrooke to Minto, 26 September 1809, Cons. of 26 September 1809, No. 2, Ben. Sec. Cons. vol. 222.

19 Vice-President-in-Coun. to the Secret Cttee, Ft. William, 6 January 1810, Ben. Sec. Letters, vol. 12.

20 Campbell to Edmonstone, 14 July 1810 and 24 July 1810, Cons. of 29 October 1810, Nos. 3 and 4, Ben(gal) Pol(itical) Cons(ultations) R. 119, vol. 17, Ind. Off. Lib.

influence in the Court.[21] The latter fear had its roots in the past and was stirred up by the abortive mission of Houssaye. In Rangoon, Canning found that Burmese trade was almost wholly with the British territories, and that the King derived a large part of his income from the port dues and trade taxes paid by British merchants. Trade with Mauritius was practically non-existent. Canning reported that no merchant would risk sending a ship to the French Islands now that notice of the blockade had been given. Arriving at Amarapura on 10 February, 1810, he found the Burmese court seething with intrigues and jealousies regarding the succession to the throne. But he found no trace of the French. The Burmese enquired about the principles and justification of the blockade and appeared to be satisfied with his explanation. In an interview on 28 February, the King of Ava refused to accept the Governor-General as his equal, and declared that he would only treat with the King of England on equal terms. The Burmese King's letter to the Governor-General was written in an objectionable style which, according to Canning, surpassed "the usual bounds of even Burmese insolence." The Heir-Apparent was given vague hopes of assistance in the coming struggle for the throne by Canning although he was not authorized to do so. The former ordered that the Lieutenant-Governor of Rangoon should not in future grant passports or protection to ships bound for the French Islands.[22] Canning's report satisfied Minto that the Houssaye affair had aroused a false alarm. He did not wish to establish British influence in the Court of Amarapura, although Canning had independently made an opening by holding out a hope of assistance to the Heir-Apparent. Minto disapproved of this part of Canning's conduct; unwilling to extend Company liabilities he lost interest in Burma once satisfied that there was no hostile European influence there.

The blockade of Java and the Moluccas begun by Rear-Admiral Drury in June 1809 on the orders of the Admiralty, however, proved to be a source of embarrassment to the

[21] Cons. of 20 July 1809, Nos. 9, 10, 11, Ben. Pol. Cons. R.118, vol. 43.

[22] Canning's Report, 8 May 1810, Cons. of 29 May 1810, Paper No. 1, Ben. Pol. Cons. R.119, vol. 4.

Company's Government. One of its objects was to prevent intercourse between Batavia and Mauritius, and to prevent Arab vessels from acting as intermediaries between the two; in effect, the blockade antagonized the Malay States, which traded with both the Dutch and the English. Being unacquainted with the European Law of Nations, they regarded the interruption to their trade and capture of their ships as acts of hostility which invited retaliation. The cessation of trade between the Company and the Malay States would adversely affect the opium trade, one of the principal sources of the Company's revenue, so Minto asked Drury not to enforce the blockade too rigorously, limiting it to the ships actually trading between the Dutch ports and the French Islands.[23] Drury assured Minto that he would interfere as little as possible with the Malay prows which, he said, indulged in piracy against all foreign vessels whenever they were sure of success.[24] However, to the Admiralty Drury complained against "that propensity which is met throughout this Country to direct the navy as a machine, which never can be permitted,"[25] and went ahead with the blockade without any modification. The fears of the Government of Bengal were soon confirmed. Few of the Malay vessels had any regular papers and their crews were hampered by language difficulties. Consequently when the annual fleet of the Bugguese prows from Borneo bound eastward to Malacca and the Prince of Wales Island fell in with H.M.S. *La Piedmontaise*, a severe encounter took place. Minto, anxious for the continuance of trade with the Malays, again requested Drury to modify the blockade to encourage them to renew commercial intercourse with the English.[26] To the King of Boni Minto sent an apology and a present of cloth and military goods.[27] Drury still refused to relinquish the blockade, which had been "the watchword for an universal outcry . . . lest political, and commercial interests of India

[23] G.G.-in-Coun. to Drury, Ft. William, 26 June 1809, Fac. Rec. Java 12; Adm. 1/182.

[24] Drury to Minto, Madras Roads, 18 July 1809, Fac. Rec. Java 12.

[25] Drury to W. Pole, Madras Roads, 17 July 1809, Adm. 1/182.

[26] Minto to Drury, Fort St. George, 18 January 1810, Fac. Rec. Java 12.

[27] Minto to the King of Boni, Fort St. George, 22 January 1810, *ibid.*

should suffer," but he found it impossible to maintain it effectively.[28] He had an extensive coast to cover, and in the course of six months the British took or destroyed only seven French corvettes. Finally, in order to lessen the number of ports to be blockaded, and at the same time to add the valuable spice trade to the Company's opium trade, Drury decided to occupy the Spice Islands. He applied to Minto, who was then in Madras, to provide about 200 British soldiers. In October 1809 Captains Tucker, Montague, and Spencer of the *Dover*, *Cornwallis*, and *Samarang* respectively, were commissioned to occupy Amboyna. The Government of Fort St. George provided 130 men of the Madras 2nd European Regiment and 46 British artillery under Captain Court.[29]

The occupation of the Spice Islands was the first step taken in the direction of British occupation of the Dutch East Indies. On 19 February 1810, Amboyna surrendered. Colonel Filz, the Dutch Commander, declared that he could offer no effective resistance due to the desertion of the Amboynese. The European garrison was largely composed of Polish and Hungarian prisoners-of-war sent there in 1803.[30] The island dependencies of Amboyna, Saperoua, Harouka, Nasso-Laut, Boure, Manippa and Gorontello were occupied soon after.[31] Captain Court took over the government of Amboyna until further orders from Bengal. Many of the former officers took an oath of allegiance to the King of England and were retained in their offices. The paper money, which was in circulation at a deflated rate, was guaranteed by the British, but not the public debt. On 10 August 1810, the island of Banda was taken by the H.M.S. *Caroline*, *Piedmontaise* and *Baracouta* under Captain Cole, with the assistance of Captain Nixon and his Company.[32] Three weeks later Ternate Island

28 Drury to J. W. Croker, Madras Roads, 22 April 1810, Adm. 1/182.

29 G.G-in-Coun. to the Court of Directors, Ft. William, 15 December 1810, Minto Papers, 201.

30 Captain Court to the Gov't. of Fort St. George, 16 April 1810; and Article of Capitulation signed by Filz, Tucker and Court, 18 February 1810, Ben. Pol. Cons. R.119, vol. 14, nos. 23 and 3 respectively.

31 *Asiatic Annual Register*, 1810-11, pp. 21-27.

32 Nixon to the Gov't. of Fort St. George, 12 August 1810, Ben. Pol. Cons. R.119, vol. 19; Captain Cole to Drury, 10 August 1810, Adm. 1/183.

was taken.[33] The question then arose of their future. Drury asked the Government whether it wanted to retain them until the pleasure of the Crown or the Court of Directors was known. Otherwise he proposed to destroy the fortifications and remove all the ships, troops, and Dutch inhabitants from the islands.[34]

Minto was in Madras with Robert Farquhar, who had been Special Commissioner at the Spice Islands during its former occupation and who was preparing to leave with a force against Bourbon. On the basis of information supplied by Farquhar, Minto decided to retain the Moluccas. The primary consideration was of course the commercial advantages. Their occupation meant not only a curtailment of Dutch trade and power but also an equivalent gain to the Company of the rich spice trade. According to Farquhar, after the disbursement of civil and military expenses, a profit of £ 200,000 per annum could be made if the spices were sold in India, and twice that sum if they were sold in Europe.[35] In the first year an advance from Bengal was necessary, as the available spices were claimed by the Navy and troops as prize. But from the second year the Company could profitably engage in the selling of the spice annually at Calcutta and Madras in the public markets. There were also political and strategic advantages in occupying the Spice Islands. They were suitable places of refuge, repairs and supplies to the Company's ships engaged in the China trade at a time when these seas were infested with privateers. Moreover, Minto had in mind the expulsion of the Dutch from Java and the creation of British authority and influence in the East Indies, and he felt that "nothing could be more unfavourable to the promotion of such views than an example of indifference to Native Interests as opposed to the Dutch and a sudden and instant abandonment of the former to the destructive vengeance of the latter."[36] It was likely that if

33 *Asiatic Annual Register*, 1810-11, pp. 27-32.

34 Drury to Admiralty, Madras Roads, 22 April 1810, Adm. 1/182; Minto to Charles Grant, Madras, 30 April 1810, Minto Papers, Box 67.

35 Farquhar's Memorandum, 25 April 1810, Ben. Pol. Cons. R. 119, vol. 4, no. 42.

36 G.G.-in-Coun. to the Court of Directors, Ft. William, 15 December 1810, Minto Papers, 201.

the Spice Islands were abandoned, the inhabitants would have to pay dearly for their disaffection to the Dutch at the time of the British attack. On these grounds Minto decided to retain the Islands. Captain Court was confirmed in his office, and was placed under the direct control of the Government of Bengal. Major Kelly was sent with reinforcements to take charge of the garrison at Amboyna.[37] Minto hoped to keep the Islands under Company control and he wrote to the Chairman of the Court of Directors:

> There can be little doubt, that the French Islands will be placed more advantageously and conveniently under the King's immediate Government than under that of the Company. I am disposed to think otherwise respecting the Moluccas, both from their local situation and from their connexion with trade.[38]

In January 1810, when Minto undertook the attack against the French Islands, the Governor-General-in-Council wrote to the Secret Committee:

> It is on the Island of Java alone that the power of the Enemy can ever become formidable. The small extent of the Territory of the French Islands, their distance from India and deficient resources impose a limit on the aggrandisement of the strength of the French and on their means of injury in that quarter. But no such limitation attends the possessions of the Dutch in the Eastern Islands.[39]

In Minto's opinion, the appointment of an officer of Daendels's celebrity and the military measures adopted by him indicated the importance which the French attached to Java.

Although Daendels had not received reinforcements from Europe, he was busy raising a local army of between 15 and 20 thousand. His aims were most probably defensive. Unlike the French Islands, Java was self-sufficient, and there-

[37] Edmonstone to Marten, 23 November 1810, Ben. Pol. Cons. R.119, vol. 19.

[38] Minto to Charles Grant, 30 April 1810, Minto Papers, Box 67.

[39] G.G.-in-Coun. to the Secret Cttee., Ft. William, 23 January 1810, Ben. Sec. Letters, vol. 12.

fore despite the blockade the troops could be maintained. Its geographical situation gave Java a particular importance for the British. It was situated closer to the Bay of Bengal than the French Islands, and it was also dangerously close to the China trade route. The anxiety of the British for the safety of the China trade is understandable, for between 1793 and 1810, the East India Company's trade with India yielded an average annual profit of £309,561, whereas with China it yielded £981,932.[40] It was not improbable that after the loss of the French Islands the French would regard Java as their only means of a foothold east of the Cape. Minto wrote to the Secret Committee on 26 October, 1810:

> Indeed from the first establishment of the French authority and even influence in Holland, we have been accustomed to regard the exclusion of the Dutch power from Java and the Eastern seas generally as one of those essential objects of national policy to which the British Arms might perhaps be more beneficially directed than to any other and it requires no argument to prove that the recent events in Europe as they have affected the United Provinces alone increase in a high degree both the importance and the urgency of extinguishing in the Island of Java, a power which is now formally as well as substantially directed by the French Counsel and the Seat of which is in fact a province of the French Empire.[41]

It was decided that operations against Java would be commenced immediately after the conquest of Mauritius. The conquest of both places was regarded by Minto as successive steps in his project for the expulsion of the French from all their footholds in the eastern seas. He wrote to Major-General Abercromby:

> It is superfluous to advert to the extreme importance of the complete expulsion of the Enemy's power from the Indian Seas. This object will be but imperfectly accomplished by

40 *Parliamentary Papers* (*House of Commons*), 1812, vii, 431.

41 G.G.-in-Coun. to the Secret Cttee, 26 October 1810, Minto Papers, 196.

the conquest of the French Islands. I have all along, however, combined the expulsion of the Dutch from their Eastern Establishments with the conquest of the French Islands as an essential part of the same plan, recommended by the same principles of policy and rendered at once more urgent and more easy of execution by success in the former enterprise.[42]

So after the successful conclusion of the Mauritius operation, Farquhar and Abercromby were requested to return with their men immediately, leaving a garrison of Cape troops at Port Louis. A force of four thousand British troops and an equal number of sepoys with a due proportion of artillery and pioneers were considered sufficient for a successful campaign. Drury's cooperation was also sought. In the meantime, it was necessary to collect more accurate and complete information about Daendels's army and fortifications than had been already received, and to find out if the Javanese and Malay Princes of the neighbouring islands were disposed to fight against the Dutch, or at least remain neutral in the coming contest.[43] Accordingly Minto employed Thomas Stamford Raffles, Assistant Secretary to the Government of Prince of Wales Island, who was then (June 1810) on a visit to Calcutta "with the expectation of still further advance in my interest with Lord Minto."[44] Minto found Raffles an expert and enthusiast about the affairs of the Eastern Islands whose services would be extremely useful, and Raffles found in Minto a patron. Of the others whom Minto consulted on Malay affairs, John Leyden's interest in the east was academic, but Robert Farquhar could have been a prospective rival for Raffles. From the French Islands Farquhar wrote about the importance of Java, enumerating its resources and

[42] Minto to Maj.-Gen. Abercromby, Ft. William, 3 September 1810, Cons. of 7 January 1811, No. 1, Ben. Sec. Cons. 236.

[43] Minto to Abercromby, 5 October 1810; Minto to the Earl of Caledon, 19 October 1810; and Minto to Drury, 5 October 1810, Fac. Rec. Java 12.

[44] Drury had recommended Raffles for Resident at Amboyna. Raffles was not interested in that appointment; nor did the prospect of a post at Penang appeal. Lady Raffles, *Memoir of the Life and Public Services of Sir Thomas Stamford Raffles* (London, 1830), p. 88.

proposing to give up his office as Governor of Mauritius for that of Java.[45] Raffles's memorandum to Minto was along similar lines.[46] He proposed that he should be authorized to go to Malacca to open communications with the Malay and Javanese chiefs. According to him the Sultan of Palembang and the King of Bantam could be easily won over. Also the Rajas of Bali, an island at the eastern end of Java, were supposed to be hostile to the Dutch. He suggested that for the sake of secrecy it should be publicized that his visit was to justify the blockade to the Raja of Linga and other eastern states. If Minto wished, he could stop at Acheen on his way to Malacca or Penang.[47] In short, Raffles requested that the diplomatic preparations for the Javanese venture be entrusted to him. Therefore for these purposes on 19th October 1810 Raffles was appointed Agent to the Governor-General with the Malay States and instructed to proceed to the Prince of Wales Island, then to Malacca and as far eastward as necessary. He was to collect charts, plans, reports, and information regarding Daendels's military establishments, the facilities for landing, the nature of the country in general, and particularly the enemy's position, the principal points at which attack should be directed, and the facilities of communication from point to point. He was to select Malay and European guides and interpreters to assist in the matter. Captain William Farquhar, Resident at Malacca, was to help in all military matters. The disaffected Javanese chiefs were to be encouraged to resist Daendels's pressures, but not aroused to commit acts of hostility against the Dutch beforehand. Raffles's suggestions regarding the relations to be maintained with Palembang, Bantam, Lampong and Bali were sanctioned by the Government.[48]

45 R. T. Farquhar to Minto, Bourbon, 21 August 1810, Cons. of 19 October 1810, No. 11; and Farquhar to the G.G.-in-Coun., Port Louis, Isle of France, 18 January 1811, Cons. of 3 May 1811, No. 1, Ben. Sec. Cons. 231 and 233 respectively.

46 Memorandum proposing capture of Java from French, 1810, by Raffles, (incomplete), Raff(les) Coll(ection), II, MSS. Eur. E. 104, Ind. Off. Lib.

47 Raffles to Minto, Calcutta, 11 July 1810 and 9 August 1810, Raff. Coll. I, MSS. Eur. C. 34.

48 Edmonstone to Raffles, Ft. William, 19 October 1810, Fac. Rec. Java 12.

In the meantime, on receiving orders from the Admiralty, Drury had independently set in motion arrangements for despatching a force to Java, with the assistance of the Madras Government. This annoyed Minto intensely. He sent strict orders to the subordinate governments of Madras and Ceylon not to make any plans without orders from Bengal.[49] Drury was politely but sternly reminded that his duty was to co-operate with the Bengal Government.[50] The tussle between the two was with regard to the departure date and route of the ships and troops from India to the East Indies. According to Drury, unless the expedition set out from India on 1 March it would be impossible to make the passage from Malacca to Java before the outbreak of the south-east monsoon which prevailed in the Java seas from May to August.[51] Minto had planned that the British troops from Mauritius were to embark at Madras while the sepoys would leave Bengal about the middle of March, rendezvousing at Malacca no later than the middle of May. Sir Samuel Auchmuty, who had arrived from England too late to command the Mauritius foray, was given command of the 4000 British soldiers, 4000 sepoys, one company of Royal Artillery, 200 Company's artillery-men and 300 pioneers. According to Minto's calculations they could reach Java by the end of June, allowing four months of dry season for the operation.[52] One serious danger was that they would run into the monsoon season. But Minto decided to take the risk rather than postpone the expedition until the following year.[53] It might appear that he was disregarding the opinion of experienced naval officers and deliberately hazarding the lives of his men. Actually Minto was depending on what first-hand information Raffles and Captain Greig, who had been sent to Malacca to examine

[49] G.G.-in-Coun. to Barlow-in-Coun., Ft. William, 8 February 1811, *ibid.*, 11.

[50] G.G.-in-Coun. to Drury, Ft. William, 8 February 1811, *ibid.*

[51] Drury to Auchmuty, 'Diomede', 23 February 1811, *ibid.*; Drury to Minto, Madras Roads, 28 February 1811, *ibid*, 12.

[52] Minto to Auchmuty, Ft. William, 31 January 1811, Minto Papers, 372; G.G.-in-Coun. to the Secret Cttee, 28 February 1811, Ben. Sec. Letters, vol. 13.

[53] Minto to Raffles, Calcutta, 11 March 1811, Raff. Coll. I; Minto to the Secret Cttee, at sea, 15 March 1811, Ben. Sec. Letters, vol. 13; Minto to Lady Minto, 'Modeste' off Java, Letter ended on 3 August 1811, Minto Papers, 39.

and survey a practicable route from Malacca to Batavia during monsoon, could provide. The Java seas had been a close monopoly of the Dutch. No charts or surveys had so far been made by the British. Drury's informant was Captain Cole of H.M.S. *Caroline*, who had been cruising in the area for two years but had made no actual survey. Drury's haste is understandable, not only because Batavia was expected to provide a rich plunder, but also because he wanted the operation well under way before his imminent retirement. His hopes were thwarted by his death in Madras, just on the eve of the sailing of the expedition.

The most remarkable feature of the whole affair was that Minto not only supervized the military and political arrangements but also accompanied the expedition. His decision caused quite a furore among the big-wigs at the seat of Government. A later critic, Lord Curzon, called it "a most undesirable proceeding, undertaken on his own responsibility and without orders."[54] Minto was away from Bengal for seven months. His main excuse was that he could not trust anyone else to take the many important decisions necessary. Since Raffles could not come to Calcutta, Minto decided to meet him at Malacca to draw up the final plans in consultation with him and Auchmuty. His object was to collect personally first-hand information which would enable him to advise the Home authorities with greater confidence. The occupation of Java was to crown his work as Governor-General. He saw in it the prospect of permanent establishment of British authority in the East Indies. In his own words, "the object we have in view is of the greatest national importance and value, and it is of infinite consequence that the first political arrangements should be made on right principles."[55] However, in the opinion of the Directors, Minto should have attended to the more important matters of his office; for instance, financial remittances to the Company were overdue. It was hinted by his enemies that he wanted a share of the prize.[56] According to some, the "Good Maharaja of Bengal"

[54] G. N. Curzon, *British Government in India* (London, 1925), ii, 184.

[55] Minto to Lady Minto, 20 March 1811, Minto Papers, 39.

[56] R. Dundas to Minto, 10 July 1811, Minto Papers, Box 72; and Gilbert Elliot to Minto, London, 2 April 1812, Minto Papers, 83; *Hansard* (1st Series), xxi, 138.

was delivering the Javanese from Dutch oppression in order to set up a benevolent government.[57] According to others, it signified the revival of the ancient connection of the two Indies and the opening of the area to trade.[58]

Two questions, however, remained unanswered: what route were the ships to follow from Malacca to Batavia; and would the natives — princes and people — welcome the British and render them assistance? With the co-operation of Captain Greig, Raffles had succeeded in answering the first, but his assurances with regard to the second were unduly optimistic. During the actual campaign all the native chiefs remained neutral, except the Susuhonan or the Emperor, who sent an army to stand by the Dutch at Samarang. Luckily for Minto, a safe route from Malacca was found through the Straits of Durion.[59] The Governor-General's ship led the fleet of a hundred ships and twelve thousand men which arrived off Batavia by 30 July, 1811.[60] A week later the British were in occupation, and on 26 August the Dutch stronghold at Meester Cornelis was stormed.[61] The Dutch Governor, General Janssens, finally surrendered Java and all its island dependencies on 18 September, 1811, after a heroic resistance.[62] The British now had an unique position in the Indian sea. The French flag was eliminated and for the rest of the Napoleonic Wars they had no rival in the area. Minto could very well congratulate himself. But this was only the realization of part of his dream. His larger aim was to add the East Indies permanently to the British Empire and to lay the foundations of Britain's commercial and political infiltration into Malaysia. Contrary therefore to the orders of the Company, Minto issued a procla-

57 Lady Raffles, *Memoir*, p. 25.

58 Raffles to Minto, Malacca, 18 February 1811, Raff. Coll. I.

59 Memorandum respecting passage from Malacca to Java presented by Raffles to Minto, Malacca, 22 May 1811, *ibid.*

60 Minto to Hewitt, Weltevreeden, 18 August 1811, Minto Papers, 174; and Minto to Lady Minto, letter ended on 3 August 1811, *ibid.*, 39.

61 Minto to the Secret Cttee, Weltevreeden, 29 August 1811, Ben. Sec. Letters, vol. 13.

62 Auchmuty to Minto, 'Modeste' off Samarang, 21 September 1811; and Articles of Capitulation, 18 September 1811, Fac. Rec. Java 9.

mation declaring the establishment of British authority over Java,[63] followed by another on 11 September, 1811 announcing the annexation of Java and its dependencies to the East India Company.[64] He did not regard himself authorized to appoint a Governor, and the appointment of a Resident would have been inadequate considering the importance of the colony. There had been an expectation among the Army that the colony might be placed under military rule, with either Auchmuty or the hero of Cornelis, John Gillespie, at the top. Minto thought a civil government more in the interest of good administration and Java's permanent occupation.[65] Raffles's knowledge, experience, and interest in the East Indies, and his intimacy with Minto's ideas rendered his claims and suitability greater than those of any other. Minto had in fact already promised him "the best attainable situation."[66]

The Java administration was formed on the model of an Indian presidency, with Raffles as Lieutenant-Governor and directly responsible to Minto. The Commander of the Forces was given the second rank and made head of the Council of three. Gillespie was appointed Commander, but clashes between him and Raffles assumed such proportions that he was soon removed. The two civil members of the Council were Dutch. The Lieutenant-Governor could overrule the Council in cases of importance or emergency, or even in times of war or internal trouble regulate military affairs without the knowledge or advice of the Council.[67] The recent army insubordination in Madras had made Minto particularly alive to the danger of a collision between civil and military. Civil authority was to be supreme. A large force was to remain to establish British authority more

63 Proclamation issued at Weltevreeden on 26 August 1811 by Lord Minto, Raff. Coll. III, MSS. Eur. E105, Ind. Off. Lib.

64 Proclamation (No. 1), done at Molenvliet, 11 September 1811, Cons. of 6 December 1811, Ben. Sec. Cons. 234.

65 G. G. to the Secret Cttee, Batavia, 18 October 1811, Ben. Sec. Letters, vol. 13.

66 Minto to Raffles, Calcutta, 11 March 1811, Raff. Coll. I.

67 G.G.'s Minute, Ft. William, 6 December 1811, Cons. of 6 December 1811, Ben. Sec. Cons. 234.

firmly and also to keep off the French. Minto had decided to employ the Dutch in the civil administration both to reconcile them to the change of government and to make use of their knowledge of Dutch and Malay and local affairs. The Dutch laws were left standing, with provisions to safeguard the rights of the British-born. The Lieutenant-Governor was given the power to promulgate laws and regulations, subject of course to the approval of the Government of Bengal.[68] Minto's intention was "to introduce as much and as early as possible an English character in the affairs of a country which cannot become English in habits and feeling too early". But although Minto would have liked the colony to be run by British officers, it was found impossible to do without the Dutch who possessed a knowledge of the Malay language and local customs.[69] Torture was abolished in Malacca and Java,[70] and slavery mitigated.[71]

With regard to the native states of the island, the British inherited the Dutch system of indirect rule. The chiefs were nominally independent, though under an obligation to sell their produce at very low prices to the conqueror. They also paid a tribute and were compelled to bow to the directions of a Minister resident at their courts. The British followed this practice, appointing Residents at the Courts of the Susuhonan and the Sultan of Mataram at a salary of Rs. 1,500 per month. A small garrison was placed at Fort Angier, which commanded the trade route between Batavia and Sumatra, under Major Yule, the Resident to the Court of Bantam. The Dutch post and factory at Macassar in the Celebes was retained; the abandoned factory at Banjermasin, on the southern coast of Borneo, reoccupied; and the direction of these and other native principalities, including the islands of Timor, Bangka and Palembang, was left to Raffles. Within the following year Raffles succeeded, with the Governor-General's approval, in strengthening British authority over the Susuhonan; in replacing the Sultans of Mataram and Djojacarta; and in

68 Proclamation (No. 2), done at Molenvliet, 11 September 1811, *ibid.*

69 G.G.'s Minute, 6 December 1811, Cons. of 6 December 1811, *ibid.*

70 Minto to Lady Minto, Malacca, 31 May 1811, Minto Papers, 39.

71 G.G. to Secret Cttee, 5 October 1811, Ben. Sec. Letters, vol. 13.

deposing the Sultan of Palembang for his brother, who ceded the islands of Bangka and Billiton, which were rich in tin, to the British.[72]

At the time of the conquest the Dutch settlements were in the grip of a severe inflation. It was therefore declared by Minto that an amount not exceeding 4½ million rix-dollars in Government paper, and 4 million of the Orphan paper, would be recognized as legal tender at the rate of 6½ paper rix-dollars to one Spanish silver dollar. To create a fund for the gradual liquidation of this debt, the paper-money was charged an annual duty of 5 per cent on the fixed value, and the resulting monies invested in government securities.[73] Perhaps a little hastily, Minto assured the Court of Directors that Java would not be a financially unprofitable venture,[74] as its resources were considerable. The finances of Raffles's government might have been stabilized with the proceeds of trade in opium, spice and timber, but in view of the larger interests of the Company the opium trade was thrown open to the Calcutta merchants. It was hoped that the Company would gain more from this arrangement, which did include the payment of compensation to the Batavian Government for the loss of revenue.[75] As the Moluccas' spice continued to be sent directly to the markets of Calcutta and Madras, there was an increase in the export of specie from the island, and acute depreciation of the value of paper money resulted.[76] The financial crisis became worse when the Government of Bengal asked the Batavian Government not to draw any more bills on Bengal.[77]

To obviate the economic stress Raffles introduced certain land reforms. Minto had found the whole system of property "vicious, and adverse alike to the interest of Government and

[72] G.G.'s Minute, 6 December 1811, Ben. Sec. Cons. 234.

[73] Proclamation (No. 3), done at Molenvliet, 11 September 1811, Cons. of 6 December 1811, *ibid.*

[74] Minto to the Secret Cttee, Weltevreeden, 5 October 1811, Ben. Sec. Letters, vol. 13.

[75] Minto to Raffles, 28 February 1812, Raff. Coll. I.

[76] J. Bastin, *The Native Policies of Sir Stamford Raffles in Java and Sumatra* (Oxford, 1957), p. 19.

[77] Raffles to Minto, 30 October 1812, Minto Papers, Box 76.

people."[78] He decided that the systems of forced coffee cultivation, contingents, and forced deliveries should be abolished and that the land system should be reformed in order to stimulate the industry of the people and to increase revenue. Under the Dutch, revenues and monopolies had been farmed out, mainly to the Chinese, who were regarded by the British as interlopers. Minto advised Raffles to end this but cautioned that "the system is too extensive to be suddenly or ignorantly attempted."[79] When land reform was eventually introduced by Raffles in October 1813, the home authorities' decision with regard to Java's future was not yet known. Gillespie's opposition in the Council to every measure proposed aggravated Raffles's uncertainty over the life of his administration. He turned to Minto for support and encouragement, saying that he wanted to receive the Government's sanction to his measures before Minto's retirement, so that all reforms could be "effected by the hand that designed it and under the superintendence of the head that directed it."[80]

Under Minto's aegis certain principles of liberal government were introduced into Java during the short British occupation. He advocated free trade and free cultivation as the best means of increasing prosperity. According to the best liberal tradition, his main object was to combine the interests of the state with the happiness of the people. Minto realized that Java might at the end of the war revert to Holland, but in his opinion "this ought not surely to prevent us from beginning to perform the first duty of Governments, in improving the condition of mankind, and of a people that has become subject to our authority, and tributary to our prosperity."[81] Furnivall writes that the Dutch themselves regard the British occupation as a turning point in their colonial administration.[82] According to K. M. Panikkar, the Dutch had never pretended that they had any moral obligation towards the Javanese. The relations between the Dutch Government and its subjects

78 Minto to the Secret Cttee, 5 October 1811, Ben. Sec. Letters, vol. 13.

79 *Ibid.*; Minto to Raffles, 26 February 1812, Raff. Coll. I.

80 Raffles to Minto, Buitenzorg, 10 July 1813, Minto Papers, Box 76.

81 Minto to R. Dundas, Weltevreeden, 6 October 1811, *ibid.*, 377.

82 Furnivall, *Netherlands India*, pp. 67, 78.

had been those of planter and coolie.[83] Minto, on the other hand, recognized the duties and responsibilities of a ruling authority. The Javanese were given the same general privileges as those enjoyed by British subjects in India, including the freedom to trade with all British territories east of the Cape, as well as with England. One perceives a mixture of humanitarian and utilitarian motives in Minto's views. He wanted to make Java an English colony as quickly as possible "by the introduction of English colonists, English capital and therefore an English interest."[84]

From the very beginning Minto had been determined to occupy the Dutch East Indies in the name of the Company rather than to place it under the Crown, like Ceylon or the newly-acquired French Islands. The fact that the orders of the Secret Committee had also the approval of His Majesty's Government was interpreted by him as "a transfer of His Majesty's right of conquest in this particular instance to the Company."[85] The Court of Directors, however, did not agree with his reasoning. They had only approved the overthrow of the Dutch; not the occupation of the area. Minto was informed that the final decision was up to His Majesty's Government. He was advised to adopt only such arrangements for the provisional administration of Java as were indispensably necessary.[86] The question of Java's future was not decided until the end of 1813. Minto wrote untiringly to both the Secretary of State for War and Colonies and to the Court of Directors for the retention of the Dutch East Indies under the Company — without success. In October 1813, Lord Bathurst, Secretary of State for War and the Colonies, informed the President of the Board of Control that Java and its dependencies should be placed on the footing of a Royal Government.[87] Before the new arrangement

83 K. M. Panikkar, *Asia and Western Dominance* (London, 1954), pp. 111, 113.

84 Minto to R. Dundas, Weltevreeden, 6 October 1811, Minto Papers, 377.

85 Minto to the Secret Cttee, Batavia, 3 September 1811, Minto Papers, 209; Ben. Sec. Letters, vol. 13.

86 Secret Cttee to G.G.-in-Coun., 23 December 1811, Board's Secret Drafts, vol. 4, No. 77, Ind. Off. Lib.

87 Lord Bathurst to the Earl of Buckinghamshire, Downing Street, 26 October 1813, Fac. Rec. Java 65.

could be made, negotiations for peace started in Europe, and the Dutch East Indies was one of the colonial conquests which Castlereagh, now Foreign Secretary, was willing to exchange for a better bargain elsewhere. The case for their retention was not very strong, because the Company had not received any commercial profits or surplus revenues despite Raffles's assurances that they would in normal times. On 19 August, 1816, the Dutch flag was once again hoisted in Batavia. The Spice Islands were restored in 1817, and Malacca and Padang in 1818. Consequently the whole eastern archipelago again came under Dutch influence, the British retaining only their posts at Penang and Bencoolen. All Minto's dreams and determination had been in vain.

Minto's expansionist policy with regard to the Dutch East Indies originally aimed at expelling all European foes of the British from the Indian Ocean. It gradually widened its scope to include the permanent establishment of the Company's rule over Java and its dependencies and visualized the establishment of diplomatic and commercial relations with the independent Malay chiefs so that the British would retain their commercial and political agreements with these chiefs even if the Dutch settlements were restored to Holland after the war. It was not until the foundation of Singapore in 1818 that the British were able once more to establish themselves at a vantage point within the Malayan Archipelago and challenge the Dutch political and commercial monopoly of the East Indies.

# THE ADOPTION DESPATCH OF 16 APRIL 1867: ITS ORIGINS AND SIGNIFICANCE

DONOVAN WILLIAMS

The Queen's Proclamation of November 1858[1] and Earl Canning's grant of adoption *sanads* in 1860 to all sovereign chiefs and princes under British rule,[2] together sought to assure Indian rulers that there would be no further annexations of territory, and that their estates would not be forfeited if there was failure of heirs. Thus Dalhousie's doctrine of lapse, that fruitful cause of the Mutiny, was officially rejected. But until 1867 it was by no means certain that the promises of the Proclamation and the intentions of the *sanads* were to be honoured. The temptations of victory included territorial aggrandizement, and not until 1867 was the principle firmly established that it was British policy to perpetuate Indian states rather than to annex them. For, in spite of Canning's professions of conciliation and the desire to instil certainty where uncertainty had prevailed, he had omitted to include the Maharajah of Mysore in the list of Princes to whom adoption *sanads* were granted. This omission deprived the Maharajah of the right to adopt a successor, and when he died his state would be at the disposal of the British Govern-

[1] A. B. Keith, *Speeches and Documents on Indian Policy 1750-1921* (Oxford, 1922) i, 383. Canning was Viceroy, 1856-62.

[2] Canning to Secretary of State for India in Council, 30 Apl. (43A) 1860, Coll(ections) to Pol(itical) Des(patches) to Ind(ia), 21/59, Coll. 1, Ind(ia) Off(ice) Lib(rary).

ment.[3] The adoption despatch of 16 April 1867 ensured that this would not happen. Thus it is a landmark in the history of British policy towards Indian states, laying the foundation for the rendition of Mysore in 1881. Further, it was a despatch which was rooted in a renewed appreciation in the India Office of the intrinsic merit of Indian polity. The denial of this merit had provided the excuse for much of the territorial acquisition which had preceded the Mutiny. The adoption despatch is usually mentioned in histories of British policy in India, but its significance has been underestimated.[4] Also, there is no detailed analysis of the policy-making in the India Office which shaped the despatch.[5] Sir Stafford Northcote (Secretary of State for India, 1867-1868) launched it in the Commons, but an investigation into activity behind the scenes reveals that he was influenced by others, and that the despatch was the outcome of several years of unremitting effort on the part of a small group of administrators under the leadership of Sir George Russell Clerk[6] who, by attrition, achieved their goal in the face of opposition from a substantial core of less accommodating officials.

These officials were the heirs to half a century of paramountcy[7] and tended to advocate excessive intervention in the affairs of Indian states, annexation and the subjection of treaty rights to political expediency. Their attitude had been shaped before Dalhousie's time.[8] Constituting two-thirds

3 Durand to Wood, 7 Jan. 1863, Mysore Papers, (in) Halifax Papers, Ind. Off. Lib.

4 Two recent publications which fail to stress the significance of the adoption despatch are T. R. Metcalf's *The Aftermath of Revolt: India 1857-1870* (Princeton, 1965), pp. 227-237, and S. Gopal's *British Policy in India 1858-1905* (Cambridge, 1965), pp. 9-10. R. J. Moore's conclusions in *Sir Charles Wood's Indian Policy 1853-66* (Manchester, 1966) do not differ substantially from my own.

5 I assume a knowledge of India Office procedure as outlined in my article "The Council of India and the Relationship between the Home and Supreme Governments 1858-1870," *English Historical Review*, lxxxi, 318 (Jan. 1966), p. 61.

6 1800-1889: in India, 1817-1848; Governor of Bombay, 1860-1862; Council of India, 1863-1886.

7 British paramountcy over India was effectively established by 1818.

8 Canning to Wood, 22 July 1861, Halifax Papers, Ind. Off. Corres(pondence), Ind. Off. Lib.

of the Council of India,[9] their reputation was such that Clerk doubted if these "reactionists",[10] the "old Rump" of the Court of Directors (as he called them), would sanction Canning's policy of granting adoption *sanads*.[11] Canning himself mentioned three of them who were likely to oppose the measure[12] — Ross Donelly Mangles,[13] Sir John Lawrence[14] and Sir John Pollard Willoughby.[15]

Despite these fears, however, the policy of adoption *sanads* was unwillingly sanctioned by the "old Rump" of the Council. There could be little active opposition in Council with Queen Victoria pressing the Secretary of State and the Viceroy for a change of policy, admiring Canning's minute on adoptions and hoping that it would be sanctioned.[16] Her interest was sufficient to silence the most vocal dissentient. Hence, although many on the Council did not like the despatch approving the measure, it was passed without opposition.[17] However, in spite of this apparent victory against the reactionists, until 1863 a cautious and even retrograde policy dominated the India Office in contrast to the spirit of the Queen's Proclamation and the policy of Canning's adoption *sanads*.[18] Sir

9 Clerk to Canning, 23 June 1860, Canning Papers, Letters from Governor of Bombay, Harewood House.

10 Henceforth I use the term "reactionist" in the Clerk sense of the word which is perhaps best defined by the *Oxford English Dictionary*, viii (1933), quoting the *Journal of Education*: "Nobody except the chronic reactionist and constitutional grumbler wants to keep back the coloured people".

11 Clerk to Canning, 23 June 1860, Canning Papers, Letters from Governor of Bombay.

12 Canning to Wood, 13 June 1860, Halifax Papers, Ind. Off. Corres. Also Canning to Clerk, 8 June 1860, Clerk Papers, Ind. Off. Lib.

13 1801-1877: in India, 1820-1839; Director, E.I.C., Chairman, 1857; Council of India, 1858-1866.

14 1811-1879: in India, 1830-1859; Council of India, 1859-1864.

15 1798-1866: in India, 1817-1851; Director, E.I.C., 1854; Council of India, 1858-1866. Canning misjudged Willoughby who was less of a reactionist than he imagined. See Willoughby to Clerk, 16 Nov. 1862, Clerk Papers.

16 Queen Victoria to Wood, 19 June 1860, Halifax Papers, Letters from the Queen.

17 Cf. Wood to Canning, 10 August 1860, Halifax Papers, Ind. Off. Corres.

18 T. R. Metcalf, in *The Aftermath of Revolt*, p. 220 says that "The Mutiny had in fact completely destroyed that self-confident enthusiasm which had led Dalhousie down the path of annexation". True enough, but it was still there, driven underground (if one may use another metaphor).

Charles Wood (Secretary of State for India, 1859-1864), the majority of the Council of India, Herman Merivale (Permanent Under-Secretary of State for India, 1860-1874) and J. R. Melville, Assistant Secretary in the Political Department, were, in varying degrees, party to it during the sixties. Rooted in paramountcy it had its attractions for an India recovering from the Mutiny and requiring, as they thought, tight control to prevent another outbreak. This reactionary attitude had to be successfully challenged before the adoption despatch of 1867 could be launched. Its greatest triumph was the rejection of the petition of the Maharajah of Mysore of 23 February 1861, for the restoration of his principality.

## II

After the defeat of Tipu Sultan the British, by the Treaty of Alliance, 8 July 1799, created an independent Hindu state in Mysore with a five-year-old boy, Kristna Raj Wodyar, as Maharajah. In 1810 he assumed the direct government of the state. Britain, however, retained the right to intervene to safeguard the welfare of the people. Maladministration culminated in insurrection in 1831, whereupon the British deposed the Maharajah. From 1834 to 1861 the state was well administered by Sir Mark Cubbon, and when he left, the Maharajah petitioned Canning for the restoration of his kingdom. Canning refused the request on the grounds that the peace and prosperity of Mysore were threatened. Lord Elgin (Viceroy, 1862-1863) continued this policy. In the India Office Wood drew strength from these decisions, and in a despatch dated 17 July 1863 he negatived the claim.[19]

The fashioning of this despatch begins with the formation of a special committee by Wood to deal with the Maharajah's request. The committee consisted of Sir Henry Thoby Prinsep,[20] Sir Henry Conyngham Montgomery,[21] William Joseph Eastwick,[22]

19 *Parl(iamentary) Papers, H(ouse) of C(ommons)*, 1866, lii, 499-504.

20 1792-1878: in India, 1809-1843; M. P. Harwich, 1850; Director, E. I. C., 1850; Council of India, 1858-1874.

21 1803-1879: in India, 1825-1857; Council of India, 1858-1876.

22 1808-1889: in India, 1826-1841; Director, E.I.C., 1846; Deputy Chairman, 1858; Council of India, 1858-1868.

William Urquhart Arbuthnot,[23] Sir Frederick Currie,[24] Sir John Willoughby and Sir John Lawrence. All except Montgomery and Arbuthnot were members of the usual Political Committee of the India Office during the years 1860-1864.

This special committee decided that the Subsidiary Treaty of 1799 authorized only the temporary assumption of the administration of Mysore. The members thought that the proceedings of the Supreme and Home Governments of India, after the assumption of the administration of Mysore by Bentinck in 1831, contemplated the restoration of the country at some future date. Such a restoration would take place when the condition of the country and the qualifications of the prince claiming to be reinstated afforded reasonable hope that the transfer of authority could be made without detriment to the people. The committee found no evidence that the Maharajah was now more capable of conducting the uncontrolled administration of his country than he was at the time of its temporary sequestration. However, subject to safeguards, Mysore could be restored. Certain administrative arrangements were essential, the most important of which was that the Resident should assist and guide the Maharajah in all departments to ensure that there should be no major change in the system which had worked so well for nearly thirty years.[25]

The decision was a compromise. It was the outcome of a struggle between the desire to annex Mysore and the recognition of the fact that there were no legal grounds for withholding the principality from the Maharajah. Willoughby, Lawrence, Currie, Montgomery and Arbuthnot were convinced that the latter was the case.[26] Prinsep and Eastwick, on the other hand, harboured sentiments which, if unrestrained,

[23] 1807-1874: in India, 1826-1858; Council of India, 1858-1874.

[24] 1799-1875: in India, 1820-1853; Director, E.I.C., 1854; Chairman, 1857; Council of India, 1858-1875.

[25] "Draft Report of Political Committee", undated, Coll. Pol. Des. to Ind. 67/48, Coll. 1. The signatures indicate that this "Political Committee" was, in fact, the special committee (the augmented Political Committee of the Council of India) constituted to deal with the claims of the Maharajah. See also Wood to Elgin, 9 Oct. (No. 1) 1862, Halifax Papers, Ind. Off. Corres.

[26] Wood to Elgin, 9 Oct. (No. 1) 1862, *ibid.*

would have resulted in retaining a European administration, if not in an outright rejection of the Maharajah's request.[27] The compromise was reached by making use of the principle that Britain was morally responsible for the welfare of all inhabitants of the sub-continent. This is clear from the minuting of the reactionists. Prinsep was steadfast in his opposition to the restoration. He maintained that it was the duty of the British Government to impress upon the Maharajah his utter dependence on Britain, as the population of Mysore must be saved from "the vicious system" which prevailed under other native governments. Bentinck had taken over the direct management of Mysore to salvage the population from anarchy and ruin. Why place faith in the promise that the Maharajah would rule well? "We can't expect him to be other now at 70 years of age from what he was at 40". Every effort should be made to deny the "weak wishes of a worthless spendthrift Raja, of tried incompetence".[28] Lawrence noted on the first draft of the despatch[29] that the only real safeguard for a stable government was to maintain Mysore under European administration.[30] Sir Erskine Perry, who was not a member of the special committee but who was obviously called upon by Wood to give an opinion which would have standing in law, minuted that " . . . the Supreme principle on which all acts of high policy rest as a sound basis — *salus populi* — forbids the restoration of Mysore;" the *status quo* should be maintained.[31] This argument, that Britain had a moral obligation in India, was advanced by the reactionists as well as their opponents, to prevent an unqualified restoration. Wood was taken by it, and his alteration to the first draft despatch[32] reflected his concern for Britain's "sacred

27 For Prinsep see his *The Indian Question in 1853* (London, 1853), p. 7, and Memo., undated, in Coll. Pol. Des. to Ind. 67/48, Coll. 1; for Eastwick, see his unsigned, undated memo. in India Office Notes on the Opening of the Civil Service, MSS. Eur. D. 557, Ind. Off. Lib.

28 Memo. by Prinsep, undated, Coll. Pol. Des. to Ind. 67/48, Coll. 1.

29 First draft despatch, Wood to G(overnor)-Gen(eral)-in-Coun(cil), 17 July (48) 1863, *ibid.*

30 Minutes by Lawrence on first draft despatch, *ibid.*

31 Memo. by Perry, 19 Nov. 1862, Mysore Papers, Halifax Papers.

32 Wood's amendment to first draft despatch, Coll. Pol. Des. to Ind. 67/48, Coll. 1. I am unable to say whether this is Wood's draft or not.

duty towards the people of Mysore, incumbent upon the British Govt." This was also the tenor of the second draft despatch[33] which rejected the claims of the Maharajah.

The second draft despatch was subjected to the patient scrutiny of Herman Merivale, lately arrived in the India Office from a similar position as Permanent Under-Secretary in the Colonial Office. He admitted that he was unfamiliar with the history of the Partition Treaty of 22 June 1799. He believed that the Partition Treaty made the Maharajah an independent sovereign, in the sense in which any other "protected" sovereign was independent. The Subsidiary Treaty of 8 July 1799 imposed certain conditions on him, which he broke; consequently he was rightfully deprived of his "independent" sovereignty.

> He does not deny all this, but says that we always promised to restore him some day or other and ought to do it now. We deny the promise and the allegations. That is our case . . . . The MR makes the fairest possible *promises*. You may believe them or not, but what *security* can he possibly offer?[34]

Merivale did not fundamentally disagree with the second draft, and in preparing the third and final draft, he merely emphasized what to him seemed the important grounds on which the case for rejection rested. He felt it was the "paramount duty" of Her Majesty's Government to ensure peace, security and good government in Mysore.

> The question finally remaining for the decision of H.M.'s Government is therefore a simple one. It was rightfully regarded in 1831 as for the benefit of Mysore that its possession should be assumed by the British Government. Would it be for the benefit of that country, that this possession should now be restored to the Maharajah?

33 By whose hand I am unable to ascertain. This is "Draft 1" (which I refer to later in this paper as the "second draft" in the Mysore Papers, Halifax Papers).

34 Minutes by Merivale, undated, on "Draft 1", Mysore Papers, Halifax Papers.

Merivale considered that the evidence before him—of Cubbon, Dalhousie and Canning—was against this. He did not doubt the Maharajah's sincerity when he stated that he would maintain the present system.

> But the question before me is, whether in justice to the people of Mysore H.M.'s Govt. could be content with such an assurance. And this is a question which, judging from the future through the lights afforded by past history, I feel compelled to answer in the negative.[35]

This was, in essence, the argument of the final despatch to India dated 17 July 1863.[36] Thus, whatever the ultimate motives for the retention of Mysore under British administration,[37] there was a strong body of opinion in the India Office which refused an unconditional restoration on the grounds of Britain's moral obligations in India, and Merivale's argument gave it legal respectability.

And the feeling was apparent not only in the India Office, but also in India. Lord Elgin, who became Viceroy in 1862, agreed entirely with Canning. He was in favour of annexation and had built up a formidable defence of Canning's policy by laying bare its true motives.[38] He warned Wood (as Prinsep had done) against abandoning the advantageous position in which Canning had placed him vis-à-vis the Maharajah by excluding him from the benefits of the adoption *sanads*.[39] Elgin's "real question"—and Merivale's minutes seem to owe something to the Viceroy's own answer[40]—was this :

> Is the Raja qualified to administer his territories well if

35 "Longer alteration draft", the bulk of which is in Merivale's handwriting, undated, *ibid*.

36 Printed in *Parl. Papers* (*H. of C.*), 1866, lii, 499-504.

37 See below, p. 231 for Merivale's disclosure in his Memorandum on the Carnatic Case.

38 Elgin to Wood, 9 Sept. 1862, Halifax Papers, Ind. Off. Corres.

39 *Ibid*.

40 In the Mysore Papers, Halifax Papers, there is a summary of Elgin's arguments, extracted by Benjamin West (Wood's private secretary) from Wood's private correspondence. It is reasonable to assume that Merivale, at least, might have had access to this. Occasionally Wood turned over his private correspondence to the Political Committee.

> we restore them to him now? Lord Canning decided this question in the negative . . . I have already pointed out to you that the denial of the Raja's fitness to govern his territory was the only effectual way of barring his right to appoint a successor.[41]

This opinion in Calcutta was pressed on Wood not only by Elgin, but also by Henry Marion Durand, the Foreign Secretary. He, too, stressed that there was no proof that the Raja was more fit to rule now than he was thirty years ago.[42]

Such arguments clearly strengthened Wood in his determination to keep Mysore. He had started off allegedly without any strong feelings on the subject[43] but basically he desperately wanted Mysore.[44] He felt that approval of the recommendation of the special committee on Mysore would perpetuate the prevailing uncertainty about the future of the principality and merely return the Maharajah to the ranks of princes to whom, according to precedent, the right of adoption was conceded:[45] thus Mysore might slip from Britain's grasp after all. How to ensure the eventual acquisition of the principality after a restoration exercised his mind exceedingly. He hoped that if he waited long enough the problem might solve itself by the death of the Maharajah.[46] Unable to come to a decision, Wood consulted Lord Stanley, his predecessor in office, who told him that "we must have Mysore".[47] And because Wood trusted

[41] Elgin to Wood, 19 Nov. 1862, Halifax Papers, Ind. Off. Corres.

[42] Durand to Wood, 7 Jan. 1863, Mysore Papers, Halifax Papers.

[43] Wood to Stanley, 19 June 1864, Halifax Papers, Ind. Off. Corres.

[44] Wood to Elgin, 9 Oct. (No. 1) 1862; Wood to Canning, 25 Dec. 1861; Wood to Elgin, 10 July 1862, *ibid.*

[45] Wood to Stanley, 19 June 1864, *ibid.*

[46] Wood to Elgin, 24 Sept. (No. 1) 1862, *ibid.* And, indeed, keeping the Maharajah happy so that he might bequeath Mysore to Britain was something of an administrative pastime with Canning, Lawrence and Wood. It could be nothing more than a pastime, for there was no contractual basis involved. (See Metcalf, *The Aftermath of Revolt*, pp. 229-230 for a fuller discussion of this).

[47] Wood to Stanley, 19 June 1864, Halifax Papers, Ind. Off. Corres. Neither Metcalf, *The Aftermath of Revolt*, pp. 228-229, nor Gopal, *British Policy in India*, p. 10, mention Wood's reliance on Stanley for the final decision.

Stanley's judgement, it "very much" determined his decision: he evasively refused the restoration "so as not to create any obstacle in the way of the future course of any Govt. which might have to deal with the question".[48] The argument of a moral obligation towards the people of Mysore provided the justification. Indeed, for Elgin, and others, it was merely a means to ensure that Mysore would eventually be annexed.

Thus, it was expediency rather than the interpretation of treaties which determined the fate of Mysore in 1863. Merivale, who varnished the final draft despatch, was the first to admit this:

> ... questions on Treaties must and will continually involve questions of public expediency. It may seem easy, in theory, to separate the question of right from that of expediency: in practice it would be found extremely difficult indeed. Look at the Mysore Case with which we have just dealt. It was substantially a question of the rights of parties under a Treaty. Yet I think most who considered were of opinion that the question of the public expediency did enter largely, and with perfect justice, into its consideration.[49]

The rejection of the Maharajah's petition appeared to be a victory for the reactionists. Yet in 1867 the Rajah was allowed to adopt a successor to the throne. This laid the foundation for the rendition of Mysore in 1881 when the young successor was considered fit to rule. A clue to this virtual reversal of policy is to be found in the dissents which were recorded against the despatch of 17 July 1863.

Montgomery was convinced that the derangement of the affairs of Mysore under the Maharajah's rule had been greatly exaggerated.[50] Willoughby stressed that there was strong evidence that a large proportion of the Mysore population, and

[48] Wood to Stanley, 19 June, 1864, Halifax Papers, Ind. Off. Corres.

[49] Memo. on the Carnatic case by Merival. 6 July 1863, Nawabs of the Carnatic Papers, Halifax Papers.

[50] Dissent by Montgomery, 13 July 1863, *Parl. Papers* (*H. of C*), 1866, lii, 505.

more particularly the higher classes, would prefer Indian to British rule.[51] Currie dissented from the proposition in the despatch "that our duty to the people of Mysore compels us to retain possession of the country"; in his view, an Indian administration adequately supervised was better adapted to the needs of an Indian state, and more acceptable than one "where the European or English modes of procedure pervade all the departments".[52] In other words, these members of the special committee and the Council of India, while agreeing that Britain had a moral obligation in India, had not been prepared to deny the intrinsic merit of Indian polity. Such a denial was the basis of one of the main arguments of the reactionists in favour of the extension of British power in India, and Willoughby had rightly pointed to its abuse :

> I am always suspicious of changes advocated on the plea of advancing civilization and such humbug, which is often only a flimsy disguise for the exercise of arbitrary power — sure to end in the extension of the red wave over the map of India.[53]

## III

The refusal to restore the Maharajah precipitated a demand from the people of Mysore for his reinstatement, and a request from the Maharajah to adopt a son. As an adopted heir had no legal right of succession, the adoption could be set aside and the state would lapse to Britain on the death of the incumbent Maharajah.[54] Sir John Lawrence, now Viceroy, received the request. As a member of the Council of India he had opposed restoration and helped to shape the despatch of 17 July 1863. Now he interpreted this — and subsequent despatches relating to the subject — as having fully disposed of any claims of the Maharajah "either by inheritance or by

51 Dissent by Willoughby, 18 Aug. 1863, *ibid.*, p. 519.

52 Dissent by Currie, 17 July 1863, *ibid.*, p. 510.

53 Minute, undated, on Wood to Gov(ernor)-in-Coun(cil) Bombay, 16 Dec. (48) 1864, Pol. Des. to Bombay, 6, Ind. Off. Lib.

54 See Metcalf, *The Aftermath of Revolt*, p. 230.

the subsidiary Treaty of Mysore".[55] Wood clearly had a strong ally in the Viceroy. In a despatch of 17 July 1865 he approved Lawrence's decision on the grounds that the well-being of the people of Mysore made it impossible to grant the Maharajah's requests.[56]

But if the reactionary trend in Calcutta was strengthened by the arrival of Lawrence, the India Office, and particularly the Political Committee of the Council of India, was leavened by the advent of Sir George Russell Clerk from Bombay. He was the perfect foil to the reactionists. His views were well-known in the India Office, where he had been Permanent Under-Secretary of State until 1859, when he left to become Governor of Bombay. Until 1863, when he returned to London, he was in touch with Willoughby, Perry, Merivale and Thomas Baring,[57] so he was aware of the attitudes in the India Office. As Governor of Bombay he had been consulted about the Mysore restoration and had been in favour of it, with adequate safeguards.[58] Deeply committed to the belief that Indian polity had an intrinsic virtue, and to the honouring of treaty rights, Clerk infused a fresh vitality into the group which opposed the policies of Wood and Lawrence. Fundamentally their platform in the Mysore affair was the rejection of the contention that Britain should denigrate Indian polity because of a self-imposed moral obligation in India towards those who would allegedly suffer under it.

Already this "Clerk group" — as it may be called henceforth—consisting of Willoughby, Currie, Montgomery and, now, Eastwick, had a cautious supporter in Sir John Kaye, the Secretary in the Political Department of the India Office. Long before the Mutiny Kaye had been sufficiently attracted by the principles of the non-annexationists, Malcolm, Metcalfe and Henry St. George Tucker, to make their lives and

55 Lawrence, *et al.*, to Wood, 31 Aug. (66) 1864. Coll. Pol. Des. to Ind. 78/57, Coll. 1.

56 Wood to Lawrence, 12 Aug. 1865, Halifax Papers, Ind. Off. Corres., Wood to G.-G.-in-Coun., 17 July (57) 1865, Pol. Des. to Ind., 9. Printed in *Parl. Papers* (*H. of C.*) 1866, lii, 556-7.

57 See Clerk Papers, *passim*. Thomas Baring, 1st Earl of Northbrook, 1826-1904; Parliamentary Under-Secretary of State for India, 1859-1861.

58 Memo. by Clerk, 22 Dec. 1861, Mysore Papers, Halifax Papers. Printed with significant alterations in *Parl. Papers* (*H. of C.*), 1866, lii, 557-9.

work better known to the public.[59] Kaye was sympathetic towards Indian polity. When the restoration of Mysore was discussed in 1863-1864, he held that the Home Government had given the Maharajah reason to believe that the sequestration was a temporary measure and that restoration would follow an arrangement for good government. He made the uncomfortably pertinent point that the British Government throughout had regarded Mysore as foreign territory, held in trust for the Maharajah.[60] This unassailable argument could only be ignored by placing faith in the all-embracing and omnipotent paramountcy of Britain on the sub-continent as a justification for over-ruling treaty rights and obligations — and this was another aspect of British policy which the Clerk group opposed, particularly during the years 1866-1867.[61]

The minutes dissenting from Wood's despatch of 17 July 1865 were vigorous. Clerk attacked the decision by ironically pointing out an inconsistency in the argument that Mysore must be preserved from the iniquities of Indian rule:

> I consider that benevolence should not be confined to a class. A Rajah, his kinsmen, his retainers, may have feelings as well as a Ryut. And with regard to the latter, there were, and still are, native Governments, where, to the minds of the Ryut and the man of the middle classes, their advantages are, perhaps, not much, but rather on the side of their native ruler.[62]

Like Willoughby, he maintained that a large proportion of the Mysore population preferred Indian to British rule.[63]

[59] Kaye's works include: *The Life and Correspondence of Major-General Sir John Malcolm* (1856); *Selections from the Papers of Lord Metcalfe* (1855); *The Life and Correspondence of Henry St. George Tucker* (1854); *The Lives of Indian Officers* (2 vols. 1867).

[60] Printed Memo., 10 Oct. 1862 and "Supplementary Note" by Kaye, undated, Coll. Pol. Des. to Ind. 67/48, Coll. 1.

[61] See p. 236 ff.

[62] Dissent of Clerk, 24 July 1865, Council of India, Minutes of Dissent, ii, 149. Ind. Off. Lib. Printed in *Parl. Papers* (*H. of C.*), 1866, lii, 557-60.

[63] *Ibid.*, dissent by Willoughby, 18 Aug. 1863, *ibid.*, 519.

Eastwick admitted that the acknowledged supremacy of Britain in India entitled her to interfere with principalities if their administration tended to be harmful to their subjects or the allies of the British Government. But he recognized that there was

> no mission confided to the British Government which imposes upon it the obligation, or can confer upon it the right of deciding authoritatively on the existence of native independent sovereignties, and of arbitrarily setting them aside whenever their administration may not accord with its own views.[64]

The giants of the past were resurrected to expound their respective doctrines through their adherents. Metcalfe's minute on adoptions (28 October 1837) and Elphinstone's views were quoted in support of the belief that the British Government was bound to acknowledge adoptions as a direct means of preserving Indian states, providing such adoptions were regular and not in violation of Hindu law.[65]

Though the Clerk group formed a vocal core of dissent, it had to contend with formidable resistance on the part of Mangles[66] and Prinsep.[67] These two grounded their arguments on the presupposition that administration deteriorated once it reverted to Indian rule. As a foil to Metcalfe and Elphinstone, they conjured up Macaulay who had said that British government in India was probably the only government in the world which was better qualified to think and act for the people than the people for themselves. "The truth of this opinion" declared Mangles "appears to me to be unquestionable, and upon this principle we are bound to act as we think for the interests of the people of Mysore"[68]

Thus in 1865 the Clerk group failed to win over the Secretary of State. Some progress had been made between 1863 and 1866 in persuading the Political Department that Indian

64 Dissent by Eastwick, 25 July 1865, *ibid.*, p. 565.

65 *Ibid.*, pp. 559-562 (Eastwick), pp. 566-567 (Currie).

66 Minute by Mangles, 22 July 1865, *ibid.*, pp. 569-574.

67 Minute by Prinsep, 1 Aug. 1865, *ibid.*, pp. 574-576.

68 Minute by Mangles, 22 July 1865, *ibid.*, p. 573.

states should be respected and not subjected to indiscreet interference which might result in annexation.[69] But it was not until Wood relinquished office that two successive Secretaries of State, Viscount Cranborne (later Lord Salisbury, Secretary of State, 6 July 1866-7 March 1867) and Sir Stafford Northcote, were convinced of the cogency of Clerk's arguments. They buried for once and for all the hopes of the annexationists that a British administration would be perpetuated there.

Towards the end of 1866 the Maharajah again petitioned to be allowed to administer his state.[70] There was a simple logic in his repetition: he regarded each change of Viceroy or Secretary of State as producing a fresh permutation which might result in a change of policy in his favour. The preparation of the papers was in the hands of Sir John Kaye. His handling of the case indicates that years of subjection to the arguments of the Clerk group had noticeably strengthened his earlier convictions.

Kaye's memorandum, prepared for the Political Committee, reveals that Clerk's arguments in favour of Indian polity had not gone unheeded. It compared Mysore with Travancore which had been restored to an Indian ruler in 1832 and which had flourished exceedingly since. Kaye quoted the British Resident in Mysore as saying that his attempt to introduce order and regularity into the administration, and to extinguish rapacity, corruption and injustice, were regarded by some classes as preparatory steps towards annexation. Also, some of the people wanted a Dewan because that office belonged to the native constitution of the country, and they regarded with dissatisfaction "the administration of a Foreigner and a stranger".[71] Here Kaye was echoing one of Clerk's minutes of 1864 in connection with a somewhat similar situation in Meywar: "Was not Eden a Foreigner?"[72]

69 I shall discuss this in my biography of Sir George Russell Clerk.

70 Lawrence to Cranborne, 31 Oct. (185) 1866, Coll. Pol. Des. to Ind. 90/69.

71 Memo., undated, *ibid.*

72 Minute, undated, on Col. E. K. Elliot, Officiating Agent, G.-G. for Rajputana, to Lt.-Col. Eden, Meywar, 24 May (660A) 1864, encl. IV in E. K. Elliot to H. M. Durand, 27 May (669-37P) 1864, *ibid.*, 77/41.

Kaye also put forward a vigorous plea for sound morality in the interpretation of treaties, basing his arguments on Clerk's view that Britain's strengthened position in India should not make her exploit treaties to her own advantage. The views of Malcolm, Metcalfe, Elphinstone and Henry Lawrence were quoted to strengthen his case.[73] This warning against the bending of treaties to suit improved conditions was in contrast to the earlier tendency towards expediency. Ever since the annexation of Satara in 1848[74] Clerk had constantly advocated non-intervention, non-annexation and restoration of Indian states. He had stressed that Britain's changed position on the sub-continent should not render treaties invalid. As one of the greatest self-appointed guardians of good faith, he considered that treaties should be scrupulously adhered to. He and his followers argued that Britain should not use her favourable position to her own advantage under the pretext of the good of the people and the interests of general tranquillity. They did not deny that sequestration should be practised when necessary; but this should be carried out through "the all-powerful influence derivable from a scrupulous adherence to the letter and spirit of our treaties". Quoting the case of Kāthiāwār, Clerk made it clear that as Governor of Bombay it had always been his practice to recognize independence which might have been either formally granted or relinquished by consent to chiefs at a time when fair dealing and conciliation were deemed to be indispensable to Britain's security and supremacy.[75] And battling from Bombay in 1862 against the rejection of the Maharajah's petition, he had argued that Britain could not afford to lose the goodwill of the Indian rulers after the Mutiny by reinterpreting treaties to suit her more powerful position.

While the Clerk group were marshalling their arguments in the India Office, Sir Henry Rawlinson,[76] on 22 February

[73] Memo., undated, by Kaye, *ibid.*, 90/69.

[74] See minute by Clerk, 12 Apl. 1848, *Parl. Papers* (*H. of C.*), 1849, xxxix, 206.

[75] Memo., 16 Nov. 1864, Wood to Gov.-in-Coun., Bombay, 16 Dec. (48) 1864, Pol. Des. to Bombay, 6.

[76] 1810-1895: in India 1827; in Persia, Kabul, Baghdad, 1833-1855; M. P. Reigate, 1858; Council of India, 1858-1859; Persia, 1859-1860; M.P. Frome, 1865-1866.

1867, asked Viscount Cranborne in the Commons whether a decision had been reached with regard to Mysore. In his view the death of the Maharajah would result in some formal act of annexation. Rawlinson argued for the perpetuation of a native dynasty. His arguments smack curiously of those of Clerk. He maintained that Indian states under sound, friendly administration were a source of strength, not weakness for Britain; they were a sort of safety valve for the exuberant "native energy" which could not find employment under British rule, and which, while idle, fermented and was a source of danger. They were also a breakwater during times of danger.[77]

Cranborne's reply was incisive and unambiguous. He did not doubt that the Maharajah had been excluded from Canning's list of *sanads* and therefore did not enjoy the right of adoption. Nor could he claim full right of sovereignty, with succession, under article 4 of the Partition Treaty. His lineal heir had no claim; an adopted son even less.[78] This argument had the ring of Mangles and Prinsep about it.[79] But Cranborne had done his homework by going through Aitchison's *Treaties, Engagements and Sanads*.[80] He had also relied on Aitchison himself who, on 10 September 1866, had drawn up a "Memorandum on the Doctrine of Lapse", which Lawrence had forwarded to Cranborne.[81] Comparing this memorandum with Cranborne's speech, it is difficult not to conclude that he drew heavily on Aitchison's reasoning in denying the Maharajah the right to adopt an heir. He concurred with Aitchison that Britain's paramountcy entitled her to make or unmake treaties by recognizing or refusing adoption in the cause of state policy.[82]

These were arguments dear to the hearts of the "old Rump", the "reactionists". But having made this point, Cranborne

[77] *Hansard* (3rd Series), clxxxv, 827-833. [78] *Ibid.*, 835-838.

[79] Dissent (or Memo.) undated, Coll. Pol. Des. to Ind. 67/48; Minute, 1 Aug. 1865, *Parl. Papers* (*H. of C.*), 1866, lii, 574-576.

[80] *Cf. Hansard* (3rd Series), clxxxv, 837.

[81] This memorandum is in a box containing letters from Sir Bartle Frere, in the Salisbury Papers, Christ Church, Oxford. See also Lawrence to Cranborne, 20 Sept. 1866, Lawrence Papers, Ind. Off. Lib.

[82] Aitchison's Memo., 10 Sept. 1866, Salisbury Papers; *Hansard* (3rd Series), clxxxvii, 1073 (Cranborne, 24 May 1867).

started on another tack, leaving the reactionists and sailing in company with Clerk and his adherents.

> But it would be a great evil if the result of our dominion was that the Natives of India who were capable of Government should be absolutely and hopelessly excluded from such a career. The great advantage of the existence of Native States is that they afford an outlet for statesman-like capacity such as had been alluded to . . . . The existence of a well-governed Native State is a real benefit not only to the stability of our rule, but because more than anything it raises the self-respect of the Natives, and forms an ideal to which the popular feelings aspire.

There was no intention to annex Mysore, but he did not feel disposed to hand it back to an Indian government unchecked and uncontrolled. Thus, when the Maharajah died, the young prince would be given the advantage of a European education and be prepared for the responsibilities which "we hope it may one day be possible to commit to him".[83]

In this speech Cranborne announced an important change in policy without consulting the Council of India.[84] The matter was further complicated by the fact that Sir Stafford Northcote succeeded Cranborne as Secretary of State before he could draft a despatch. When Northcote consulted the Council he found the majority against Cranborne's policy and in favour of annexation.[85] It is not unreasonable to suppose that the resistance of the "old Rump" was considerably stiffened by Cranborne's disregard for the Council,[86] a dis-

[83] *Hansard* (3rd Series), clxxxv, 839-841.

[84] Dissent by Perry, concurred in by Mangles, 15 Apl. 1867, *Parl. Papers* (*H. of C.*), 1, 580; Northcote in the Commons, 24 May 1867, *Hansard* (3rd Series), clxxxvii, 1063.

[85] *Hansard* (3rd Series), clxxxvii, 1063-1064.

[86] The pique is evident in memos. by Perry, 23 March 1867 and Prinsep, 25 March, 1867, Northcote to G.G.-in-Coun., 16 Apl. (69) 1867, Pol. Des. to Ind., 10. Throughout the Mysore affair Wood never succeeded in bringing out nine recorded dissents, as Cranborne did (*Parl. Papers* (*H. of C.*), 1867, 1, 574-587). Ten Councillors were actually against the measure. *Hansard* (3rd Series), clxxxvii, 1047.

regard which possibly set some of the uncommitted against the Secretary of State. Nevertheless, as a member of Lord Derby's government, Northcote felt himelf bound to press on with a despatch embodying Cranborne's views, in spite of the Council. In any case, he agreed with Cranborne that an Indian state should be maintained in Mysore. It was essential to refuse any claim on the part of the Nizam and with due regard to the people of Mysore it was impossible at present to restore the present Rajah to the throne. A new arrangement could only be made with the adopted son when he attained the years of discretion.[87]

Ignored as they were by both Secretaries of State[88] the majority of the Council objected strongly to Northcote's draft despatch.[89] Prinsep pointed out that it omitted reference to the subject of the expiry of the treaty and the freedom of the British Government to make new arrangements when the Maharajah died. Instead of this, there was a paragraph referring to Lord Wellesley's policy which established an Indian prince in Mysore under subsidiary engagement, guided by the advice of a British Resident. This policy was eulogized and the intention was stated that the present government desired to maintain and continue it.[90] The reactionists stressed that the territory governed in the name of the Maharajah was actually annexed to the Company's dominions, that the entire sovereignty passed to the British at the transactions at Seringapatam, and that the Maharajah and his ministers could only be regarded as Vice-Regents at will. Perry quoted Lord Wellesley and James Mill's *History of British India* in support of this view.[91]

There were four councillors who did not join in the clamour against Cranborne and Northcote, and who remained silent even about the fact that the Council had been ignored: Clerk, Currie, Willoughby and Eastwick. They formed the

87 *Parl. Papers* (*H. of C.*), 1867, 1, 571-574; printed memo. by Northcote, 2 Apl. 1867, Coll. Pol. Des. to Ind. 90/69.

88 Dissent by Perry, 15 Apl. 1867, *Parl. Papers* (*H. of C.*), 1867, 1, 580.

89 Draft des. by Northcote to G.G.-in-Coun., 16 Apl. (69) 1867, Pol. Des. to Ind., 10. Printed in *Parl. Papers* (*H. of C.*), 1867, 1, 566-567.

90 Dissent by Prinsep, 15 Apl. 1867, *ibid.*, p. 576.

91 Dissent by Perry, concurred in by Mangles, 15 Apl. 1867, *ibid.*, p. 578. See Mill, *History of British India* (3rd ed.) iii, 140.

majority of the Political Committee and were the core of resistance against Prinsep and Mangles. Prinsep was in the minority on the Committee, but commanded a great following in Council. The two Secretaries of State had acted unconstitutionally by not consulting the Council. Their action was made more culpable by Northcote overriding the Council. But, as Rawlinson pointed out in the Commons on 24 May 1867, a mere numerical majority of Council was not of essential consequence. The majority of the Political Committee were the only councillors who had served in Indian courts, and who were therefore supposed to be conversant with Indian feeling. They had been in favour of perpetuating an Indian state.[92]

Of the Political Committee, Sir George Russell Clerk was the most vocal and persistent advocate of the doctrine that Britain should pay the utmost regard to the spirit in which treaties were made. There is no doubt that his persistence and sincerity, coupled with the cogency of his arguments, had influenced Northcote.[93] Speaking in the Commons, the latter pointed out that the right of inheritance was not to be decided merely by the technical construction of the clauses of the treaty. He had tried to ascertain the spirit of the arrangement which had originally been made by Lord Wellesley. If possible he wanted to carry that into effect irrespective of any special pleading with regard to the exact wording of the treaty, and thus, in fact, to treat the matter as a question of broad national policy.[94] The similarity to Clerk's reasoning is hardly coincidental. Also, Northcote's entire agreement that Britain's policy should be to maintain, as far as possible, the existence of separate Indian states[95] is directly attributable to Cranborne's influence,[96] and Cranborne

92 *Hansard* (3rd Series), clxxxvii, 1047-1048.

93 Metcalf, *The Aftermath of Revolt*, p. 232, attributes the preservation of an Indian dynasty in Mysore to the change of administration. In doing so he underrates the influence of the Clerk group in the India Office.

94 24 May 1867, *Hansard* (3rd Series), clxxxvii, 1064. 95 *Ibid.*, 1068-1069.

96 Memo., 2 Apl. 1867, Coll. Pol. Des. to Ind., 90/69. Northcote admitted in March 1867 that he was not very familiar with the Mysore question (Memo. 19 March 1867 in Wood to G.G.-in-Coun., 16 Apl. (69) 1867, Pol. Des. to Ind., 10) and his first draft came directly from Cranborne (Dissent by Perry, 15 Apl. 1867, *Parl. Papers* (*H. of C.*), 1867, 1, 580.)

himself admitted his indebtedness to Clerk. Speaking in the Commons on 24 May 1867, he pointed out that British administration in India had grave disadvantages. He listed "Its tendency to routine; its listless, heavy heedlessness, sometimes the result of its elaborate organization; the fear of responsibility; an extreme centralization". Opposed to this

> In cases of emergency...the simple form of Oriental Government will produce effects more salutary than the more elaborate system of English rule. I am not by this denying that our mission in India is to reduce to order, to civilize and develop the Native governments we find there. But I demur to that wholesale condemnation of a system of government which would be utterly intolerable on our own soil, but which had grown up amongst a people subjected to it. It has a fitness and congeniality for them impossible for us adequately to realize, but which compensates them to an enormous degree for the material evils which its rudeness in a great many cases produces. I may mention, as an instance, what was told me by Sir George Clerk, a distinguished Member of the Council of India, respecting the province of Kattywar, in which the English and Native Governments are very much intermixed. There are no broad lines of frontier there, and a man can easily leap over the hedge from the Native into the English jurisdiction. Sir George Clerk told me that the Natives having little to carry with them were continually in the habit of migrating from the English into the Native jurisdiction; but that he never heard of an instance of a Native leaving his own to go into the English jurisdiction. This may be very bad taste on the part of the Natives; but you have to consider what promotes their happiness, suits their tastes, and tends to their moral development in their own way. If you intend to develop their moral nature only after the Anglo-Saxon type, you will make a conspicuous and disastrous defeat.[97]

Clearly Clerk had been assiduously at work in his campaign of conversion to the merits of Indian polity as opposed to

97 *Hansard* (3rd Series), clxxxvii, 1074.

direct British rule. The growing strength of this doctrine throughout the Mysore deliberations, coupled with the plea for scrupulous morality in interpreting treaties, lay at the heart of the reversal of policy in 1867. To this reversal Clerk had contributed generously by unflagging energy behind the scenes. In 1867 a few adherents held key positions and could thus ignore the majority in policy-making. This defeat of the reactionists paved the way for the rendition of Mysore in 1881. The fulfilment of the benevolent intentions of the Queen's Proclamation of 1858 therefore owes more to one man than is generally conceded. To Sir George Russell Clerk falls the honour of not only being an important contributor to a turning-point in British policy in India; in 1853-1854 he had been responsible for implementing a major change in British policy in southern Africa.[98] The consequences of these major shifts in policy are with us today. Few British administrators during the 19th century could lay claim to having participated in such remarkable decisions in two continents.

[98] On 16 January 1852 the Transvaal Boers received their independence by the Sand River Convention, signed on behalf of Britain by Commissioners Owen and Hogge; in February 1854 Clerk signed the Bloemfontein Convention which recognized the independence of the Orange Free State. These Conventions mark a watershed in the history of British policy for southern Africa. I shall discuss Clerk's contribution in my biography of this colourful character.

# APPENDIX

*(List of Oxford students who have completed research degrees under the supervision of Dr. C. C. Davies.)*

| *Degree* | *Name* | *College* | *Subject* |
|---|---|---|---|
| | | 1965 | |
| B.Litt. | Prince M.A. Naim | Christ Church | Anglo-Afghan relations from 1809 till 1839. |
| D.Phil. | Z. Ahmad | New College | Life and conditions of the people of Bengal (1765-85). |
| | | 1964 | |
| D.Phil. | R. J. Bingle | Balliol | The Governor-Generalship of the Marquess of Hastings 1813-23, with special reference to the Supreme Council and Secretariat, the Residents with Native States, Military Policy, and the transactions of the Palmer Company. |
| | | 1963 | |
| D.Phil. | E. D. Potts | Regent's Park | British Baptist missions and missionaries in India, 1793-1837. |
| D.Phil. | K. E. Verghese | Balliol | The development and significance of transport in India (1834-82). |
| | | 1962 | |
| D.Phil. | Mrs. A. Das (née Majumdar) | Lady Margaret Hall | Lord Minto's administration in India (1807-13), with special reference to his foreign policy. |
| D.Phil. | Mrs. A. Siddiqi | Somerville | Land revenue administration in the North-Western Provinces, 1819-33. |

| *Degree* | *Name* | *College* | *Subject* |
|---|---|---|---|
| D.Phil. | V. Mazumdar | St. Hugh's | Imperial Policy in India, 1905-1910. |
| D.Phil. | D. Williams | New College | The formation of policy in the India Office 1858-66, with special reference to the Political, Judicial, Revenue, Public and Public Works Departments. |
| | | 1961 | |
| D.Phil. | B. De | Nuffield | Henry Dundas and the Government of India, 1773-1801. |
| | | 1960 | |
| D.Phil. | Munir-ud-Din Chughtai | Magdalen | Muslim Politics in the Indo-Pakistan sub-continent, 1858-1916. |
| | | 1959 | |
| D.Phil. | K. J. Crowther | Lincoln | Portuguese Society in India in the Sixteenth and Seventeenth Centuries. |
| | | 1958 | |
| D.Phil. | I. M. Habib | New College | The Agrarian System of Mughal India (1556-1707). |
| D.Phil. | Miss B. Hjejle | Lady Margaret Hall | The social policy of the East India Company with regard to Sati, Infanticide, Slavery, Thagi, and Human Sacrifices, 1772-1858. |
| | | 1957 | |
| D.Phil. | B. J. Hasrat | St. Catherine's | Anglo-Sikh relations, 1799-1849. |
| | | 1956 | |
| D.Phil. | T. Raychaudhuri | Balliol | The Dutch in Coromandel, 1605-1690. |
| | | 1953 | |
| D.Phil. | Miss C.E. Barrett | St. Hilda's | Lord William Bentinck in Bengal, 1828-35. |
| | | 1952 | |
| B.Litt. | Miss M. Sharadamma | St. Anne's | Sati and its abolition. |

| Degree | Name | College | Subject |
|---|---|---|---|
| | | 1951 | |
| B. Litt. | A. S. Bennell | Corpus Christi | Southern India under Wellesley, 1798-1805. |
| D.Phil. | S. Gopal | Balliol | The Viceroyalty of Lord Ripon, 1880-4. |
| | | 1948 | |
| D.Phil. | K. Ingham | Keble | The Achievements of the Christian Missionary in India, 1794-1833. |
| D.Phil. | S. Gupta | Balliol | British Policy on the North-East Frontier of India (1826-86). |
| D.Phil. | K. P. K. Pillay | St. Catherine's | Local Self-Government in the Madras Presidency, 1850-1919. |
| | | 1939 | |
| B.Litt. | A. W. Mahmood | St. Catherine's | The Governor-Generalship of Sir John Shore, 1793-8. |
| D Phil. | L. E. Frechtling | Queen's | British Policy in the Middle East, 1874-1880. |

*We should like to thank the Oxford University Registry for compiling this list. It is impossible to mention by name the many students who attended Dr. Davies's admirable lectures on "Warren Hastings and British India" which he taught as a Special Subject. However, they are represented by several of the contributors to this collection.*

# INDEX

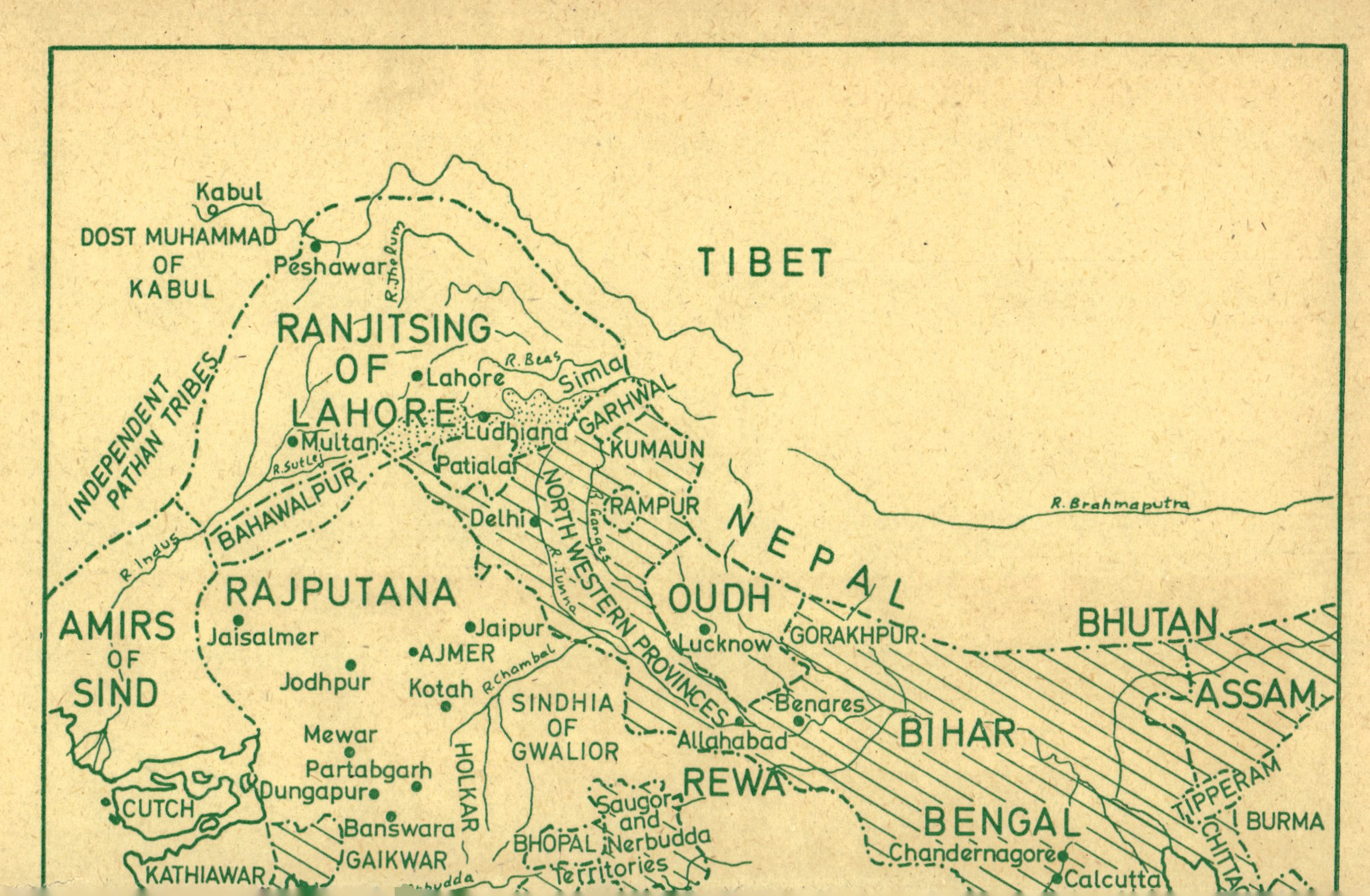
TIBET
Kabul
DOST MUHAMMAD OF KABUL
Peshawar
R. Jhelum
RANJITSING OF LAHORE
Lahore
R. Beas
Simla
INDEPENDENT PATHAN TRIBES
Multan
Ludhiana
GARHWAL
KUMAUN
R. Sutlej
Patiala
BAHAWALPUR
RAMPUR
R. Ganges
Delhi
R. Brahmaputra
NEPAL
R. Indus
RAJPUTANA
R. Jumna
NORTH WESTERN PROVINCES
OUDH
AMIRS OF SIND
Jaisalmer
Jaipur
AJMER
Lucknow
GORAKHPUR
BHUTAN
Jodhpur
Kotah
R. Chambal
SINDHIA OF GWALIOR
Benares
ASSAM
Mewar
Partabgarh
Dungapur
HOLKAR
Allahabad
BIHAR
REWA
CUTCH
Banswara
Saugor and Nerbudda Territories
BENGAL
TIPPERAM
BURMA
GAIKWAR
BHOPAL
Chandernagore
KATHIAWAR
Calcutta